Walking in Cities

This book brings together an international group of artists and writers to respond to the question of how our new world orders force us to reconsider urban walking and urban spaces in ways which extend into the digital sphere of online dialogue and screen sharing. In their reflections on walking cities in lockdown, the artists and writers contributing to this book share a number of complementary themes. Key to this is the question of how we walk in post-pandemic cities and how such walking might motivate or be motivated by transgressive, atomised or collective thoughts, affects, relations and experiences. Here we see how navigating cities in lockdown requires us to re-territorialise, improvise, create and de- or re-politize. There is, for example, a clear distinction between the severe lockdown measures that were introduced in Cape Town and the liberal appeal to good citizenship that northern hemisphere cities such as Stockholm chose to rely on. These measures impact on the way we experience urban walking and, in each case, lead to deeper reflections about the heightened presence of ideological structures embedded within the urban.

Jaspar Joseph-Lester is a London-based artist. His work explores the conflicting ideological frameworks embodied in representations of modernity, urban renewal, regeneration and social organisation as a means to better understand how art practice can redefine master plans and regeneration schemes that determine the cultural life of our cities. He has exhibited his work internationally and is author of *Revisiting the Bonaventure Hotel* (Copy Press, 2012). Joseph-Lester is Professor of Critical Spatial Practice at the Royal College of Art.

Ahuvia Kahane is Regius Professor of Greek (1761), A. G. Leventis Professor of Greek Culture (2017) and Fellow of

Trinity College Dublin. His research interests include temporality, complexity theory, ancient literature and the relations between antiquity, modernity and contemporary critical thought. His book *Epic, Novel and the Progress of Antiquity* (Bloomsbury) is in press. Forthcoming work includes (ed.) *A Cultural History of Time in the Ancient World* (Bloomsbury), *Orality and the Formula* (de Gruyter), and "Ancient Narrative Time" (in *A Handbook of Ancient Literary Theory*, Oxford).

Simon King is a London-based writer and walking artist undertaking a practice-based PhD at Birkbeck, University of London. His research investigates the infrastructures of creative and critical practice in relation to walking, dialogue and social engagement. He is the co-founder with Jaspar Joseph-Lester of the cross-disciplinary Walkative project at the RCA and has worked collaboratively since 2017 with the artist Corinne Noble to create participatory group walks that have an overarching theme or narrative and a distinctive methodology.

Esther Leslie is Professor of Political Aesthetics at Birkbeck, University of London. Her books include various studies of Walter Benjamin, *Hollywood Flatlands: Animation, Critical Theory and the Avant Garde* (2002); *Synthetic Worlds: Nature, Art and the Chemical Industry* (2005); *Derelicts* (2014), *Liquid Crystals: The Science and Art of a Fluid Form* (2016) and *The Rise and Fall of Imperial Chemical Industries: Synthetics, Sensism and the Environment* (2023). Work on the biopolitical economy of dairy, with Melanie Jackson, includes *Deeper in the Pyramid* (2018/2023). A study of anti-fascist radio pioneer Ernst Schoen (written with Sam Dolbear) appeared in 2023: *Dissonant Waves: Ernst Schoen and Experimental Sound in the Twentieth Century.*

Walking in Cities:

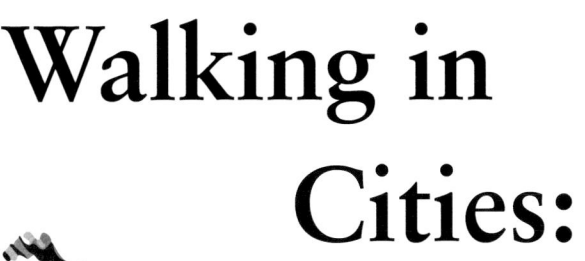

Navigating Post-Pandemic Urban Environments

Edited by
Jaspar Joseph-Lester
Ahuvia Kahane
Simon King
Esther Leslie

First published 2024
by Routledge
605 Third Avenue, New York, NY 10158

and by Routledge
4 Park Square, Milton Park, Abingdon, Oxon, OX14 4RN

Routledge is an imprint of the Taylor & Francis Group, an informa business

Library of Congress Cataloging-in-Publication Data
A catalog record for this title has been requested

ISBN: 9781032412603 (hbk)
ISBN: 9781032412610 (pbk)
ISBN: 9781003357056 (ebk)

DOI: 10.4324/9781003357056

Typeset in Akzidenz and Sabon
by Samuel Jones

All images in this volume are subject to the terms of copyright

Publisher's Note: This book has been prepared from camera-ready copy
provided by the author.

Contents

Introduction

For this book, we have invited an international group of artists and writers to respond to the question of how our new world orders force us to reconsider urban walking and urban spaces in ways which include the digital sphere of online dialogue and screen sharing. *Walking in Cities: Navigating Post-Pandemic Urban Environments* sets out to describe how we might think of 'being within' as opposed to 'moving through' a city.

The idea of representing the inner space of the urban is inspired by our shared experience of walking in lockdown. Here we became familiar with the virtual space of walking and how the experience of the urban environment in its several modalities: digital, cognitive and the imaginary, can transport us into a global context free from physical borders and political boundaries.[1] However, at the height of the pandemic, walking in cities was characterised by global restrictions to designated times and spaces. We soon came to appreciate the act of walking as a valuable resource for seeing and understanding local environments – and we gained a heightened awareness of the immediate surroundings.

In *Walking Cities: London* (Joseph-Lester et al., 2020) we make reference to the French aristocratic writer Xavier de Maistre's 1790 fantasy 'A Voyage Around My Room', written when the author was serving a 42-day sentence of imprisonment in Turin. The theme of de Maistre's book, eventually published in 1794, is the pleasure that can be found in one's everyday surroundings; his regret was that he needed to return to the spaces of everyday society. Little did we know in early 2020 that this philosophical notion of walking would become a reality.

The potential for new ways of walking is elaborated through 'sympathetic' affect and participation, through the exchange of individual perspectives and the overcoming of traditions oriented more-narrowly in the West. What we have sought to capture in *Walking in Cities: Navigating Post-Pandemic Urban Environments* is an insight into the changing conditions of the urban. Through this collection of writings on global, digital, phenomenological and physical space we ask: How do we walk in a post-pandemic city? How does this change in the way that we navigate and negotiate the urban environment help us to rethink cities? What have we learned from walking cities in a digital context? How does this group activity allow us to consider critical spatial practices? And if urban walking impacts on the way we think about research, how has lockdown led to new ways of working? What potential, if any, does the changing condition of the urban have for collaboration and dialogue with other practitioners?

POLITICS OF SPACE

Through the book, we move from one 'global city' to the next to consider how a range of approaches to the enforcement of restrictions embodies broader political, economic and cultural differences. There is, for example, a clear distinction between the severe lockdown measures that were introduced in Cape Town and the liberal appeal to good citizenship that northern hemisphere cities such as Stockholm chose to rely on. These measures impact on the way we experience urban walking and, in each case, lead to deeper reflections about the heightened presence of ideological structures embedded within the urban.

Esther Leslie's essay investigates the resonances of streets under lockdown in her local residential area in London. As the nearby streets emptied of people in the absence of work and usual outdoor activities, discussions on fifteen-minute cities took place, while the process of demolition, privatisation of social space and other brutal punctuations of the cityscape occurred busily, almost unseen.

Ahuvia Kahane's *Political Geometries* considers the politics of habitable space and the implications of movement within and across cities in time and within spaces of conflict and constraint. Aspects of the relation between time and geometries of the political, between freedom and constraint, sovereignty and resistance, are considered through the monumental architectural landscapes of the city of Dublin and their historical resonances. Lockdown 2020–21 provides an instructive critical heuristic, a conceptual modality of constraint, against whose background Kahane explores the limits of political sovereignty, authority, freedom, identity and change.

Robin Kirsten's *Fear and Loathing in ZA* proposes an analysis of neo-liberal militarily enforced biosecurity through aspects of the legacy of apartheid policies of urban spatial planning and the decimation of industries in relation to a site: a security grille fronting a homeless shelter on a public square: This allows multiple viewpoints into the everyday conditions of political and economic life in ZA under lockdown, where security features protect selected bodies, their possessions, social interactions and home .

F.C. Wilfred's *Hong Kong: An Uneasy Walk* developed out of the transcription of an online walk and talk during lockdown, in a city that was also the location of street protests against the Hong Kong Extradition Bill. The Bill led to the imposition of the 30 June 2020 national security law from China, which subjected Hong Kong's citizens to both increasing sanctions on movement and assembly, and escalating police brutality; a state of affairs in which the very act of walking is both precarious and political. Against a backdrop of the ubiquitous Pepe the Frog meme—a symbol of defiance—and through navigating the sites of resistance in the city's shopping malls and metro stations, Wilfred sets out to make a film about walking as a way of revealing the original face of Sha Tin, their neighbourhood community, in a time of danger.

DIGITAL WALKING
This section considers how the pandemic has forced us to approach urban walking in ways which extend into the digital

sphere of online dialogue and [screen-sharing]. Online walking has allowed for a connection in the *here and now* and enabled a mode of communication via the Zoom platform, that is conducive to a dialogic exchange of experiences, attitudes and preoccupations.

In *Isolated Together*, Anna Ådahl explores how, as a result of the pandemic, a socially distanced choreography became inscribed into the daily habits of people living in Stockholm; a new normalcy of collective behaviours which for many was hard to accept. Ådahl considers how those around her quickly adapted to a new situation; how digital lives intensified to allow for continuous work modes and communication while at the same time being isolated and under stress. Ådahl points out that even when we are connected, we are atomised online. To think of the pandemic as a temporary phenomenon, even if its existence has changed parts of our lives forever, gives hope as our urban and social life is not built or sustainable according to the social behaviours that were determined by the virus. For coming pandemics and climate change, Ådahl argues that we need to rethink our cities.

In *Traversing the New Byzantium: How Los Angeles was Remade by a Changing Economy*, Norman Klein takes us on a helicopter ride across the LA basin to ask: what precisely is a crossroads city, in broader historical terms, as a trend that will last generations? We understand crossroads implies multi-ethnic, usually due to trade patterns and migration; often across continents. Crossroads means a relative independence, a new sovereignty—a New Byzantium. LA's version of Byzantium is overwhelmed by contradictions that would have been unthinkable fifty years ago. Crossroads implies a freeport within a neo-mercantilist globalisation, crenellated, like its many canyons; an archipelago of tiny neighbourhoods—a freeport, the eastern capital of the Pacific, a northerly haven for Latin America. Meanwhile, its public sector must confront failing schools, a patchwork health care system, and a gig economy. Crossroads cities are layered more than simply vertical. The future of LA is like a deep mapping project, a MultiPlan of realities.

Ryan Bishop and AbdouMaliq Simone's text begins with a consideration of the preposition 'in' with regard to walking in cities during lockdown and engaging with tele-technologies reliant upon our collective exoskeletal, planetary ring of telecom satellites, modes of data generation and sensing the earth as a planet. Where and what is 'in' spatially, experientially and noetically in such a situation? The essay draws from an MCI commercial from the 1990s (which makes reference to the web by saying that information (and us) would no longer need to travel from here to there): '... there would be no more there; we would all only be here'. Through playing with the metaphysics of eliminating space (in relation to the internet, as articulated in the ad) and duration (with real-time tele-technologies), but looping back to the 1990s and, further, to the Cold War, our present is placed in a historically contextualised moment prefigured from the middle part of the twentieth century. All of this forms a context from which to discuss infrastructures and logistics of urbanism across a planetary space and, thus, also, the varieties of technological sensing that define such space.

Prior to lockdown, Duncan Hay, in common with many academics, commuted between his home in the North West of England and his work in London. As with so many things which had been taken largely for granted, the pandemic brought this to a halt, and regular access to the capital was rendered unavailable. This has had concrete effects on the way the author has been able to conduct his research, which had been bound up with the material business of the capital. The *virtual* experience of London—something which had previously been a supplement to an embodied experience of the city— has come to supersede it. In *London Experienced at a Safe Distance*, Hay considers this shift from the embodied to the digital, asking: what scope do digital representations have for allowing the city and its history to be experienced as difference?

ART AND THE URBAN

Focusing on walking cities in lockdown allows us to rethink contemporary art practice, we consider how navigating and negotiating cities urgently requires new thinking around re-territorialisation, city-making, creativity and political awareness. In *Lockdown Art Practice: Twelve Months in Berlin* (March 2020 to March 2021), the Berlin-based artist Antonia Low describes the gradual changes in the urban environment and social behaviour that resulted from the pandemic. The text starts with a hasty return to desolate streets, empty shop shelves and Low's uncertain feeling of boredom. The diary continues with a close observation of the changing life of the city, the differing attitudes towards wearing masks, the novel experience of breathing fresh air in the city and the phenomenon of secret outdoor parties. As time passes, the claustrophobic tension in the streets palpably increases. When exhibitions are postponed or cancelled, Low starts exploring new formats in her art practice: lecture performances via online conference tools, streaming on social media platforms and outdoor venues for reaching out and connecting to others. Projects travel virtually.

The premise of Jaspar Joseph-Lester's photo essay *The Rise of the Infinity Pool* builds on Fredric Jameson's observation that the cultural products of our time reflect the broader logic of what he terms 'late capitalism'. The Sky Pool in Embassy Gardens, Nine Elms, appears, in almost every respect, to be the most advanced material expression of the ideological forces that constitute capitalism today. The old perceptual tricks that only partially disguised the inner workings of the system have been replaced with acrylic, water and sky. The unveiling of this spectacular feat of engineering in May 2021 (which followed the second wave of the pandemic) speaks of transformative developments in urban space that require a new understanding of political territories, physical boundaries and cultural critique.

In *Wanderlust Brixton*, Virginia Nimarkoh considers six 'sculptural' interventions/ installations in public space—public statues, street furniture, guerrilla/community gardens. They each highlight the big themes that touched Nimarkoh most during the pandemic—identity politics and the environment and where they intersect. Some offer a sense of hope for the future, others less so. Nimarkoh's various creative practices stem from walking alone, exploring the neighbourhood for inspiration, for connection, for the hell of it. During the pandemic, we were forced to reassess these freedoms as the home became a necessary place of safety from the virus. But Nimarkoh, as a woman and person of colour, the right to walk freely in public space became ever more contentious. Ultimately, every step taken, became a small act of defiance. Nick Ferguson's photo essay *Pandemic Landscape: Fieldnotes from London Heathrow* presents a personal account of Heathrow Airport under the first national lockdown in England, March–June 2020. Ferguson brings together photographs, planetary social thought and aesthetic reflections on the modern ruin. He asks: What is on view at the deserted airport, and what might be learned from it?

DIALOGUE AND COLLABORATION

In this section we focus on how we increasingly posit technology and communication as vital factors, specifically, through the possibility of local, technologically-unmediated networks and a rethinking of our relationship with the city. The potential for new ways of walking dialogically and collaboratively, brought into sharp relief under lockdown, is elaborated through empathy and participation, through the exchange of individual perspectives and the overcoming of western informed traditions.

At a time when restrictions were placed on international travel, friends and fellow artists Jasone Miranda-Bilbao and Ashish Sahoo combined text and image that juxtaposed Ashish's 'lived from within' experience of the lockdown in the neighbourhood of Chhatarpur, Delhi with Jasone's enforced temporary exile in London. *A COVID-19 Crisis: From a Delhi Perspective and a Half Way between London and Delhi* explores the idea that the time-space distance between Delhi and London compensated for the dislocation created by the pandemic and generated a third space for sharing knowledge and supporting each other. The images work as evidence of the abstraction of reality that took hold of the situation and which inspired them to imagine new projects and collaborations in a post-pandemic future.

In *Swimming in Venice*, Andreas Philippopoulos-Mihalopoulos and Katarina Rothfjell argue that Venice in lockdown was not Venice. While lockdown had a major impact on the cities in which it was enforced, Venice was a city that has been removed from its *essence*: a city whose heavily made-up face has been turned towards the global tourism for the past few centuries, and has increasingly relied almost absolutely on it, shedding all other aspects of a city, has found itself without a mirror. What happens to a city when there is no-one around to live in it? What happens to a celebrity when there is no one around to admire them? This is a guided tour of a city deprived of its *élan vital*, explored through performative walking and walking as performance, aimed at unveiling a deeply buried essence of Venice: an ontology of a city beyond humans, given to atmospheric elements.

Realised as a letter-form dialogue drawn from an online and IRL correspondence, and structured performatively as an inquiry around a legal glossary, *Court Circular SE11* is an account of the creation of a place-responsive public art walk in June 2021 between artist Corinne Noble and writer Simon King (collaboratively, Noble & King). Invited to create a traversal in relation to a decommissioned civil court building in south London as part of a group exhibition, the imposition of lockdown required the pair to resolve fundamental questions, including how to make socially engaged work in isolation from others, and whether working remotely and walking singly can be an effective substitute for walking together. As part of the post-lockdown group show in June 2021, the writing here featured as an installation piece that complemented the themes within the final walk.

NIGHT WALKING IN LOCKDOWN

This section is a meditation on night walks in London and Melbourne during the COVID-19 lockdowns. The texts explore how night walks are compromised by context and the (evolutionary) history of the body but remain unique, creative and distinct. At a time when night walking has provided a release from lockdown rules and regulations, this section offers political and provocative insights into the way that global cities and the structures that lurk in the shadows become more visible at night.

Walking at night in his South West London neighbourhood, Jonathan Skinner examines through careful reflection and distillation, the chaos of the inner monologue crowding in on the walker as they pursue the ostensibly simple action of putting one foot in front of the other. The suggestion is that no two walks are the same whether it be external gait, or internal conversation with the self interrupted by reactions to external stimuli. More explicitly, *Meditations on a Night Walk* engages with the superficial visual stereotypes of walking projected upon subjects as place-making dispositions of the body, illustrations of an urban or peasant habitus, and examples of allegedly socially-sedimented practices in the body. The night walks are compromised by context and the (evolutionary) history of the body but remain unique, creative and distinct.

On the night of 25 January, 2021 a walk through the Accor-owned Mantra Bell City Hotel, Melbourne was shared live on Zoom to an international community who, via a split screen, could also see footage from past walks at the Hotel—secret investigations—undertaken since October 2020.

In *Melbourne: Mantra Bell City Hotel*, Jacqueline Felstead gives an account of furtive walking, within a constrained allowable travel radius during the COVID-19 lockdown. The walk took place in response to the indefinite detention of approximately 60 refugees on the Hotel's third floor for over a year. This essay investigates the mechanics of refugee detention for a functioning private hotel, while virtually and communally skirting its periphery in the dark.

Samuel Jones' design of *Walking in Cities: Navigating Post-Pandemic Environments* embodies the notion of walking 'in' digital spheres, screen-based mediascapes and mental spaces. The repeated use of the line, that at first glance appears pixelated, is simultaneously shown to be composed of smooth vectors. The play on perception, scale and proximity is also demonstrative of how, under the circumstances of a pandemic, we became aware of the more subtle and often overlooked realities of our surroundings.

Jaspar Joseph-Lester
Ahuvia Kahane
Simon King
Esther Leslie

ENDNOTE

[1] As the world went into lockdown due to COVID-19, Jaspar Joseph-Lester and Simon King organised a series of international city walks in a virtual sphere. The group walks took place in Berlin, Cape Town, Stockholm, Toronto, the Marshall Islands, Hong Kong, Santiago, San Francisco and Los Angeles. In each city, we saw how the pandemic had changed the way artists engage with public space and how this new relationship with the city had impacted on their practice. See Walking Cities: In Lockdown (YouTube channel): https://www.youtube.com/channel/UChp00VbIiwCv3IiA6BkXmCw

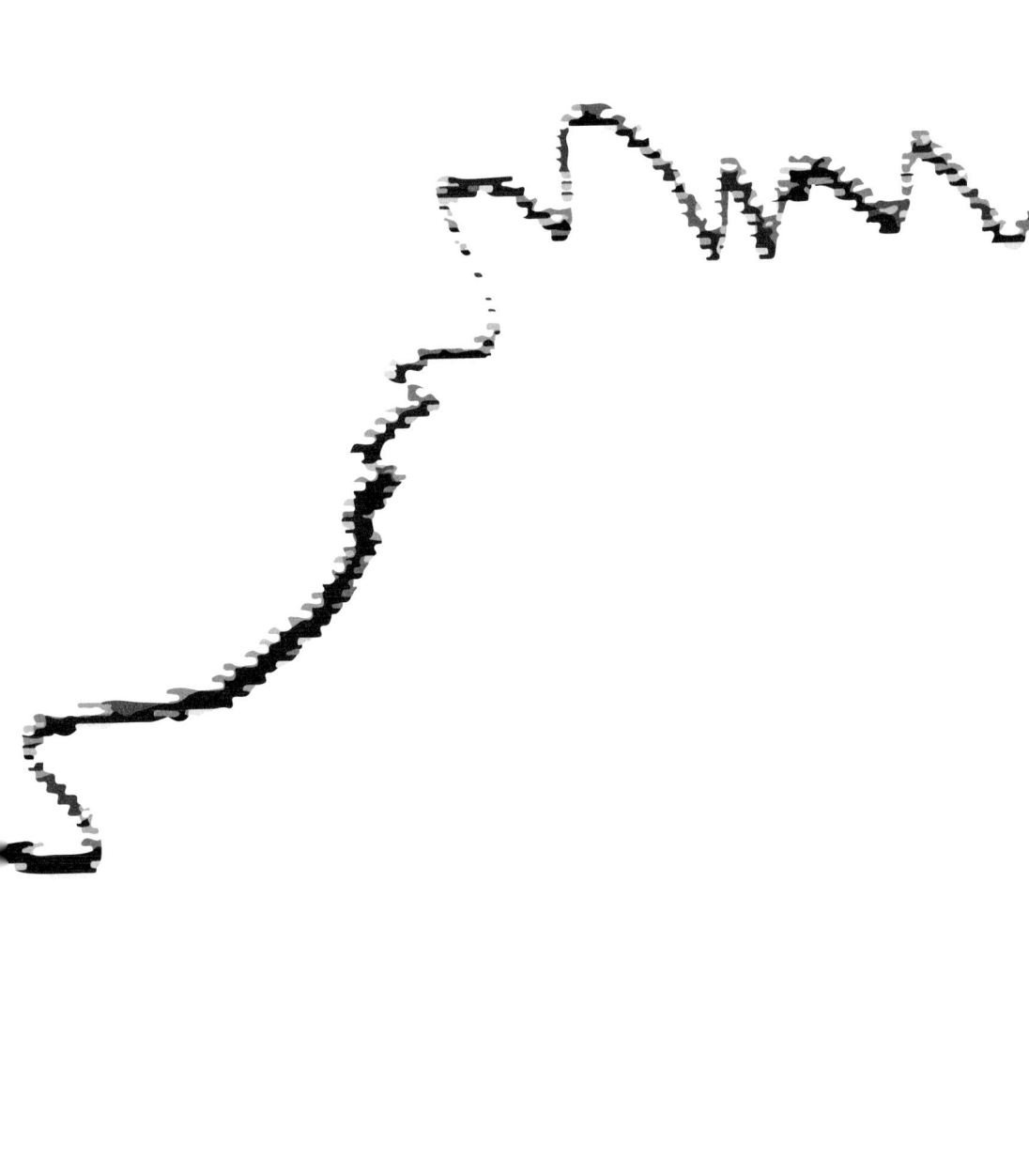

Politics
of Space

Development and Standstill:

Pandemic Energies in Somers Town

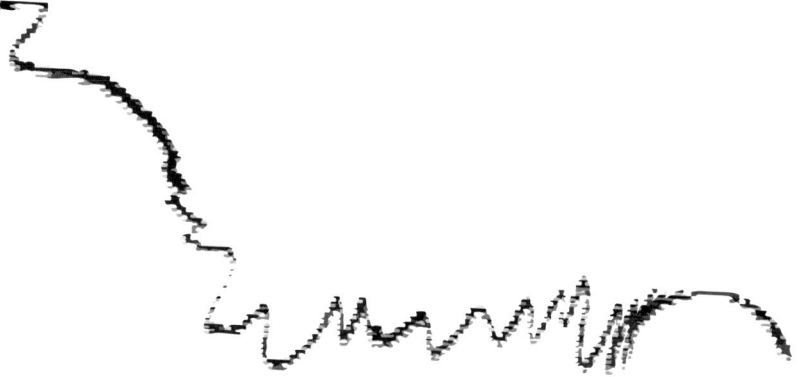

ESTHER LESLIE

DEVELOPMENTS

In *Walking Cities: London* (Joseph-Lester et al., 2020), I explored a history of squatting in my local area, in two periods when it lay in virtual abandonment, the early 1970s and the mid 1980s. In what follows, I return to those same streets in the present, in lockdown and during the pandemic. While the streets are quiet, the idea of the streets has not been. Across this period there have been lively debates about locality, the fifteen-minute city and revitalising a dying shopping street and its market, a main thoroughfare through an area that is in the top fifteen percent on the UK deprivation index. While there is liveliness of concept, in the face of deserted streets – where only Pinners café, with its lucky ability to use the broadness of what was once a grandly conceived street, draws in customers – there is also another business that has not ceased and has, in fact, ramped up over the past months. Development has been brutal during 2020. In this small area, demolition and building has occurred at 42 Phoenix Road for a large complex of student flats, on the main park, for a twenty-seven- storey 'luxury' tower block. There are consultations going on for the half a billion pounds commercially oriented British Library extension – and the new Moorfields hospital adjoins the area. My essay draws attention to the multiple developments that are reshaping the area, making it available to the 'Knowledge Quarter', a combination of educational institutions, for profit journals, biotech startups, Google and other platform capitalists and local councils. Somers Town is increasingly bound in to the adjoining private development at King's Cross. That new area of London is accessible by a bridge named Somers Town Bridge–in the first lockdown, it was locked, barring access between the two areas, and reminding us of the fact that Argent's development was conceived of as gated. What military-style management is afforded to privatised city managers? What seepages come from them? What is exceptional in these times, but also becoming a 'new normal', as the odious phrase puts it?

MADE OF...

'Made of King's Cross'. What does it mean to state that
a luxury development is made of somewhere? And what
does it mean when that somewhere it claims to be made of
is not the place where it is? What does it mean to take the
name of a part of town and displace it, let it land in another
area? It means real estate. It means the state of the real.
It means that the other place, a quarter of a mile east, is
now a brand – King's Cross, The King's Cross Estate, N1C.
And the place whose earth is being churned up to provide
the foundations for an alien structure, a luxury tower block
that ranges 28 storey above all the other homes, and each
selling off plan, 5 years in advance for a couple of million
pounds, is a place that is not a brand, has no buzz in its
consonants, no extra added value. It will be on the map,
perhaps, only once the tower is built, but it will go under
the cover of another name.

The JCBs stir up the earth of the park. The operations
take place behind thick hoardings that, along with the
building's claim to be 'Made of King's Cross', advertise
aspirational luxury living in the centre of London, in a block
unimaginatively named 'Grand Central Apartment'. The park
is eaten up by the new development. The council insists there
will be no net loss of green space, once it is all finished, for
they will introduce green elements in boxes and along walls,
but the locals know, unlike the park where they could play,
relax, deal drugs, or where the homeless could camp, the
new 'greenings' are not for them, but for the passengers
who move between Euston and St Pancras, wheeling their
suitcases, sipping their coffees.

There are few wheeled cases under lockdown. The streets
are empty, have been empty for much of the year of the plague.
The Somers Towners go to the last remaining stragglers
of the market on a Friday, on Chalton Street, and some of
the older people meet for chips and tea on the wide avenue
outside the Pinner Cafe built into the fabric of Levita House.

Levita House is part of the Grade II listed Ossulston Estate, a dilapidated but striking council housing estate from the 1920s, one flat of which is marketed right now at a sizeable price by an upmarket estate agent and logged as located in Marylebone.

Marylebone, King's Cross – anywhere but here. Indeed here, Somers Towners have worried about their continuing presence on the map – their own and that of the bricks and mortar that has mouldered here awhile. Without a name, it is easier to eradicate a place. The last years in this area have seen many broken promises, shifting goalposts, the trauma of demolition and closure, all this fuelling an increasing sense that the people of Somers Town are in the way of something much bigger, better and shinier. People joke, heavy heartedly, that the area is being renamed East Euston, King's Cross West, or, as the venture capitalist hub, Local Globe, which took over the old trade union building on Phoenix Road, put it, 'a new Palo Alto'. Local Globe, adjacent to the new twenty-plus storey sky-stealer block, with sixty-eight private flats, inhabits a blue building with a cotton-cloud ceiling with rainbow chairs on yellow flooring. From here, they dream up, through mirrored windows, a prospective Silicon Valley on the spot of a once hustling, unregulated market called The Brill. This club for free marketeers designates itself a hub for venture capitalists. Here they incubate dreams of pixels and Clouds. Another Silicon Valley here, at the heart of the Knowledge Quarter (another branding of the local environment). The local knowledge economy began with the British Library (ejected from Bloomsbury) and was joined by the Francis Crick Institute, a biomedical research centre. Soon it will be joined by the massive, commercially oriented Alan Turing Institute, which goes under cover of the British Library. Along one street amasses a weighty collation of brain power. What shadows do these cast across the deprivation that is its neighbourhood? What leaks out? What is walled out? What projects are worked on in this environment – and what mysteries are to be solved? Those long stuck here watch on as land is claimed and eaten up by HS2, Crossrail, The Crick, the British Library, UCL, Moorfields. So many institutions, chip away at the centrally placed area. It feels as if a new clearance is underway, as the looming luxe-tower block at Brill Place consumes even more of the insufficient green space of the gardenless families, as the new 'flat whiters' surge through the green trails of the estates, an embodiment of the networks they run for themselves. And those who dream of pixels bring all too material pollution into being – LocalGlobe brought Cazoo to Chalton Street in Somers Town and found venture capitalists to fund their online used car dealing business. Cazoo became, in 2020, during the pandemic, the fastest-ever British company to date to become a unicorn, a billion-dollar company. Here, in Somers Town, of all places, where hardly anyone has a car and where the streets are empty, because nothing is supposed to be happening.

BUSY NOT BUSY
Some incredible wealth has been amassed while everything was supposed to be on hold – on hold the little shop selling Pastéis de Nata, on hold the cheese shop and the July festival, and all the after school clubs. Busy only the food banks. But what is most tangible – because assets and shares and profits are not visible – is the development, which should be named as its opposite: destruction. Number 42 Phoenix Road, a structure that has sat on the corner from 1931 – Pevsner noted its canted oriels with swept roofs and arched windows – was pulled down in August 2020. It began existence as a nursery for 'fatherless children', as if any of us were, as such. It was one of a plethora of reformist institutions in Somers Town that targeted families, childcare, maternity and welfare services, to alleviate the miseries of poverty for the many thousands who were crammed in here. In more recent years, it was Hopscotch, a project initiated by Save the

Children to support Bangladeshi women who had come, with their children, to join husbands in the UK. Even later, it hosted a tutoring service, with a makeshift prayer room in the basement, selling the chance of better GCSE grades to those determined that their children were able to get somewhere else. 42 Phoenix Road was demolished to make way for a new building for children without parents, that is to say, for student accommodation. Another corner disappeared. Somers Town is used to it. Everywhere has layers. Everywhere develops and regresses and develops again. Before the day nursery, the corner was occupied by Evesham Buildings, where the main landlord and investor in Somers Town, Jacob Leroux, lived, in 1791, and William Godwin, in 1797. On the other side of Phoenix Road, the fifteen sided Polygon, built as the jewel of a speculative development in the 1780s, was replaced by another building that took the name Polygon in 1894. These dwellings, four barrack-like blocks, were erected by the Midland Railway, as recompense for the huge loss of homes brought about by construction, in 1887, of its station and goods yards, the Midland Railway Somers Town Goods Depot at St Pancras. Midland Railway employees lived here and the caretakers sported the Midland Railway's livery on their uniforms. That building lasted until the 1970s, a period through which Somers Town was tarnished by the soot of the neighbouring railway termini. The second Polygon was replaced by the building that stands there today: Oakshott Court, first designed by S.A.G. Cook, the Borough Architect, and Peter Tábori, with working drawings by Roman Haller, and, when Haller's practice folded, James Gowan. Oakshott Court, with its strata of pedestrian streets in the sky, is constructed such that the maximum hours of daylight enters each flat, and thus, each dweller, each council tenant might borrow every day a portion of the skies, might cast an eye into the environment, and fancy themselves in a greater world than this bounded enclave. Here and elsewhere. Development again, now, under lockdown, in the pandemic of 2020–21. But this time, the developmental energies were directed more outwards, to privatised populations, to new enclosures for private accumulation.

GATES

In the early days of the pandemic, terrified of the air and its particles of poisons, I resolved to set out only rarely for food and to walk along the canal as that had fewer pedestrians than the high road. Once there, I could climb the steps to the wide expanse of Granary Square, its fountains stilled. I could take my place in a long, well-policed queue to get into the large and overpriced supermarket and buy food for two weeks. I set out one day, crossed through the graveyard and turned to the right, to cross the bridge that had recently appeared there. Strangely, it does use the Somers Town name. It was built to connect this back road, which runs between the railway line and the canal, and is soon to be redeveloped, to Argent's development at King's Cross. The sixty-seven acre King's Cross Estate, the new NC1, is a vast brownfield site development and home to a hub of digital and platform capitalism. It has been designed for leisure, shopping, learning, working and exclusive living amongst private security guards who patrol Pancras Square, Granary Square, Lewis Cubitt Park and Gasholder Park. When their eyes are averted, extensive monitoring is operated by CCTV. I approached the bridge and saw its gate (what bridges have gates?) was locked. Access to the development was cut off, at least from this route, over the Somers Town bridge. Another route could be scrambled, much further down the road and via the new steps at the Co-op, where the student housing is located. But it felt as if the way was blocked specifically to those who might be using this route, the low-income undesirables. It was a sudden reminder of the capricious largesse that determines our access to what are effectively gated communities, when conditional on Section 106 agreements and their clauses, such as entitling the 'Developer or any person, firm or other body authorised by the Developer' 'to prevent public access to the Development Estate Realm Areas and in such a manner so as to prevent the Development Estate Realm Areas from becoming public highway by prescription'. Only the existence of the canal as public highway compromises that. The extensive security systems are an ever-watchful border that remedy the potential results of incursion. On such privatised estates, the rules are opaque and seemingly arbitrary – young people from Somers Town rarely go here, for if they do, just to sit amongst the boxed plantings, they say they get chased away. This is a city inside the city. It is an enclave, with an art school and an upmarket supermarket, simultaneously forces and signs of urban regeneration or gentrification.

RUNNING

Lockdown changed my relationship to the streets. For a while, at the start of the confinement, I started running – to move through them quickly, heeding government admonishments about exercise. To do something. Before that, I never used to run. I hate running. I hate being seen running. Running makes me exhausted and overheated and I get bored as I run. I had often seen a banner advertising the Somers Town Striders and wondered if it would be agony or fun to join them, to run as a band, some fit, some struggling, through the streets. I had read too of the fitter group of runners who combine their exercise with delivering medicines to those who are housebound. Idly I had wondered if that could make me feel like running was useful, because it had a purpose. But I never pursued these things, never had the will to, or the time. But, when everything was turned upside down in the lockdown of 2020, which came from nowhere and transformed work into home and school into home-school and a banal shopping trip into an exposure to risk that had to be carried on from behind a mask. For a while, the only way of being outside with the sun on one's face and wind in one's hair, was to run. So I ran.

Every morning, with my daughter, for around 15 minutes through the streets of Somers Town, we ran. At first we would run three times around the blocks on Crowndale Road, where we live. No-one else was around. There were next to no cars on the road. The 214 bus passed by with a single passenger now and again. I took in the details, the rosemary bushes near Godwin Court, the mural on the wall by the slip road off the estate, the fact that the launderette was open only every other day. There was a woman who would often stand outside it, her face masked, as so many are masked. I wondered why she was so often there. One day I saw her slip inside a block of flats and crouch on the floor, observing Ramadan. I watched as the contents of the newly arrived outside-library – neatly placed at the top of a set of steps on Godwin Court, which led nowhere – as it changed its assortment of books. I passed the bins, three times a day, where I once saw some discarded suitcases, old heavy brown ones from the 1960s or 1970s that had covered some distance, were plastered with labels and had the words 'From Delhi' written on them. Sometimes, as we ran along the back path behind the school, we would have to wait for someone else to pass through the narrow gates that stop cyclists tearing through. I worried about being in the slipstreams of others' breath – the news was contradictory, information changed each day – 2 metres, 1.5, airborne, only in coughs, wash your surfaces, disinfect your shopping, wash hands, for 20, for 30 seconds, masks protect you, protect those around you, do nothing. After a few days, a man appeared, tucked away in the back corner of our estate's communal garden. He stood by the rose bush with its vivid pink blooms, and began to grow some marrows in a large pot. We smiled at each other as we ran by, each alone, each doing something we had not done before.

Eventually we grew bored of the ritual of running three times around the estate and so we ventured off into the streets behind. Somers Town was now our running ground.

The lockdown meant the streets were empty. There were no people, no cars. Or there were people, but they were invisible, sheltered, as so many sheltered, as much as we could inside our homes, unless compelled to go out to work or to care for others. The streets were free for lumbering runners and shy cats. Each day we tried to run a different route – to traverse the roads, which I have known for 25 years and my daughter for 14, in ways we had not done before. And anyway, how we saw things was different now. The empty streets made our attention turn to the emerging signs of summer, the colour of cars, the differing paving stones, a dead pigeon, its body damaged by one of the cats, a man sleeping in the now little used bus stop, some tatty bunting hanging off a lamppost. Soon, what emerged into visibility, as we sought new routes around the small network of streets, were the barriers, the places that were closed, inaccessible: Polygon Open Space playground, the Cock Tavern, Fine Tutors at no 42 Phoenix Road. And then, in the quest for new routes, surprising elements to brighten up our journeys, we realised that there were open gateways onto the estates, that we could gently run through the narrow alleys and stairways of Oakeshott Court, through the lush vegetation of Coopers Lane, through parts of the Sidney Estate with the balconies that overlook courtyards which are strewn with tricycles and little tables, not used now, and we thought of all the sociable communal lives that have been lived here, in these beckoning enclaves, and were no longer.

CLOUDS

I stopped running, out of boredom with the routine. Sometimes, I walked the streets of Somers Town to get a little air. But the confines shrank down and hope dwindled. I saw fewer routes through and more and more destruction. I retreated behind a screen. My clouds were more often the ones we upload into and download from. As the COVID-19 pandemic affected life on the planet, it was cloud infrastructure, with its switches, routers, firewalls, load balancers, storage arrays, backup devices, servers, hypervisors, that swelled, becoming the means by which 'work from home', with its 'remote-work-model', was made possible, as well as home education, online shopping, social meet-ups via Zoom and Google Hangouts and everything else. And on my sky, through my window, not just my screen, the tangible results of this commitment to concrete immateriality loomed into view, as a massive new building for Google UK is built in King's Cross, designed for 7,000 employees, should they be tempted back into the city, after the public health crisis. It is a real sky-stealer, from my low-point perspective, even if it is proclaimed widely as low-rise (with only eleven storeys), as long as the sky-piercing Shard, but horizontal. There will be clouds above it, just as there always are on Google's own images of the outsides of its data centres.[1] Only a lift shaft has been built so far in late 2020 and that alone already blots out the sun. The building is located here to be proximate to Alphabet's DeepMind, another eleven storeys and Facebook's three buildings of up to twelve storeys. Here, where there were once warehouses and markets, a dense cloud covering gathers. The vagueness of the Cloud and its institutions is countermanded by the concretion of its infrastructure. Our highways turn virtual. It is safer, or rather, it is all about security.

POTEMKIN CITIES

The place round here is crammed with virtual cities and towns – front organisations that promote the city or the quarter as brand on social media: Euston Town, Camden Alive, Coal Drops Yard, Camden Town Unlimited, Camden Highline, Visit King's Cross, King's Cross, Gasholder, KXStPancrasBP, Urban Partners, King's Cross N1C, Knowledge Quarter, Love Camden and more and more. City quarters as little businesses, burgeoning brands – self-promoters. Value enhancements through social media engagement. The streets are dead, except for the sounds of diggers and wrecking balls. But the webways are busy, promoting, branding, chattering.

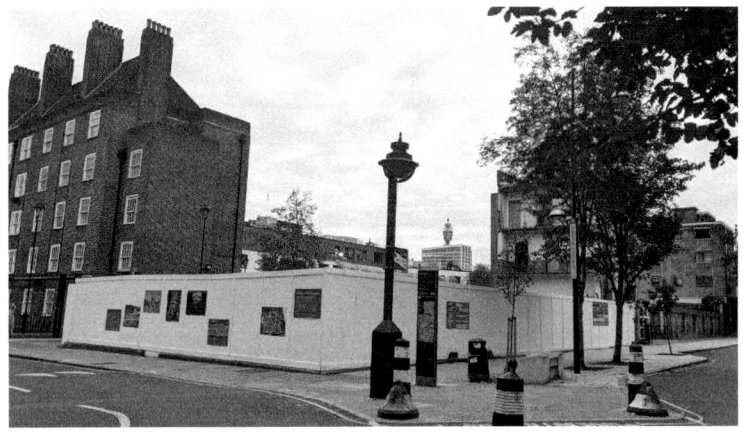

I try to turn my attention elsewhere. While the streets are quiet, the idea of the streets has not been. Across this period, amongst little pockets of disgruntled Somers Town people, there have been debates about locality, about the death of the main street and how it could be revitalised, but not by chain stores and top-down institutions. There have been discussions of the 'fifteen-minute city' idea for revitalising a dying shopping street and its market, a main thoroughfare through an area that is in the top 15% on the UK deprivation index. Can these notions, promoted by councils but carried out on the terms of institutions and quangos – with their blaring social media presence – be combined with some sort of democratic, community-led, from below governance of public space? There is consultation fatigue in Somers Town – endless questionnaires and webinars that leave nothing tangible – from HS2 and Crossrail 2 and the British Library Extension and the new Moorfields and the Community Investment Plan and more.

Somers Town is crammed with stories, but the material traces are disappearing and it is as if the time when we were shut away, kept under lockdown, business as usual in unusual times took off. The buildings crumble in front of us. HS2 and Crossrail will cut under and through this place, here where every type of social housing and various types of experimental living have occurred, in this patch where reformers and meddlers have looked out on the poor, in this enclave where artists and fabulists have flourished, where communities have experienced joy and tension, as well as indifference, in this area that threatens to become just a passageway between two railway termini, or a cleft, a new Silicon Valley Those of us still clinging on here ask, why not a space for us, a room of our own, a museum, a history room, a memory shop, a reminiscence cafe; a shelter to gather up what is threatened, what has no place, what stories can be found, and to use the past as stimulus for a better future, one not frequently predicated on forgetting?

When the hoardings appeared around the luxury tower block development site, and access to the park was restricted, there was anger. In August 2020, HS2 protesters had just set up camp at Euston, in protest at the removal of a park and trees to provide room for a temporary car park in front of the station. Links were made. One of them climbed one of our trees, whose days were numbered, and unfurled a banner: 'Our Trees Not Your Profit'. It was swiftly removed. When the slick marketing images, 'Made of King's Cross' appeared there, we screamed and growled and then took practical steps to reclaim something in streets that had not only been mis-located, but was also being sold as locations for those with many millions, who likely would barely live here. We, some local people, plastered other hoardings along the road with photos of local people, holding images of all that has been lost here, not just during lockdown, but ever more rapidly through it. Emulating the font used by the marketeers, we named the exhibition 'Made of Somers Town'.

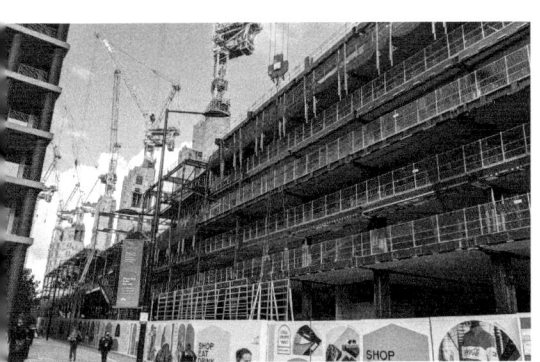

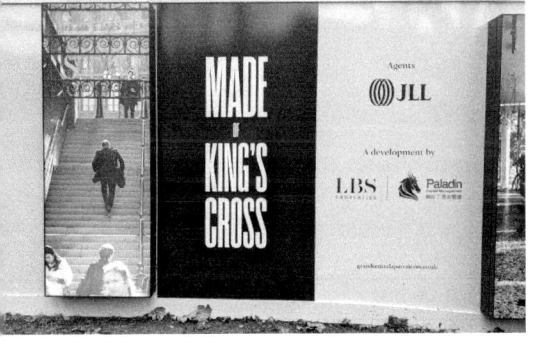

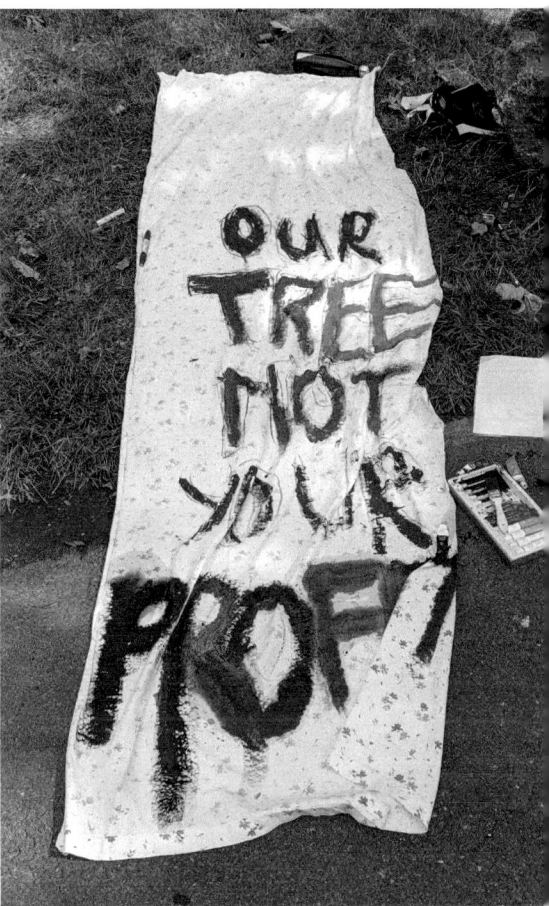

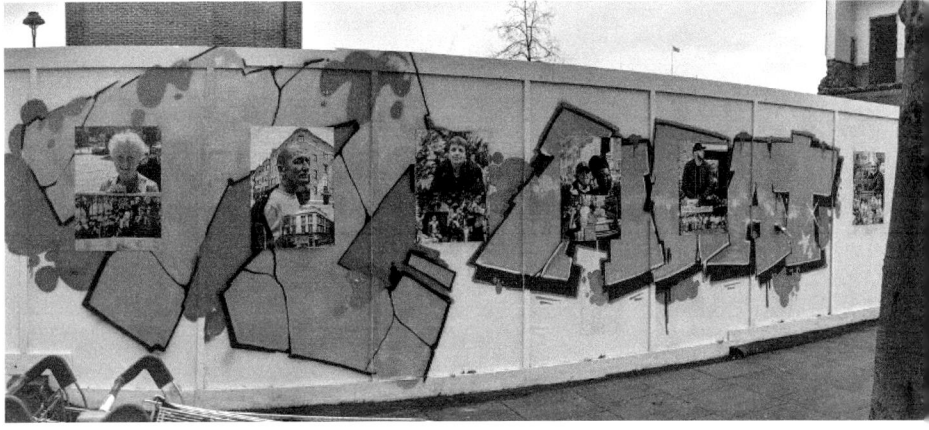

Political
Geometries

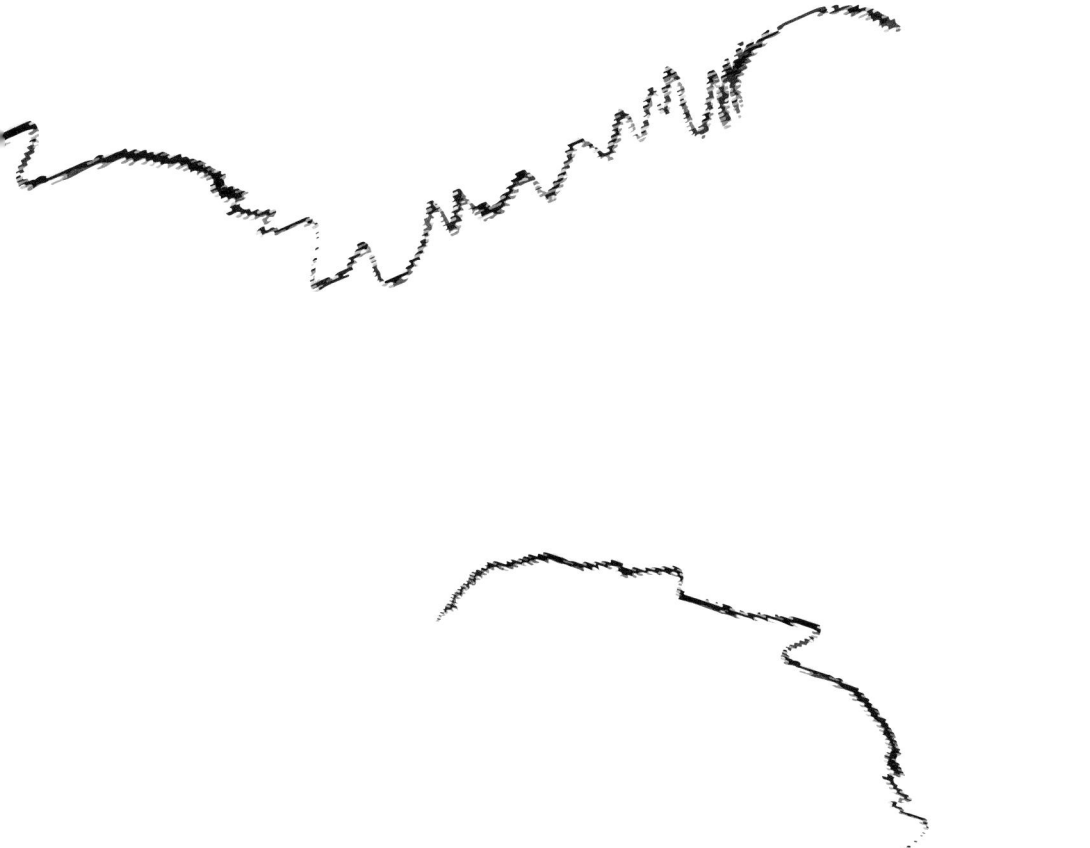

AHUVIA KAHANE
WITH AN ENVOI BY FIACHRA MAC GÓRÁIN

Now let us make the fantastic supposition that
Rome were not a human dwelling-place, but a
mental entity with just as long and varied a past
history: that is, in which nothing once constructed
had perished, and all the earlier stages of
development had survived alongside the latest. ...

... There is clearly no object in spinning this fantasy
further; it leads to the inconceivable, or even
to absurdities. If we try to represent historical
sequence in spatial terms, it can only be done
by juxtaposition in space; the same space will not
hold two contents. Our attempt seems like an
idle game; it has only one justification; it shows
us how far away from mastering the idiosyncrasies
of mental life we are by treating them in terms
of visual representation.
        S. Freud, *Civilization and Its Discontents*

1. CENTENARY WALKS

On the north bank of the River Liffey, stands a stately eighteenth
century neoclassical building known as the Custom House.
Commissioned by John Beresford, the British Commissioner
of Revenue in Ireland, it was completed in 1791, with some
protestations from the burghers of Dublin and Dublin
Corporation who at first tried to disrupt its construction.
The Custom House was built in perfect geometrical symmetry,
decorated with emblems of Ireland's rivers, and was once
the seat of the Her Majesty's Custom Office and later the centre
of the British Local Government in Dublin.

During the Irish War of Independence, on 25 May 1921,
at about 1:10 pm or shortly afterwards, the Custom
House was set alight. It burned for five days. The decorated
interiors were completely destroyed. The building's dome

collapsed. An exterior shell remained. Inside, fire consumed three hundred years of Irish historical records.[1]

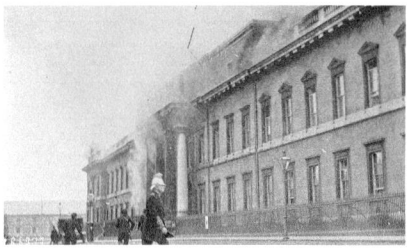

In 1928, the Custom House was restored by the Irish Free State. The dome was rebuilt, albeit using Irish Ardbraccan limestone (like the stone of Leinster House, formerly the home of the Duke of Leinster and since 1922 the home of the Irish Parliament) rather than the original English Dorset stone.[2]

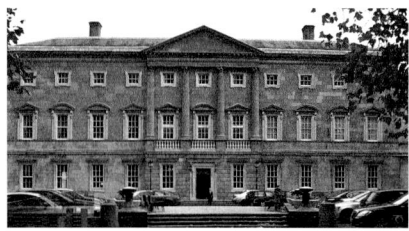

Today, the Custom House holds the Republic of Ireland's Department of Housing, Local Government and Heritage.[3]

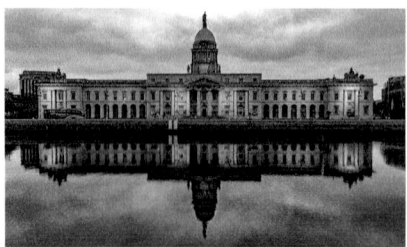

Not far from the Custom House, on the north bank of the Liffey stands another stately neoclassical building known as the Four Courts. Completed in 1792, it housed the four British high courts in Ireland.[4]

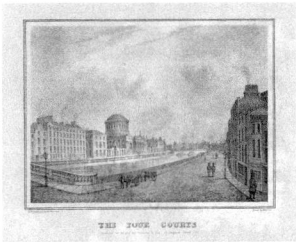

During the Irish Civil War, on 30 June 1922, either at 11:30 am or perhaps at 2:15 pm, one, or perhaps three large explosions destroyed the building, which also held the Irish Public Record Office, along with, inside, almost seven hundred years of Irish historical documents.[5]

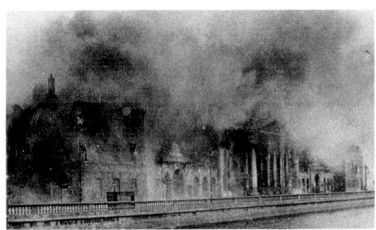

The Four Courts was rebuilt in 1930, although the design of most of its ornate insides is lost to oblivion. The building is now home to the Supreme Court of the Republic of Ireland, the Court of Appeal, the High Court and the Dublin Circuit Court.[6]

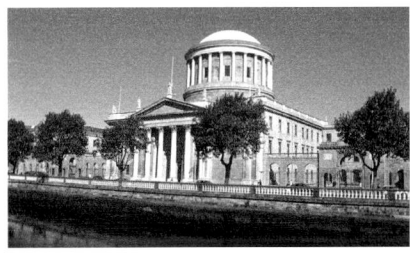

2. WE WALK, OR STAY INDOORS… WE SEE THE LIVING AND THE DEAD

The matrix of these images and the space they occupy brings together the linear geometries of a neoclassical frieze, a column, a peristyle and an architrave, the fractals of smoke, flame, ash, gunpowder, bone and blood, toruses and Möbius strips of history and time. This matrix holds a Tax Office and a Visitor Centre, a Duke's private Home and two Houses of the Irish *Oireachtas*, four of the King's Courts and four of the Republic's Courts.

What's more, as Freud knew well, our attempts to represent this matrix in spatial terms, whether in Rome or in London, in Dublin or elsewhere, are *not an idle game*. Yet *pace* Freud, the same space, indeed the same visual representation, *can* and *does* 'hold many contents'. Our attempts to represent historical sequence in spatial terms, whether in Rome or London or in Dublin, or elsewhere, whether walking or staying in the confines of our room, whether we roam freely or are constrained by public lockdown orders, are part of the real, the *non dit* we observe, for example, when walking along the pathways of the Tiber or the Thames, or the Liffey, or when we are not walking at all, when we look at pictures or are reading a book in the Long Room in Trinity College Dublin, which today is visited by many, but which in lockdown stood empty and unobserved but which, *pace* Freud, *secundum* Freud, is precisely a representation: not a picture of reality, but reality itself,[7]

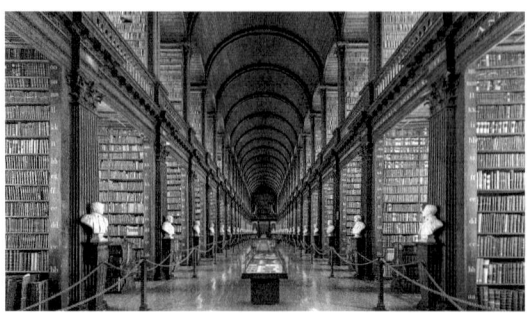

and likewise the dome of the old Reading Room in the British Museum,[8]

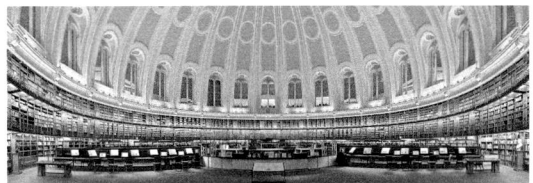

where Marx wrote *Das Kapital*, but which holds no books today, has no old leather Readers' seats, and is now a visitor centre and café, held together by its complex geodesic geometry.[9]

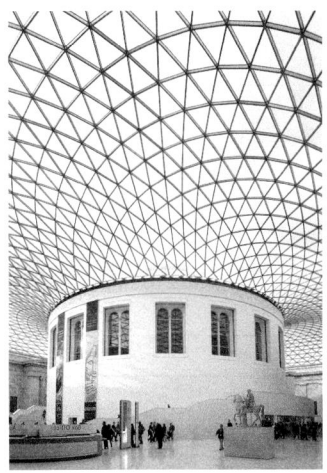

These real spaces hold many *contents*. Their geometry is traced by spectres of the living and the dead, and of the futures to come.

Dubliners, and those who have never been to Dublin, know this well. As James Joyce writes:

"The morning was still dark. A dull yellow light brooded over the houses and the river; and the sky seemed to be descending. It was slushy underfoot; and only streaks and patches of snow lay on the roofs, on the parapets of the quay and on the area railings. The lamps were still burning redly in the murky air and, across the river, the palace of the Four Courts stood out menacingly against the heavy sky".

We walk, or stay indoors, and when we do, we see the living and the dead, redly, menacing ghosts of the past that make up the present, and joy, and love, like Gabriel Conroy in what is perhaps Dublin's most famous short story by Dublin's most famous Dubliner:

"His soul had approached that region where dwell the vast hosts of the dead. He was conscious of, but could not apprehend, their wayward and flickering existence. His own identity was fading out into a grey impalpable world: the solid world itself which these dead had one time reared and lived in was dissolving and dwindling".

Places we have seen and have not seen, open spaces and spaces in lockdown, interiors and exteriors, these are, in fact, spectres of time that we can see: "neo-classical" architecture, new images of classical antiquity, forcefully defended and/or blown to rubble by colonial powers, projecting and enforcing their claims to authority, and by forces of resistance seeking independence. The geometries of such places collapse and decay, align and defract in the course of political time. We see repositories of local government records carefully collected at the centre, brought to Dublin from country parishes over centuries of British rule, from places where we have never been, places that have witnessed the rise and fall of those who lived and died there and who agreed and disagreed about the "freedom to achieve freedom". We see these pasts right up to the present, in the present, right up to the rowdy stag and hen parties stumbling and sprawling late at night in the cobbled streets of Temple Bar, silenced and stopped by lockdown, by a pandemic, always political, even when they seek nothing but the good times of oblivion: political precisely because of time and the tension between what is allowed and what is not, between where one can go and where one cannot.

In Dublin, we can see (Joyce again) "a covey of gulls, storm petrels" as it "rises hungrily from Liffey slime with Banbury cakes in their beaks". We "can't hear with the waters of. The chittering waters of. Flittering bats, fieldmice bawk talk". "Ho!", we say, "Are you not gone ahome? What Thom Malone? Can't hear with bawk of bats, all thim liffeying waters of".

3. THE FUTURE TO COME

On such walks, mobile and stationary, the past, the present and the future-to-come rise and collapse, like digital tomographic images of the world that appear onscreen and recede. Such images are cut (in Greek, *temnô,* thus *tomo-graphy*) and sliced for diagnostic purposes. Yet "as soon as the image is replaced by a statement, the image is given a false appearance, and its most authentically visible characteristic, movement, is taken away from it", says Gilles Deleuze of cinema. This is the cinematic reality of the world, how we see reality as a political image, an image whose politics resides in its geometry.

The Irish Records Treasury in the Four Courts was destroyed in 1922.[10]

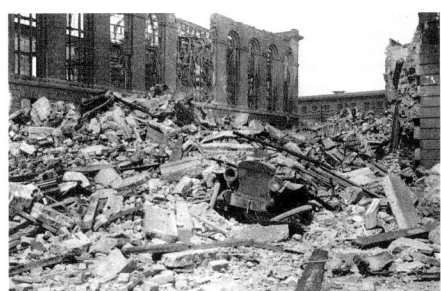

Today, we can see not a few of those reconstructed records,
painstakingly collected from copies around the word, set
in a digital inside space which opens up onscreen to reveal
floors, walls, ceilings, shelves and enclosed repositories,
moving forwards and backwards, wholly reversible, wholly
consonant with the order and the rubble of the past,[11]
in three-D ("D" for "digital") spaces online, observable
from wherever we are in the world, whenever we are,
without ever having to have been in Dublin, observable
even when we are confined to our closed indoor spaces,
locked-down.

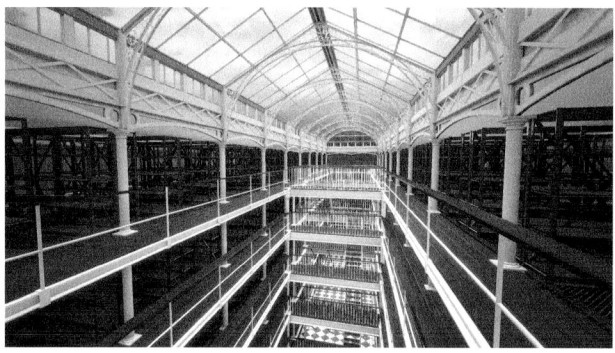

The substance of rubble, water, smoke and fire lies in the
reality of memory and affect, in fear and hope, in despair
and dream, in conflict and in reconciliation, in photographs
and paintings, in cinematic time (in the movement of images
whose stillness is false), in public records, in ledgers scrawled
in the parish priest's hand, in printed documents, in short
stories and novels, in flyers and notices, torn and discarded,
burnt to ashes or neatly shelved and stacked, or digitized
and ready for use. This substance is not a relation between
objects or between representations and reality or between
what we say and what we see, or between the intelligible
and the visible. Yet this substance can be observed in the
perfect geometric order of what is unequal to itself and
equal to the real.

Foucault, we recall, famously reminds us (and Deleuze and others assert), that

> … between the figure and the text we must admit a whole series of crisscrossings, or rather between the one and the other attacks are launched and arrows fly against the enemy target, campaigns designed to undermine and destroy, wounds and blows from the lance, a battle … images falling into the midst of words, verbal flashes crisscrossing drawings … discourse cutting into the form of things.

Such crisscrossing drawings are always there, always in time, always political, between the Custom House, and the Four Courts, and Leinster House, and the Liffey, in the history of the Irish struggle against British rule and the war between the proponents of the Anglo-Irish Treaty of 1921 (like Michael Collins, for example) and its opponents (perhaps like Éamon de Valera), in youthful photographs of Pádraic Pearse or of the General Post Office as it looks today[12]

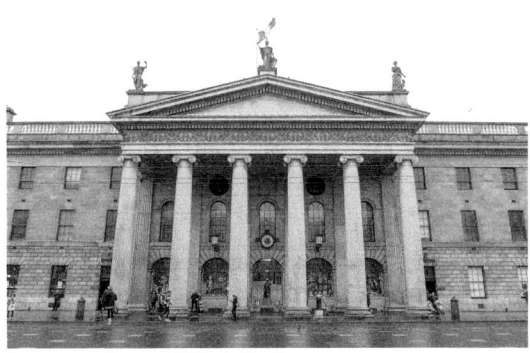

and Nelson's Pillar (the one in Dublin, not the Column in Trafalgar Square in London), which is not there anymore because it was destroyed by a blast in 1966, as these monuments looked after the Easter Rising,[13]

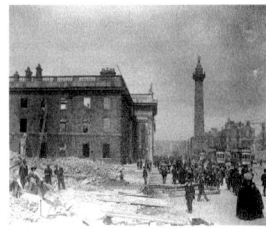 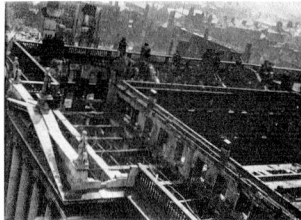 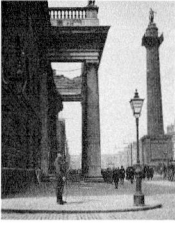

or the bare stone yard in Kilmainham Gaol in Dublin,
in which there was nothing to burn, because it was all made
of stone,[14]

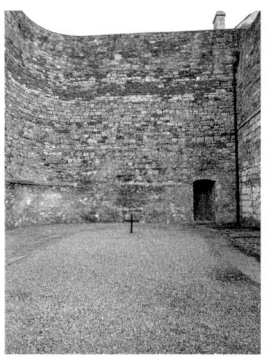

the place, that is, where Pearse and fifteen other leaders
of the Rising were executed by firing squad on orders from
General Maxwell, and which is now a Museum part of the
Office of Public Works,[15]

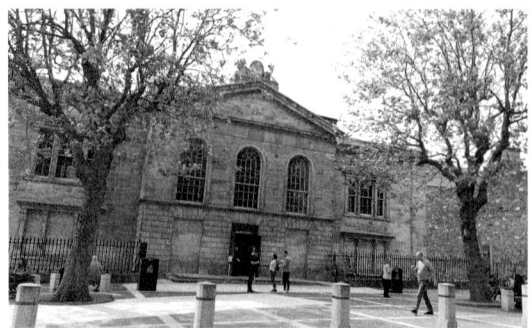

or the crossroads at Béal na Bláth, where Michael Collins died in 1922.[16]

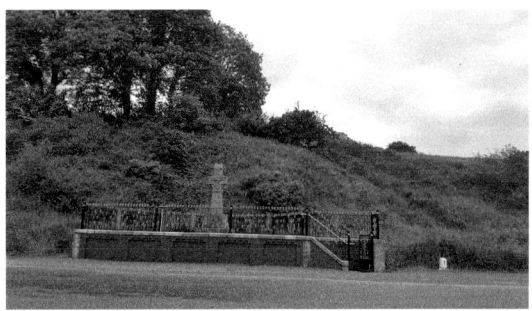

4. VECTORS, CURVES, AND FRACTALS

Attacks and campaigns, or "risings" and "fallings" (as Georg Simmel, writing on the ruin, for example, called them long ago), these are not *idle play*. They are the substance of time and are (to turn Derrida's famous phrase on its head) "the element of *visibility itself*". They reside in the many complex geometric *contents* of the world, in the political *form* of the world, its Cartesian axes and Newtonian curves, its fractals, topologies, entanglements, leaps and superpositions, its constant material movement, bound by the flow of the Tiber, and the Arno, and the Liffey, on the banks of which we walk and from which we are, in times of a pandemic, forced to stay away.

It is difficult to walk thought the dense urban landscapes of everything that has ever been constructed and has perished, the earlier and later stages of development, the sites where the very same building rises from the marshes by the Liffey (like the Custom House, for example) and decays, or goes up in flames or down in piles of rubble, and is in time rebuilt. And yet such landscapes, their materials and images, accrue, thrown up by storms, piling up at our feet in a heap (as Benjamin and others knew). These landscapes mark the geometric form of time, and history, and the real.

5. *L'ESCAMOTAGE PHILOLOGIQUE*

Some of us don't walk that much in any case. We are *philologists*. We look at the world, mostly, through its words, its language and perhaps through its thought, these days sometimes more frequently by force of global constraint.[17]

The geometry of words, language and thought is limitless, of course.

> There is not one language but a multiplicity, not a stable multiplicity but a permanent multiplication of languages,

as Werner Hamacher says. And he adds:

> The relation that the many languages within each individual language, and all individual languages, entertain to one another – their restrained inclination toward repetition, advocacy, contestation, supplementation – is philology. Philology is the continued extension of the elements of linguistic existence.

Philology is nothing more than an affinity with words and with the multiplicity of things in the world. It is the art of walking slowly through the space of thought.

Space itself (*khôra* in Greek, as, famously, in Plato's *Timaeus*), of course, and things in space, and representations of things in space are subject to the same geometry. They too incline towards "repetition, advocacy, contestation, supplementation". This isomorphism is no accident:

> Metaphysics is rooted in an implicit geometry
> which – whether we will or no – confers spatiality
> upon thought.

As Gaston Bachelard points out. Dublin's space reveals this to us even as we move through a city whose history has so often gone up in flames. Dublin's geometry, built and in ruins, digital, material, multiple, is the measure of politics, identity and truth.

6. REAL SPACE

Gaston Bachelard, and many of those he influenced, Foucault, Althusser, Bourdieu, Derrida, Latour, Daston and others, knew this geometry. In *The Poetics of Space,* he quoted the poem 'L'espace aux ombres' from Henri Michaux's collection *Nouvelles de d'etranger* (1952).

> *L'espace, mais vous ne pouvez concevoir, cet horrible en dedans en dehors qu'est le vrai espace.*
>
> *Certaines (ombres) surtout se bandant une dernière fois, font un effort désespéré pour "être dans leur seule unité." Mal leur en prend. J'en rencontrai une.*
>
> *Détruite par châtiment, elle n'était plus qu'un bruit, mais énorme.*
>
> *Un monde immense l'entendait encore, mais elle n'était plus, devenue seulement et uniquement un bruit, qui allait rouler encore des siècles mais destiné a s'éteindre complètement, comme si elle n'avait jamais été.*
>
> [Space, but you cannot even conceive the horrible inside-outside that real space is.

Certain (shades) especially, girding their loins one last time, make a desperate effort to "exist as a single unity". But they rue the day. I met one of them.

Destroyed by punishment, it was reduced to a noise, a thunderous noise.

An immense world still heard it, but it no longer existed, having become simply and solely a noise, which was to rumble on for centuries longer, but was fated to die out *completely,* as though it had never existed.]

'Shade-Haunted Space' (*News from Abroad,* 1952)

ENVOI: THE INFINITE VIEW
FIACHRA MAC GÓRÁIN

Well, perhaps what you see depends on where your gaze begins – and how it has been (in)formed. Georgian Dublin is impressive and monumental: it does indeed direct the mind to Anglo-Irish history and the struggle for freedom. In this respect, Dublin is more concentrated architecturally than Freud's Rome, for example, but in the imagination the concertina is infinitely extensible. In primary school, we learned about Viking and Norman Dublin (795, 1169, Diarmuid MacMurrough, Laurence O'Toole; my generation learned this. Do they still teach all this in primary schools?).[18]

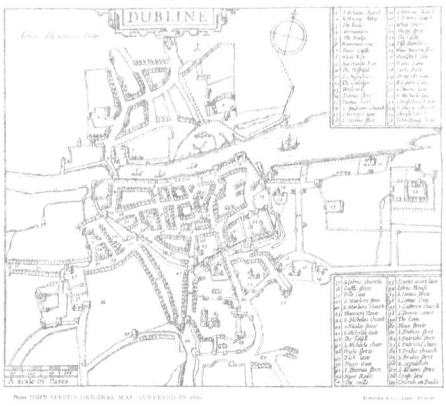

45

The point: it primed us to see certain things even before we were in the habit of walking in the city centre, shades from history, from even before the more pointed Anglo-Irish conflict of the long nineteenth century, and also the prehistory of that conflict. Some of us felt that Norman Dublin at the other end of Dame Street was the vital kernel of Dublin, more so than Trinity College and Georgian Dublin. (I exaggerate, but ...).

We also learned about the Celts, the Iron Age, the Tuatha Dé Danann, why Dublin has two names (Dubh Linn = black pool/marsh) and Baile Átha Cliath (town of the ford of hurdles), and Dublin was part of Leinster and only one of many counties and Leinster only one province in dialogue with all the others.

All these things are on Joyce's radar, and he takes refuge in them because as we know from stifling table-talk in *Portrait*, he wearied early of the nationalist discourses of Parnell and the Land War. The shadow of St Michan (which takes us from the Vikings to Handel's *Messiah*, with all the layers between and since) launches this exuberant run of catalogues:

> In Inisfail the fair there lies a land, the land of holy Michan. There rises a watchtower beheld of men afar. There sleep the mighty dead as in life they slept, warriors and princes of high renown. A pleasant land it is in sooth of murmuring waters, fishful streams where sport the gunnard, the plaice, the flounder, the mixed coarse fish generally and other denizens of the aqueous kingdom too numerous to be enumerated. In the mild breezes of the west and of the east the lofty trees wave in different directions their first class foliage, the wafty sycamore, the Lebanonian cedar, the exalted planetree, the eugenic eucalyptus and other ornaments of the

arboreal world with which that region is thoroughly well supplied. Lovely maidens sit in close proximity to the roots of the lovely trees singing the most lovely songs while they play with all kinds of lovely objects as for example golden ingots, silvery fishes, crans of herrings, drafts of eels, codlings, creels of fingerlings, purple seagems and playful insects and heroes voyage from afar to woo them, from Eblana to Slievemargy, the peerless princes of unfettered Munster and of Connacht the just and of smooth sleek Leinster and of Cruachan's land and of Armagh the splendid and of the noble district of Boyle, princes, the sons of kings.

And there rises a shining palace whose crystal glittering roof is seen by mariners who traverse the extensive sea in barks built expressly for that purpose and thither come all herds and fatlings and first fruits of that land for O'Connell Fitzsimon takes toll of them, a chieftain descended from chieftains. Thither the extremely large wains bring foison of the fields, flaskets of cauliflowers, floats of spinach, pineapple chunks, Rangoon beans, strikes of tomatoes, drums of figs, drills of Swedes, spherical potatoes and tallies of iridescent kale, York and Savoy, and trays of onions, pearls of the earth, and punnets of mushrooms and custard marrows and fat vetches and bere and rape and red green yellow brown russet sweet big bitter ripe pomellated apples and chips of strawberries and sieves of gooseberries, pulpy and pelurious, and strawberries fit for princes and raspberries from their canes. [More catalogues follow.]

ENDNOTES

1 Image: Agence Rol, Public domain, via Wikimedia Commons.

2 Speaking at Leinster House on 23 June 1963, Robert F. Kennedy said: 'This elegant building, as you know, was once the property of the Fitzgerald family, but I have not come here to claim it. Of all the new relations I have discovered on' this trip, I regret to say that no one has yet found any link between me and a great Irish patriot, Lord Edward Fitzgerald'. Image: Ardfern, CC BY-SA 3.0 <https://creativecommons.org/licenses/by-sa/3.0>, via Wikimedia Commons.

3 Image: Bernd Thaller from Graz, Austria, CC BY 2.0 <https://creativecommons.org/licenses/by/2.0>, via Wikimedia Commons.

4 Image: British Museum, Public domain, via Wikimedia Commons via Wikimedia Commons.

5 Image: National Library of Ireland on The Commons, Public domain, via Wikimedia Commons.

6 Image: Johnckarnes, CC BY-SA 4.0 <https://creativecommons.org/licenses/by-sa/4.0>, via Wikimedia Commons.

7 Image: Diliff, CC BY-SA 4.0 <https://creativecommons.org/licenses/by-sa/4.0>, via Wikimedia Commons.

8 Image: Diliff, CC BY-SA 3.0 <http://creativecommons.org/licenses/by-sa/3.0/>, via Wikimedia Commons.

9 Image: Andrew Dunn, http://www.andrewdunnphoto.com/, CC BY-SA 2.0 <https://creativecommons.org/licenses/by-sa/2.0>, via Wikimedia Commons.

10 Image: Irish Architectural Archive 010_035_X.

11 Image: VR model of the Public Record Office of Ireland showing the interior of the Record Treasury. Created by the 'Beyond 2022: Ireland's Virtual Record Treasury' research project, hosted by Trinity College Dublin.

12 Image: CraftyCaedus, CC BY-SA 4.0 <https://creativecommons.org/licenses/by-sa/4.0>, via Wikimedia Commons.

13 Images: Keogh Brothers Ltd., photographers [1], No restrictions, via Wikimedia Commons; Thomas Johnson Westropp, CC0, via Wikimedia Commons.

14 Image: Eweht, CC BY-SA 3.0 <https://creativecommons.org/licenses/by-sa/3.0>, via Wikimedia Commons.

15 Image: Regier, CC BY-SA 4.0 <https://creativecommons.org/licenses/by-sa/4.0>, via Wikimedia Commons.

16 Image: Frabjousone, CC BY-SA 4.0 <https://creativecommons.org/licenses/by-sa/4.0>, via Wikimedia Commons.

17 Image: SriMesh, CC BY-SA 3.0 <https://creativecommons.org/licenses/by-sa/3.0>, via Wikimedia Commons.

18 'Dublin as published by John Speed' in *Remains of St. Mary's Abbey, Dublin. Their Explorations and Researches, A.D. 1886.* Dublin, Forster and Co. 1887. BL HMNTS 10390.h.14, BL HMNTS 4735.g.4 p. 10. Image: The British Library, Public Domain.

Fear and
Loathing in ZA

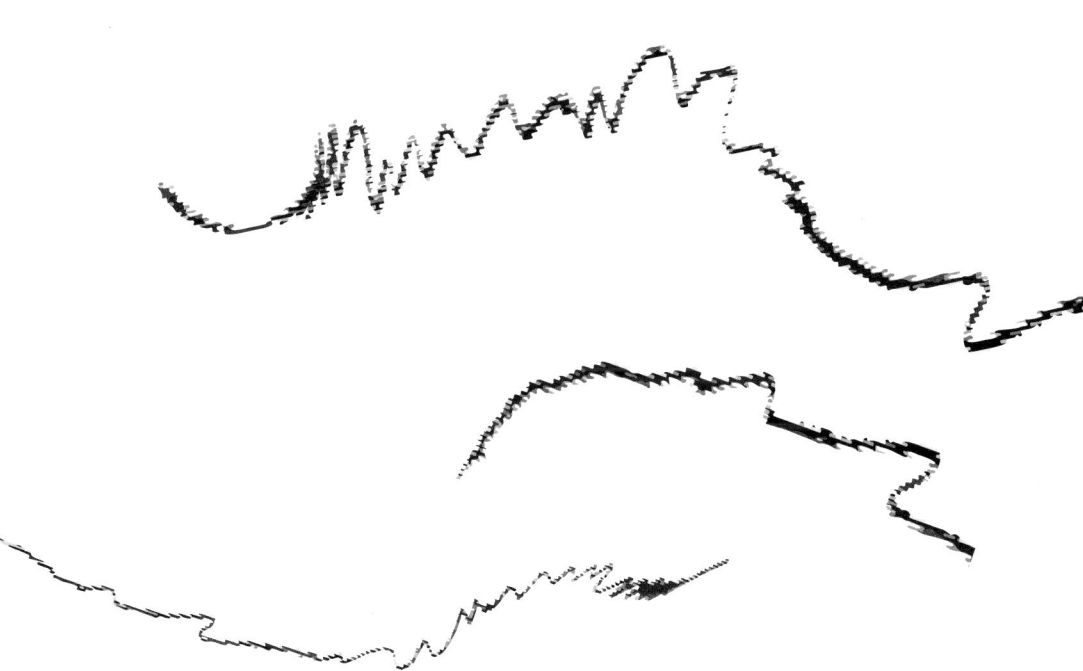

ROBIN KIRSTEN

1.   Expedia's 2017 travel guide for Cape Town parachutes the viewer down from the stratosphere along a spiralling vortex, landing straight into the Victoria and Albert Waterfront shopping and entertainment complex, named after Queen Victoria of the United Kingdom of Great Britain and Ireland, and her husband, Prince Albert of Saxe-Coburg and Gotha. As you journey into 2020's Best City in the World (for the seventh year running according to *The Telegraph*), the narrator sketches broad strokes of the Cape's history – from Portuguese postal station (1500), to the establishment of the Dutch East India Company's supply station (1652), the French Huguenot religious refugees (1687–1706), the British Settlers (1820), through Apartheid (1948–1991) and into the birth of Nelson Mandela's "Rainbow Nation" (1994) – drawing his audience into the ultimate dream holiday, in "the best setting in the world", Cape Town, South Africa (ZA).

2.   The Cape of Good Hope awaits you dear traveller, under an eternal azurean sky. Swim with the endangered penguins on the world's best beaches, lunch and dine to commuter jazz amongst the vineyards that stretch along the cities edges, set in iconic landscapes of crags and crystal clear waterfalls. And of course, there's Table Mountain, with its foothills blooming with suburbs named by the colonisers, like Rondebosch (Dutch), Claremont (French) and Bishopscourt (British), and the suburb of Observatory, named after the Royal Observatory, completed by the British in 1828, and my neighbourhood during lockdown level five. Victorian mansions, semis and arcades abound, freshly painted in *macaron* moods of salmon, turquoise, lavender, lime and butter yellow. Magnolia and bougainvillea, jasmine and geranium, frangipani and gardenia, buzz in the morning light with swarms of honey bees, butterflies and singing starlings. Charming and boho, Observatory signals the end of the city centre and the beginning of the southern suburbs, AKA 'The Muesli Belt' due to its lush and verdant abundance, synonymity with manor homes, high class, opportunity, success, ambition, wealth, health, Waldorf schools, the President and Cape Governor's homesteads, the National Gardens of Kirstenbosch, and an English-speaking international elite.

3. Bounded on the east by the Liesbeek River, Observatory is where several major roads join to funnel traffic into the city centre. Across the river to the north is Ndabeni, the first proto-apartheid Black township created during British rule to house Africans during the bubonic plague of 1900, who were considered by local authorities to be lethal spreaders of the deadly virus.[1] And south east, the Cape Flats, a formerly desolate and windswept, barren flat land with beach sand for soil, whose terrain was bisected latitudinally by the ox-wagon trails of the Voortrekkers (the Dutch Settlers or Free Burghers of the Dutch East India Company), who eventually colonised ZA all the way from Cape Town harbour to the far northern territories. Voortrekker Road, running from west to east, split the Cape Flats into white areas above, and non-white areas below the parallel railway line, during Apartheid.[2]

4. Expedia's travel guide sells the city via drone footage of dream spots dotted along the coast line. Of snow-white beaches, idyllic scenery and a cornucopia of fusion cuisine served in monstrous proportions. Leisure and pleasure and abundance available at a mere snip, but don't look any further than those white beaches and vineyards and big shopping malls, as the true story is really something else. So Expedia skips over the largest area, the Cape Flats, accounting for it simply as the 20 minute drive between two luxury wine farms at its eastern and western edges.

5.　When you fly in you'll enter from the north of the Cape Flats into the tenth Most Violent City in the World (according to a 2020 study compiled by the Mexican Council for Public Security and Criminal Justice), along a highway that passes by Observatory. The highway of your short journey is flanked by thousands of tin shacks without basic services (water, gas, electricity, sewerage), crumbling government-owned dense housing stock, and a row or two of blue plastic portable outdoor toilets for everyone.

6.　But it's lockdown level 5, and no one is welcome anymore. The city is dead. Cape Town has been ghosted. We are all confined to our homes, unless we need to obtain essential medical services, basics and food. The Year of the Great Pause has exposed a new reality, irradiated by the gamma rays of the government's response. The National Coronavirus Command Council, created through the declaration of a State of Disaster, comprising cabinet ministers no longer part of the democratic process, have effectively created a parallel government unaccountable to parliamentary oversight.[3] Outdoor exercise and travel is prohibited, but we can journey to the nearest outlet for essential supplies, which for me is a 12 minute return walk to the local supermarket, Kwikspar, always ensuring to keep the purchase receipts in case I am stopped by security forces, who are entitled to ask for them to validate my presence on the street. Deep memories of brutal Apartheid-era police oppression strategies, like my non-white friends Pass Law experiences which limited their movement into white suburbs, or my own *détournements* into the 'wrong' non-white suburbs, persist. A practice repeated in the return of roadblocks and news images of militarized urban spaces, whose cadets brutally enforce COVID-19 lockdown regulations and laws, like Ritalin-infused droogs.

7.   As the economic fallout of the lockdown takes hold
– blighting the meagre incomes of the plethora of pre-
lockdown beggars and low-income labourers who remain
permanently disenfranchised from any financial gain,
promised or achieved, by the New Republic of post-Apartheid
South Africa – homelessness swells. Plastic-covered cardboard
box shelters and hovels of wood off-cuts replicate across
the city. Under bridges and below trees. On greens, parks
and squares, homeless dwellings become the mushrooming
leitmotif of failing neo-liberal economic policies, exacerbated
by wholesale corruption of service delivery budgets, and
they grow exponentially. Any suburban open space is claimable
by a swelling army of previously unseen destitution, normally
only found in the shantytowns, ghettos and highway curbs
that trail into this city, the Cape of Storms.

8.   Opposite Kwikspar in Observatory is the Village Green
where multiple homeless shelters had, and have, duplicated
themselves like the virus. Made of scavenged tarpaulin,
black bin-liners, planks of broken fencing, wads of
unidentifiable materials, cardboard and old bricks for weights
all tied together with bits of twine, the temporary shelters
are inhabited by an increasing number of destitute people,
invisible to the state or other support structures.

9. The most prominent of these shelters is fenced with a potted garden of more-or-less surviving plants, which appear to be damaged or weak rejects from any one of the neighbouring, grand old Victorian homes. The dweller is brave, as the City of Cape Town Council, with help from the Red Ants,[4] is ordinarily adamant about evicting the homeless and destroying informal settlements which spring up near secure places of potential riches for beggars and the eternally unemployed, all of whom are without access to state welfare resources, of which there is, in any case, basically none. The clientele of Kwikspar is the closest they can get to a revenue stream of charitable donations. During hard lockdown, no cars were on the street, so traffic light junctions – the normal location for their daily labour – had ceased to be places to work. Kwikspar's clientele was, and is, their only lifeline.

10. And neatly placed in the opening to that brave dwellers home, is a found flat object made of steel. An object no more than 80 × 80 cm, with thin uprights and horizontals mapping a grid of equal 5 cm squares. It's a security feature, a front gate, to keep the occupants safe. It's uncanny how this home, with its potted front garden and steel security feature, resembles every other house and home that encircles the Village Green, and which extends across the entire nation. Suburban homes where every wall, window, door, opening and alley, glistens with sharp, hard steel security features.

11.   Leagues of barbed wire cascade across every possible entry point in ZA, national borders included. The crossing with neighbouring Zimbabwe at Beitbridge is largely to protect the failing state of ZA from an influx of immigrants fleeing the already failed state of Zimbabwe, where 2020's inflation sat at 319.04% – the highest in the world. Across ZA, metal spikes that are often the shape of the *fleur-de-lis* heraldic symbol associated with the French crown and seen in slave trading areas, for example, on the flag of Baton Rouge, Louisiana, USA, or which were branded into the skin of errant Mauritian slaves, line boundary walls and windowsills. And if not spikes, then chunks of broken glass bottles are cemented into the top of walls. Plus, if fear of crime is high, or fear because of exposure to crime is higher, then 10,000-volt electric fencing supplements barbed wire, spikes and broken glass-bottle barriers. The electricity is pulsed on and off through the wires at one-second intervals, otherwise if they didn't pulse off, and you touched them, you'd never let go.

12.   And in ZA, life is cheap. The eighth cheapest in the world. Averaging 58 murders per day, or 21,170 per year, and five times the international average.[5] Other daily averages include 113 rapes, 587 robberies, 44 car jackings and 605 house burglaries.[6] Consequently all windows on all buildings have burglar bars, and these should be dense and small enough to prevent children from entering the house on behalf of older controllers of crime syndicates and gangs. CCTV is optional, and ordinarily limited to your own domain, unless you live in a fortified security cluster 'Garden City' home. Doors and windows can be wired with magnetic sensors, which when activated by forced entry, sounds an alarm and flashes up directly to a nearby control centre manned by a private security firm. When activated, they will urgently attend and inspect the property, checking in on the owner to ensure it's not a false alarm. Additional optional features include rabid, gnarling, barking dogs, or the Sublethal[6] system of perimeter turrets fitted with cameras and remote controlled gun barrels linked to a CCTV system or mobile phone, which can rapid fire rubber bullets with sniper precision at any target that appears.[7] All property in ZA, be it a house, a block of flats, a shop, a restaurant, a head office, a warehouse, a manufacturing plant, a government compound, an entertainment complex, a mall, school, yacht, car, farm or church, has to have at least a few combined security features to lower insurance premiums and to keep the owners, occupants or users, safe. Fear of crime is palpable, and fear in ZA is a big and growing industry.

13.   But not as large as the private security firms that patrol upper and middle class income areas across suburbia, and the business districts in and around them. Bigger than the army and police force combined (in 2018), private security started to boom at the end of Apartheid, led by the exiting of white officers and conscripted and voluntary service men from the National Defence Force. They brought with them transferable skills gathered from years of experience patrolling, controlling and suppressing at flash point areas during the years of "the troubles". A time marked by the African National Congress' non-commitment to peaceful struggle against Apartheid, declared on 16 December 1961, and the formation of its armed wing, the *uMkhonto we Sizwe*, after the Sharpeville massacre on 20 March 1960, where unarmed Africans in the township of Sharpeville were ruthlessly gunned down for peacefully protesting against the Pass Laws. On this day, 69 people were killed, 180 injured, of which many were shot in the back as they tried to flee the security services aggression.

14.   Townships are peri-urban unregulated informal settlements on the outskirts of the city and suburbs, lacking basic amenities and services. Cheek-by-jowl shacks of corrugated tin, boards and materials often stripped from local buildings, and measuring no more than a bedroom, are clustered in thousands, like barnacles on the shipwrecks of the Dutch East India Company now wallowing beneath the Atlantic.

15. The shacks can accommodate entire families, with some even shared amongst as many as eight, which is denser than a prison cell. Rural labourers stream into these townships, expanding them into urban spaces which constantly morph their shape, by spilling out of any perceived boundary. *Spazas*, *shebeens* and barbers proliferate, and trade is predominantly curb side wares. Jobs are hard to find, if at all available, and many people wait outside the nearest city centre's DIY outlets, or other choice spots, to be picked up daily to labour for a sub-minimum, cash-in-hand wage, without bank accounts, or employment benefits and protections, tax benefits or further developmental opportunity. It's bleak, but ZA was built exactly on that.

16. Township public space is minimal, with unkempt narrow alleys un-serviced by refuse removal or sanitation systems, and where security is nil. No CCTV, no electric fencing (electricity comprises largely illegal connections criss-crossing the airspace), no barbed wire or subscription-based patrols. And biosecurity is practically impossible. With multiple occupants in each shack, whose water supply is a single shared tap a walk away from their homes, and with outdoor portable toilets servicing several hundred each, the lockdown legal requirements for social distancing, sanitisation and access to PPE becomes farcical.

17. To enforce biosecurity during lockdown, the military weaved its way in columns along the highways, and were stationed in close proximity to the townships. The day before lockdown those images circulated on social media. Images not seen since the Apartheid era's State of Emergencies (1985 and 1988) declared by the government in response to protests and violent uprisings in the struggle against the continued and legally enshrined oppression of the non-white majority in South Africa, giving the President the right to rule by decree.[8] The only discernible difference now is the colour of the servicemen's skins. The army and security force's DNA remains unaltered.

18. Public humiliation for contravening the lockdown regulations is broad. Men are caught on camera being forced to do push-ups in the street as punishment for contravening a regulation, videos of people claiming to have been beaten by police batons for the same are released on YouTube. The police confiscate all vegetables and fruits being sold by the self-employed pavement micro-traders because trading is now illegal. Army combatants with AK47's stand guard in the lowest income ghettos, pointing them at the heads of anyone caught illegally out on the street. Violence is flaring up across the country. A supermarket food delivery truck is hijacked and filmed being stripped of its contents by mobs of hungry people, whose jobs have been cancelled, mostly without compensation or resplendent furlough schemes. Their desperation to secure supplies is acute, and the footage attests to their frenzied fear of a future without food. Shops are looted and more army recruits are brought in. Tyres are burnt in the streets, replicating the scenery from the worst acts and images of the uprising during Apartheid, when necklacing (forcing a car tyre over someone so they cannot run, and setting it alight until they gruesomely melt together into the tarred streets, watched by an applauding audience) was the ordinary form of punishment meted out to anyone considered an enemy of a community, in a nation in flames. That was the 1980s during the State of Emergency. Now during the State of Disaster, behaviour is on repeat.

19. Violence and aggression, fear and loathing, is palpable. Again. Rising to the surface of our screens as identikit versions of the worst that ZA's urban spaces has to offer as indicators of the gross inequalities of our society. The truest picturing for decades of the status quo between the "haves" and the "have-nots". And a status quo that clearly appears now to have become endemicl, exacerbated by the security forces whose abuse is considered by the ruling party's state apparatus, as being a reasonable response to the impossibility of communities in destitution to comply with lockdown regulations designed by the elite.

20. But something else is brewing. Something appearing as pure theatre, replete with choreographed disobedience, slick and astute marketing strategies and communication plans executed and coordinated on point by a cast of diehard enablers, with unfettered belief and determination.

21. Enter stage very far left, the "radical militant" Economic Freedom Fighters, the EFF. Headed by Julius Malema *à la Guevara* (replete with jaunty red beret and workers overall), who carves his role as Son of the Soil, in emulation of Nelson Mandela's nomination as Father of the Land. Malema is not the prodigal son, but he takes up the mantle of carrying out the Father's vision for a just and fair democratic state, with antithetical, radical Marxist-informed slogans based on intolerance, and commodified hate.[9] Posters, speeches and banners proclaim: "Kill the Farmers"; 'Honeymoon is Over for White People in South Africa"; "A Revolutionary Must Become a Cold Killing Machine Motivated by Pure Hate"; "The only white man you can trust is a dead white man", and "The EFF: Our Last Hope of Getting Our Land Back". The EFF's cross-hairs are also on the burgeoning Black political elite and middle classes, the "tenderpreneurs" and entrepreneurs.[10]

22. Land in ZA is the, and their, major issue. The right
to own some, build a home on some, till the ground, have
essential services and basic security, and close enough to
areas of economic opportunities for business, industry and
jobs, and for emancipation from continued enslavement
to the forces of global capitalism. A right for *all* the people
of ZA to live in dignity in a land of extraordinarily bountiful
resources, and not to have to construct rudimentary illegal
dwellings on Observatory's Village Green, or to live in high
density, shanty townships which flood with sewerage after
the rains, waiting for the Red Ants to evict you to nowhere.
The EFF's *Land* manifesto clearly states their points
on reclaiming land without compensation.[11] A *vox pop*
of declarations usurped by the ruling ANC party's absorption
of these into their own manifesto. And there are many
variations of land ownership in ZA.

23. On the western coast of the Cape Peninsula, set on the
slopes of Table Mountain are the most expensive properties
in Africa, with views towards Antarctica. Mansions exchange
hands at impossible prices only available to international
property consortiums, the elite, old colonial money, celebrities,
crooks and the new 0.5%. A mere 30 minute drive in
a collective taxi carrying 15 plus tightly packed passengers
from the peri-urban sprawling township of Khayelitsha
on the eastern side of the Cape Flats, who labour to clean and
tend to those properties. These taxis plough the route from
east to west along Voortrekker Road, all day and all night
long. During lockdown these routes were shut down, depriving
the workers of access to their incomes from these colossal
homesteads of absurd wealth. Now abject poverty is their
new reality. And the now reinstated, jam-packed, collective
taxi service, where workers sit thigh-to-thigh will, and does,
expose them to the virus, bringing it back to their small tin
shacks, families, townships and communities.

24.   On the other side of the Rainbow Nation spectrum
is Orania, in the middle of the semi-desert. A pneumatic
town, a private community with lots of hot air, a kind of
a Bantustan,[12] with its own parallel currency equivalent
to the Rand, the Ora. An expansive place created by white
Afrikaners after the end of Apartheid, ostensibly set up to
preserve and celebrate their own culture.[13] A place without
non-white labourers or non-white residents, who are *not*
not welcome. That would be unconstitutional and illegal, but
in practice is the case, although Article 235 of the constitution
does allow for self-determination, which enables Orania
to proliferate and expand. Orania has privately owned land
for everyone, lots of it, and it expands through acquiring
neighbouring farms, and has privately-funded new universities,
hospitals, houses and public facilities, all built without
exploiting Black labour. Instead, poor white citizens who might
arrive with their belongings in a plastic bag, are offered
subsidised housing and loans in exchange for their labour
to build this new "crime free" "state" within a state. Crime
statistics are zero – except for one rape case – as they keep
their own tribunal system. Murder is unheard of, and no
one locks their doors and windows. Nor are there barbed
wire fences or Sublethal[◊] turrets primed to fire rubber
bullets in the town. It's a spacious hotspot in the blistering
dessert, so biosecurity must be a breeze.

25.   And very hot spots have now flared up across ZA,
again, and the security apparatus is back in town, again. To
enforce, to punish, and to turn everyone into a criminal. It's
now illegal and punishable to not report someone to the
police for not wearing a face mask. We are all compelled
now to be snitches and grass people up. Chinese whispers
abound, and the police are onto us, they say.

26.   And they'll punish us all, again.

27.   We'll be imprisoned and fined. We'll all be criminalised by the state's fascist ambitions, and so you'll never be able to get a visa to travel overseas to get the hell out of Dogville. But if you have a wine cellar and a fully stocked private bar in your rambling mansion overlooking the Atlantic, with a view "absolutely to die for" you can continue to stir Martinis and party with the setting sun waiting for the Milky Way to appear.

28.   The two-faced rules change depending on who you are and how much money you have.

29.   And as warned by ZA's Minister of Police, Mr Bheki Cele, "There is no December 31st. By 9 o'clock everyone should be in bed… Our [police] stations may be full, but we will make room [for you]…".[14]

30.   However, our corrupt officials won't miss out on celebrating at midnight on New Year with Moët no doubt, whilst those who are always threatened by the militarised elite continue to live in fear and loathing in ZA.

ENDNOTES

1 Tembeka Ngcukaitobi, "The Land is Ours: An extract from Tembeka Ngcukaitobi's new book", *Mail & Guardian*, 15 March 2018, https://mg.co.za/article/2018-03-15-the-land-is-ours-an-edited-extract-from-tembeka-ngcukaitobis-new-book/.

2 Non-white includes Black Africans, Coloureds (mixed race) and Indians.

3 Marianne Merten, "Who is in charge – the NCCC or the Cabinet? Ramaphosa unveils the blurring of democratic practice at the highest level", *Daily Maverick*, 10 June 2020, https://www.dailymaverick.co.za/article/2020-06-10-who-is-in-charge-the-nccc-or-the-cabinet-ramaphosa-unveils-the-blurring-of-democratic-practice-at-the-highest-level/.

4 The Red Ant Security Relocation and Eviction Services is a private company, employed by private land owners and the state, whose aim is to deliver "a one stop all encompassing Urban Management Support Services for Human Settlements". An example of their highly regarded work destroying people's homes can be read about in, Dan Meyer, "Tears flow as Red Ants demolish hundreds of shacks in Cape Town", *Times: Live*, 25 April 2019, https://www.timeslive.co.za/news/south-africa/2019-04-25-tears-flow-as-red-ants-demolish-hundreds-of-shacks-in-cape-town/.

5 Michael Cohen and Paul Vecchiatto, "South Africa Murders Increase to Highest in More Than Decade", *Bloomberg: Politics*, 31 July 2020, https://www.bloomberg.com/news/articles/2020-07-31/south-african-murders-increase-to-highest-in-more-than-a-decade.

6 "South Africa's crime statistics for 2018/19", *The Citizen: Factsheet*, 12 September 2019, https://citizen.co.za/news/south-africa/crime/2178462/factsheet-south-africas-crime-statistics-for-2018-19/.

7 See, Sublethal, https://www.sublethal.co.za/.

8 See, South African History Archive: A State of Emergency, https://www.saha.org.za/ecc25/ecc_under_a_state_of_emergency.htm.

9 "Yep, it's hate speech, says SAHRC on Julius Malema's 'dead white man' tweet", South African Human Rights Commission, 17 September 2019, https://www.sahrc.org.za/index.php/sahrc-media/news/item/2138-yep-it-s-hate-speech-says-sahrc-on-julius-malema-s-dead-white-man-tweet.

10 Tenderpreneurs is the local ZA term given to individuals and companies who have enriched themselves on the government tender system for goods and services.

11 See, Economic Freedom Fighters Manifesto, 2019, PP. 28–9, https://effonline.org/wp-content/uploads/2019/07/2019-EFF-MANIFESTO-FINAL-1.pdf.

12 "The Bantustans or homelands, established by the Apartheid Government, were areas to which the majority of the Blacks population was moved to prevent them from living in the urban

areas of South Africa". See, 'The Homelands', South African History Online, https://www.sahistory.org.za/article/homelands.

13 Rebecca Davis, "Everyone in Orania is woke": A journey to SA's most notorious town', *Daily Maverick*, 21 January 2020, https://www.dailymaverick.co.za/ article/2020-01-21-everyone-in-orania-is-woke-a-journey-to-sas-most-notorious-town/.

14 Mluleki Mdletshe, "Be home by 9pm on New Year's Eve or Bheki Cele will 'make room' for you", *Times: Live*, 30 December 2020, https://www.timeslive.co.za/politics/2020-12-30-be-home-by-9pm-on-new-years-eve-or-bheki-cele-will-make-room-for-you/.

Hong Kong:
An Uneasy Walk

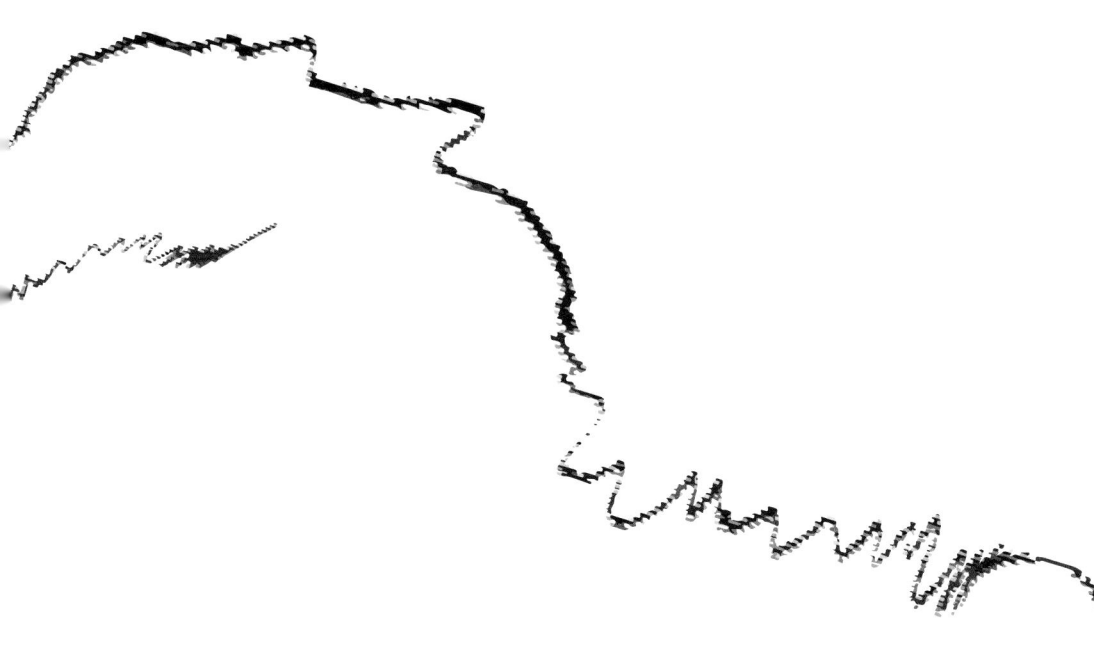

F.C. WILFRED

FCW: In the past twelve months, Hong Kong has been experiencing massive political unrest, a nervous and confrontational social atmosphere which gives me the title of the short film that I present here: *An Uneasy Walk*. The film is a record of the changes in my hometown Sha Tin, particularly to its community over this period. It's a virtual walk that witnesses the confrontations between protesters and police. When making the film, I was moved by the news coverage of the Black Lives Matters movement in the United States and the Yellow Jacket movement in France. It was also clear to me that shooting a virtual walk of the social unrest in Hong Kong at this time would be an 'uneasy' matter.

SHA TIN NEW TOWN AND PASSIVE CIVIC AWARENESS

I've lived in Sha Tin for ten years and before this shifted between the New Towns[1] in the New Territories in Hong Kong. Before Sha Tin became a new town it was a network of agricultural villages. The British Colonial Government later built the Lion Rock Tunnel and the Tolo Highway to connect traffic between the Northern New Territories and the border between Hong Kong and China. I am one of the first generation of Hong Kongers who grew up with the experience of horizontal urban planning, which includes residential, industrial, commercial, recreational and social services in the New Towns. The rationale for this programme was a self-reliant urban planning scheme, aimed at providing job opportunities and a better quality of life for local people. Sha Tin, as a role model of the New Town,[2] attracts a lot of middle-class professionals and is an important example of Hong Kong urban planning. This horizontal urban planning has cultivated what I would call a passive civic awareness[3] in Sha Tin's inhabitants who expect and celebrate a holistic local government administration to bring the 'good life' rather than promoting political engagement that contributes to a better community life. In the past thirty years, I have rarely seen Sha Tin residents publicly organising themselves in order to voice their demands, whereas the government and commercial sectors have always used public spaces. For example, the parks or the Podium of Sha Tin New Town Plaza are often used to organise concerts or variety shows to celebrate National Days, Chinese Lunar New Year or the Mid-Autumn Festival.

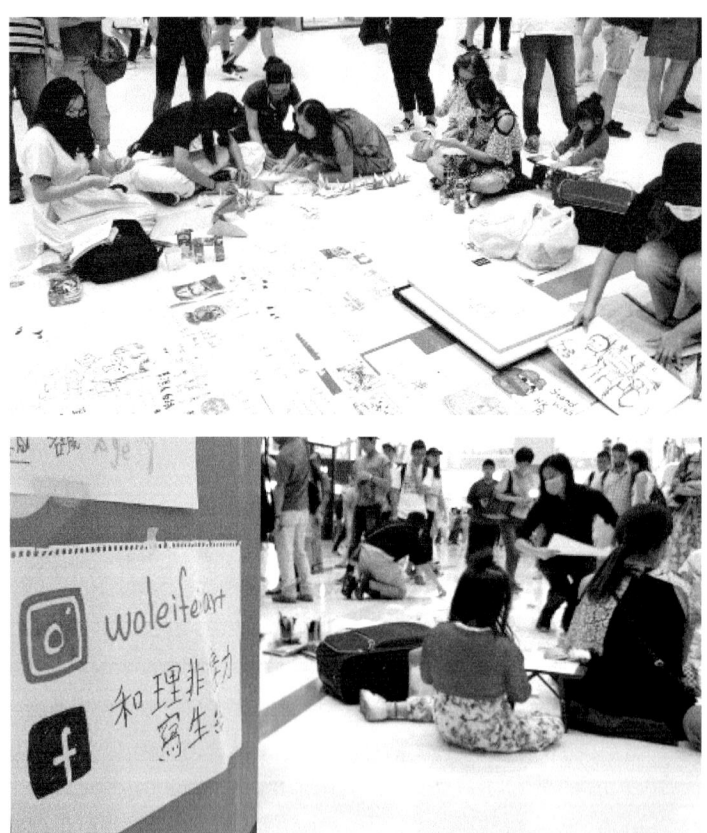

THE SHA TIN NEW TOWN PLAZA – FROM SHOPPING MALL TO 'DEMOCRATIC SQUARE'

An Uneasy Walk is about the big storm that has changed the Sha Tin community since 2019. It was filmed during the first anniversary of the police using rubber bullets and tear gas on demonstrators during the protest by a million or so citizens against the Hong Kong Extradition Bill on 12 June 2019.

The bill would allow the Hong Kong Chief Executive to approve an extradition request before an arrest warrant is issued. Such a move prompted Sha Tin residents' concerns over eroding freedoms in the Hong Kong Special Administrative Region. People feared that they could end up with a mainland legal system where the Communist Party routinely prosecutes dissidents and others for political reasons. *An Uneasy Walk* records the protests of Sha Tin residents in July 2019, and the dramatic scenes which show patrolling police officers in the podium of Sha Tin New Town Plaza starting a violent confrontation with protesters. The police use of pepper spray and batons on the crowd were broadcast on TV and social media with journalists first-person narration making the protests appear as if they were a virtual walk. Families with children and the elderly was also caught up in the violence in the mall. For me, it represented a demolition of the collective memory. The modern, civilised and peaceful Sha Tin was replaced by an autocratic environment that violently prohibited free speech and peaceful protest.

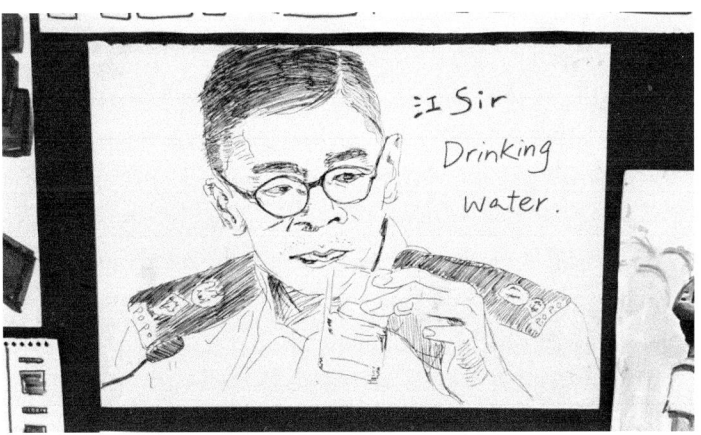

This protest was the first time that Sha Tin residents took over the podium and transformed it into a democratic square where their voices could be heard. For example, they organised drawing and painting workshops for children, they also used the public space as their Lennon Wall.[4] This drawing titled 'Drinking Water', shows Kong Wing-cheung, the former Senior Superintendent of Police (Media Liaison and Support, Public Relations department), hesitating to answer journalists' questions in a press conference and nervously drinking water from a glass – 'How many rubber bullets and tear gas canisters did the Hong Kong police force fire yesterday?' Such scenes, inspiring the anonymous child who made this drawing, were repeated over and over again in the daily live broadcasts. Apart from art and crafts, the Sha Tin residents had also begun a consumer campaign against the corporations that have publicly supported police brutality and displayed it on the wall of the podium. These included the boycott of Starbucks and the Mass Transit Railway (MTR) and other well-known commercial enterprises.

PWSW: The frog we can see in this image is called Pepe who is quite an important icon for Hong Kong protesters because it has become a symbol of progressive resistance against authoritarianism. Pepe was originally designed by an American cartoonist called Matt Furie in 2006. In Hong Kong, people love the Pepe character because he looks both sad and smart, funny but also angry. Graphic designers in Hong Kong have added protester characteristics like a yellow helmet and so on. It somehow shows the sub-culture and the phenomenon of a borderless internet and online media. A lot of us are also aware that Pepe has been used by right-wing movements in the States but the figure which has been reinvented in Hong Kong is probably closer to the original intention of Matt Furie who has had a lot of trouble with the right-wing usage of the icon (at one point, he tried to kill off Pepe in his work).

FCW: I'm interested in the question of what the arts can do during such a political crisis. The artists who organised the drawing workshop helped to reduce the stress and anxiety

Sha Tin residents were under by inviting them to paint and draw. During this period the residents of Sha Tin were able to follow the frequent updates on social media platforms every day. A sensory overload of violent and provocative images which need a peaceful and quiet space for them to rethink, digest and express negative emotion.

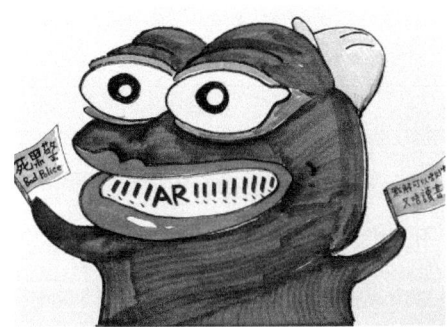

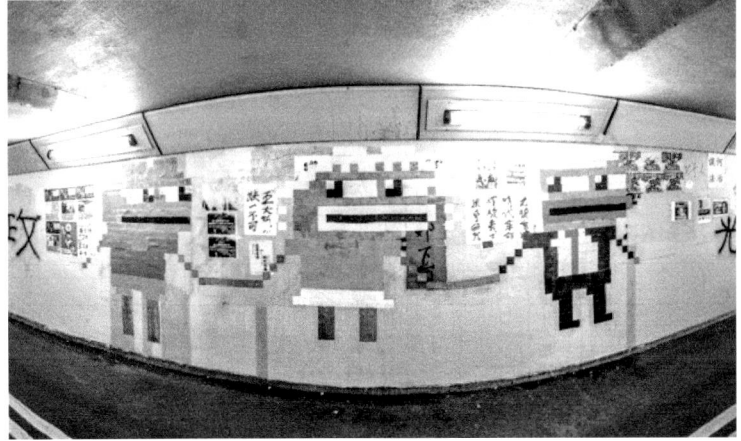

THE POLARISATION OF SPACE AND THE SHA TIN COMMUNITY

JJ-L: In your film I was most struck by the extreme position of the police. You can assume the police themselves also live in Hong Kong, but how is it possible for there to be such a polarisation between the police and the people?

ACAB: I think the police force is like a system, it has a mechanism. I think all the brutality was encouraged and allowed by the government and by Carrie Lam, the Chief Executive. It's a systemic problem and the same thing is also happening in the States. You can ask them the same question: 'How come the police are like that?' Because it doesn't happen overnight, it's accumulative. Since 1997, a lot of the police have been trained in China and they've already developed this mentality of us versus them. The protesters are believed to be evil; they have their own logic that we cannot understand. Remember, there was the Umbrella Movement in 2014, and at that time I think a lot of police thought that they had been humiliated. There was a recording leaked on 12 June last year (2019) which showed the police watching what was happening, and they were saying things like 'Okay, this is our time to get revenge. We (The Hong Kong Police Force) got defeated in the Umbrella Movement, now it's a shining moment to shoot. We can do whatever we want!' This kind of hatred is similar to what's happening now.

JJ-L: It makes sense, It's just so striking. As you say, you see this again and again in different places around the world, but the Hong Kong police must be part of the same community, living alongside the protesters. It's difficult to understand exactly how this polarisation has become quite so distinct. It's not only the polarisation between the police and the protesters, it is the division through Hong Kong society as a whole.

ACAB: We are also very polarised. We have the blue camp and the yellow camp. The yellow is pro-democracy and pro-protesters and the blue camp is pro-establishment and pro-police. In one family the parents could be very blue and the kids could go out to protest every day. It causes a lot of trouble in families and the community and people stop talking to each other. I have friends who I've never spoken to since the protests began.

THE IMPACT OF THE VIRTUAL WALK

FCW: In 2020, the main reason for us doing a virtual walk like this is the restrictions on travel and social distancing. However, in Hong Kong people was experiencing virtual walks before COVID. Such 'tours', including the Sha Tin rally, were broadcast live by journalists.[5] Most Sha Tin residents did not directly witness the physical confrontations between protesters and police close up but watched live broadcasts day and night at home. I call these live broadcasts 'virtual walks' because the journalists 'take' their audience with them to witness the events that are unfolding. These virtual walks were not edited documentaries but rather a full record of a walk to experience unprovoked confrontation and violence. When police misconduct and violence went viral, it would be immediately circulated and re-edited to keep the public properly informed. I think it was the tipping point in making Sha Tin residents active and later transforming the podium into a democratic square.

SK: I have a question from someone in the audience about walking in Hong Kong which is such an integral part of life there. How has walking changed with the increasing boycott of MTR (Mass Transit Railway) and in terms of navigating public and private space?

ACAB: I think ever since the protest. I've been walking a lot more than before, like walking from one end of the city to the other end and going back is not that difficult anymore. During the protests, that's what we were doing every weekend. That sort of changed me and we also still try to avoid taking the MTR. We're trying to download apps that promote alternative routes of travelling like buses or something called the yellow economic circle[6] to support businesses, taxis and restaurants that are pro-democracy. There's an app that tells you where you can go and what taxi to take for example, so it gives you a new perspective or understanding of the city. Don't forget about the airline too. Talking about the experience of the protest, wherever I go now I have images of tear gas or police violence so it keeps reminding me of these horrible scenes. I don't know how long this impression will last but it's changed my view of the city.

AUDIENCE MEMBER: Can I add to that, about working in Hong Kong now because we are so heavily dependent on the MTR system. It's so convenient and clean. It's designed that way because you use the MTR and then you go to your apartment, it's all connected to your building, shopping mall and bridges and you don't even need an umbrella if it rains. Then, you do your shopping after work and go straight to your flat. The whole movement is making a lot of Hong Kongers re-examine this way of life. I haven't been using the MTR, I just intentionally do not use it anymore and I know many of my friends who would rather walk. In terms of walking, it has just changed the way we navigate the city.

JJ-L: I thought it was amazing the way that you, Fredie, started with the images from your childhood, wonderfully mundane images of the shopping mall and then you show it again, transformed through the battles between protesters and the police. What do you think now about this space? Is this no longer a space where people can come together?

FC: That is an interesting question! The podium itself was supposed to be a public space when the Sha Tin New Town Plaza was built. The design emphasised that the mall connects the subway and it and the podium connects with the corridor. If you remember there's one shot, a long take from the podium, of walking into the subway station, and people swiping their cards. So, it's supposed to be a public space. But people just don't have the awareness that urban planning can shape our personality and logic of thinking. My parents' generation might believe that the urban planners of Hong Kong's New

Towns had already designed a 'good life' for us and activism was not necessary. Where spaces like Sha Tin New Town Plaza podium are public spaces to consume and relax – and, when I was young, this was part of our family weekend,[7] but I believe that Sha Tin residents must have become aware of the relation between design and civic action.

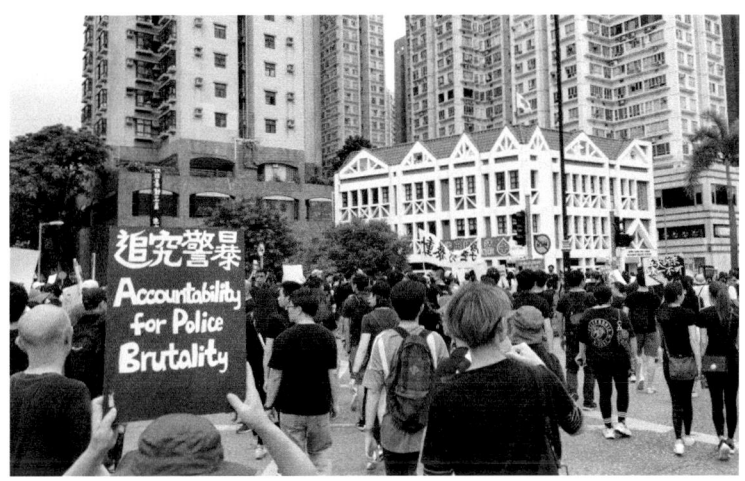

ENDNOTES

1 The Hong Kong government started developing new towns in the 1950s to accommodate Hong Kong's booming population. New Town was a concept borrowed from the United Kingdom, of which Hong Kong was a colony.

2 Urban geographer Roger Bristow's book *Hong Kong's New Towns: A Selected Review* covers the development procedures, the active role of the colonial government and the private sector in catering to the public need in Sha Tin and other New Towns communities.

3 Indeed, cultural geographers have observed that Sha Tin community inhabitants are proud of the colony's good governance and administration rather than celebrating bottom-up political engagement that contributed to Sha Tin's good quality of life. The article concluded that British rule successfully managed locals without helping them to build an independent citizen subjectivity.

4 The Lennon Wall is a wall in Prague, Czech Republic. Since the 1980s, this once typical wall has been filled with lyrics from Beatles' songs, and designs relating to local and global causes. Inspired by the original in Prague, many thousands of people posted colourful Post-it notes expressing democratic wishes for Hong Kong. The wall was one of the major arts of the Umbrella Movement 2014 and Anti-Extradition Bill Movement 2019.

5 Most live broadcast video was narrated by journalists, the audience also witnessed journalists and camera operators being attacked by the police force and other violent groups with pepper spray, batons, and rubber bullets.

6 Proponents of the yellow economic circle frequent 'yellow shops' and boycott 'blue shops', the former supporting the protesters and the latter supporting the Hong Kong Police Force. The yellow economic circle is a system of classifying businesses in Hong Kong based on their support or opposition to the 2019–2020 protests in the city.

7 Family days are an important part of Hong Kong culture. Such days are opportunities for busy working parents to take time away from the workplace to spend the day with their children and other family members.

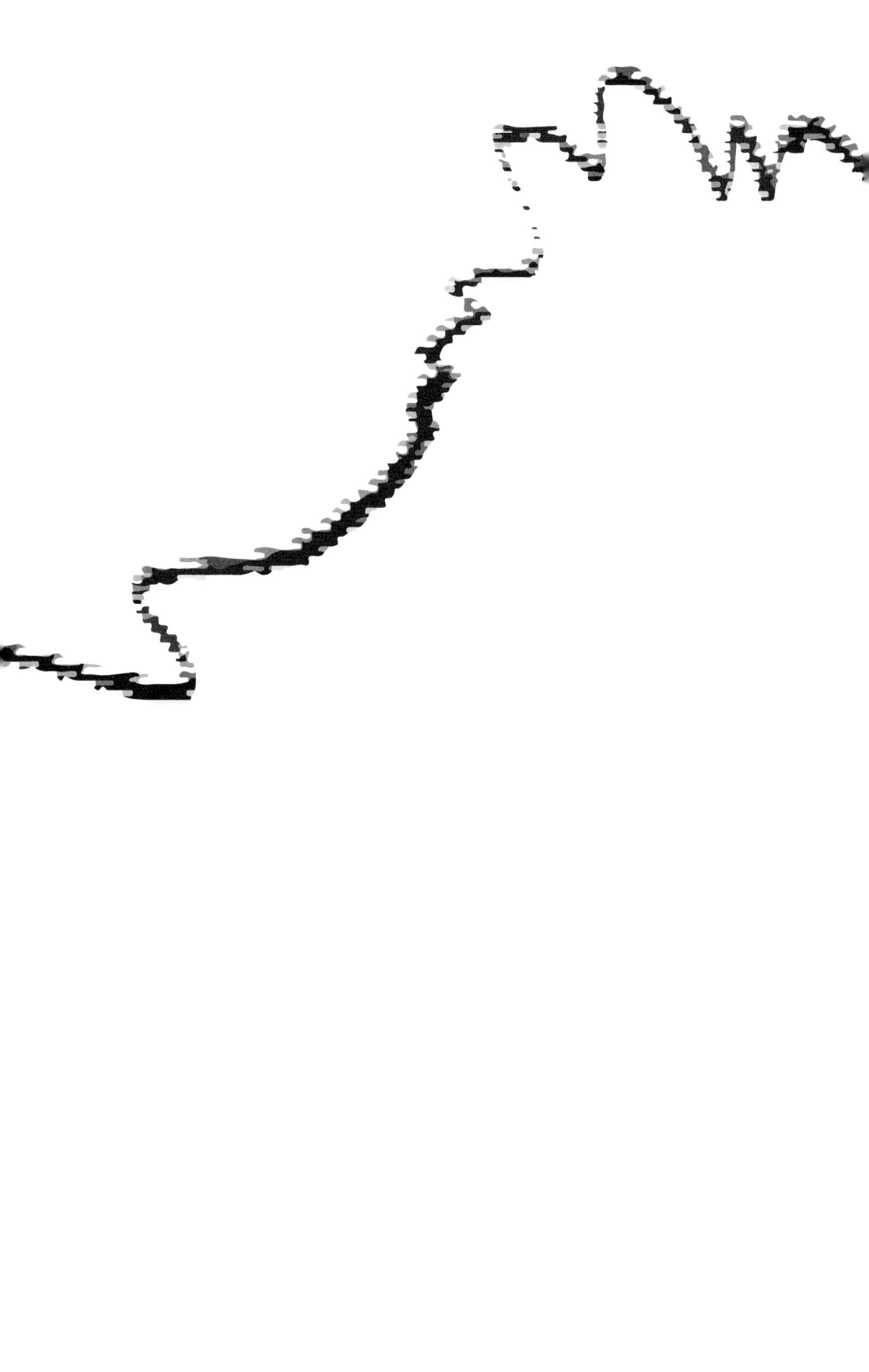

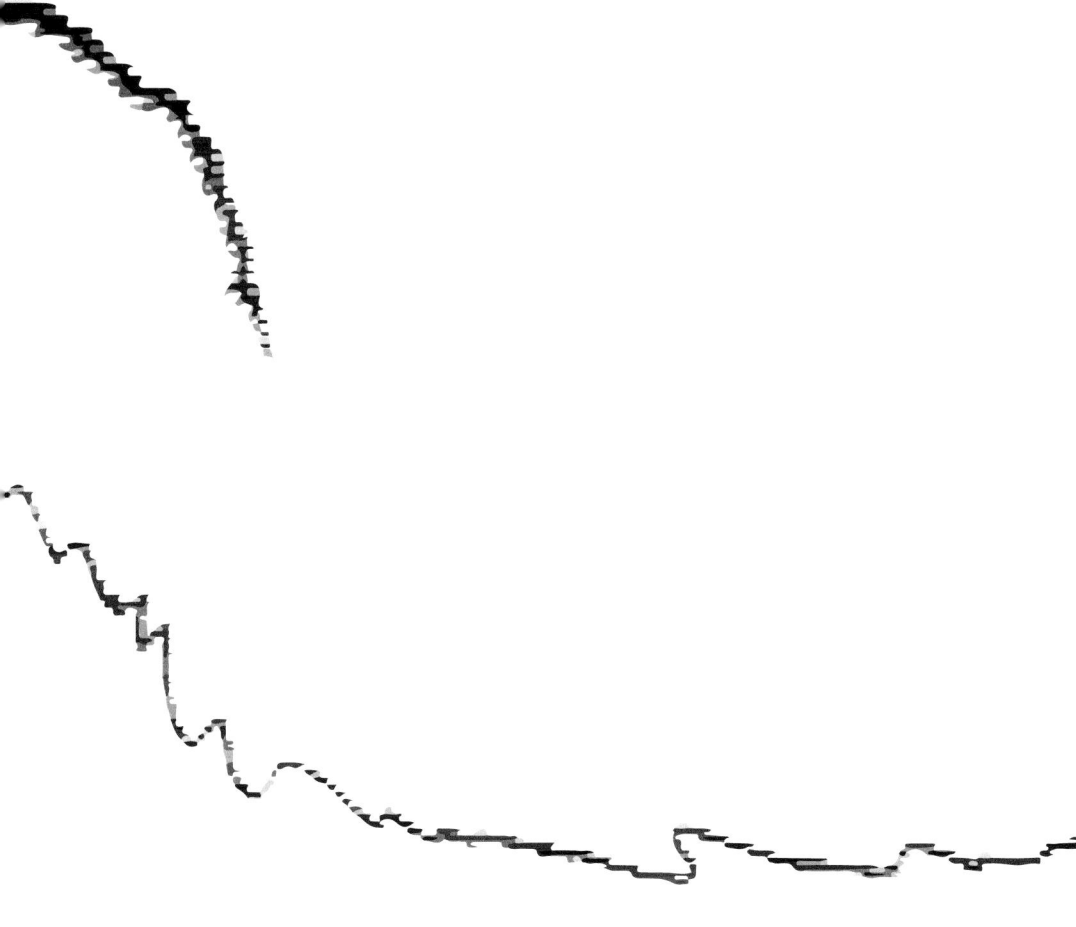

Digital
Walking

Isolated
Together

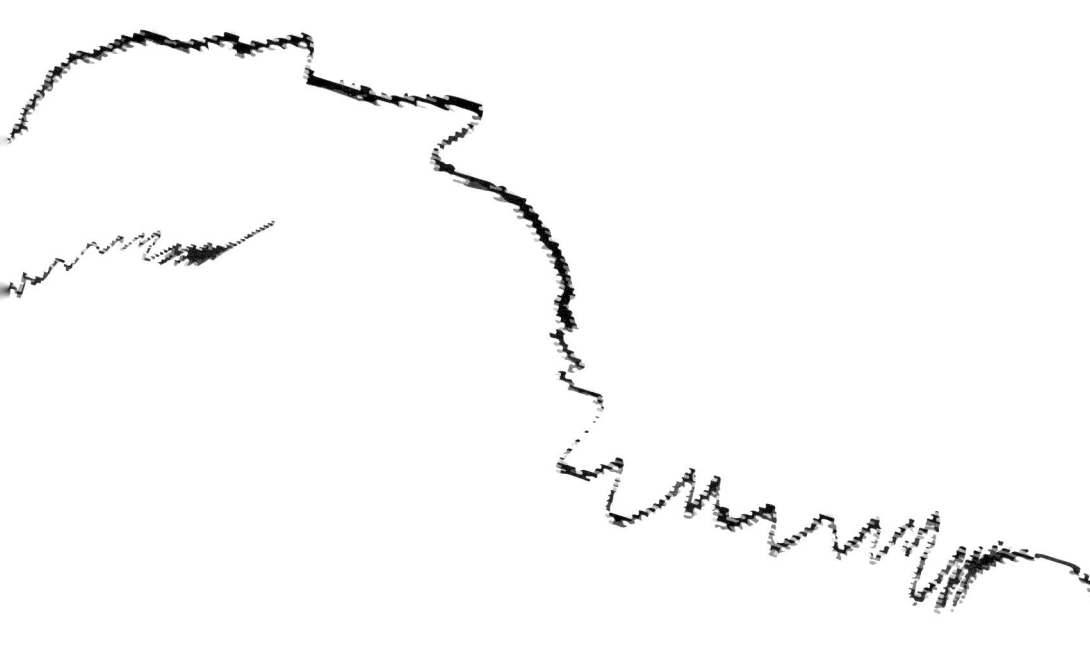

ANNA ÅDAHL

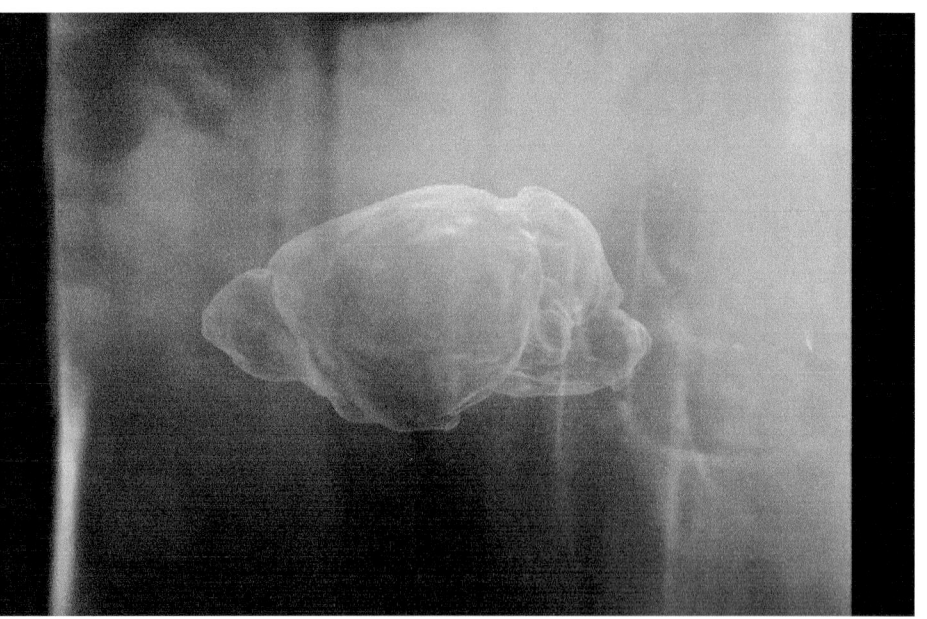

A year has passed with the pandemic. The socially distanced choreography has been inscribed into our daily habits even if hard to accept. No one wants this to be our new normalcy of collective behaviours. It needs to be temporary. As when being ill we have difficulty seeing beyond the predicament the illness has put us in. We start to adapt our lives to the new situation. Most of the time the illness goes away, and we go back to how things were. The pandemic as a temporary phenomenon, even if its existence forever has changed parts of our lives, gives us hope as our urban and social life is not built or sustainable according to the virus. For coming pandemics and climate change, we need to rethink our cities.

Today the fear of the virus has turned into hate. We do not fear it but despise it. We wish we could fight it, but we have to avoid it. No possible confrontation. We can only sit and wait impatiently for the vaccine to neutralise its effects. Spreading immunity among us.

We had a small moment of relief during the summer which gave us false hopes and broke the inhabited choreographic patterns the spring brought along. The summer has become a distant dream. Yet dreaming has become a state close to reality. We dream at night of a world before the pandemic or have nightmares of the virus. As we wake up from the dream in the morning, it takes us a couple of seconds to be reminded of the horror movie we are presently living. Normally we wake up, on a good day, in hopes of new possibilities. Now we wake up from a dream we want to go back to or a nightmare which does not end.

As in the spring, we still have to navigate the streets with caution. Applying the COVID choreography of avoidance and distance. We still have to navigate others, outside of our household, as skiing down a steep slope where we need to avoid a possible fatal crash. A slope that today appears more like a mudslide as our bodies are weary of constantly being tense and on guard from other bodies.

Our cities are built for us to be together – densely. Initially constructed by the arrival of settlements and technologies which replaced nomad life. Cities are a social phenomenon but also places of governance and markets. The buildings its symbols. The skyscraper towering over the urban horizon is the emblem of the vertical crowd a visual of economic hierarchy, the top ruling the urban landscape below and beyond.

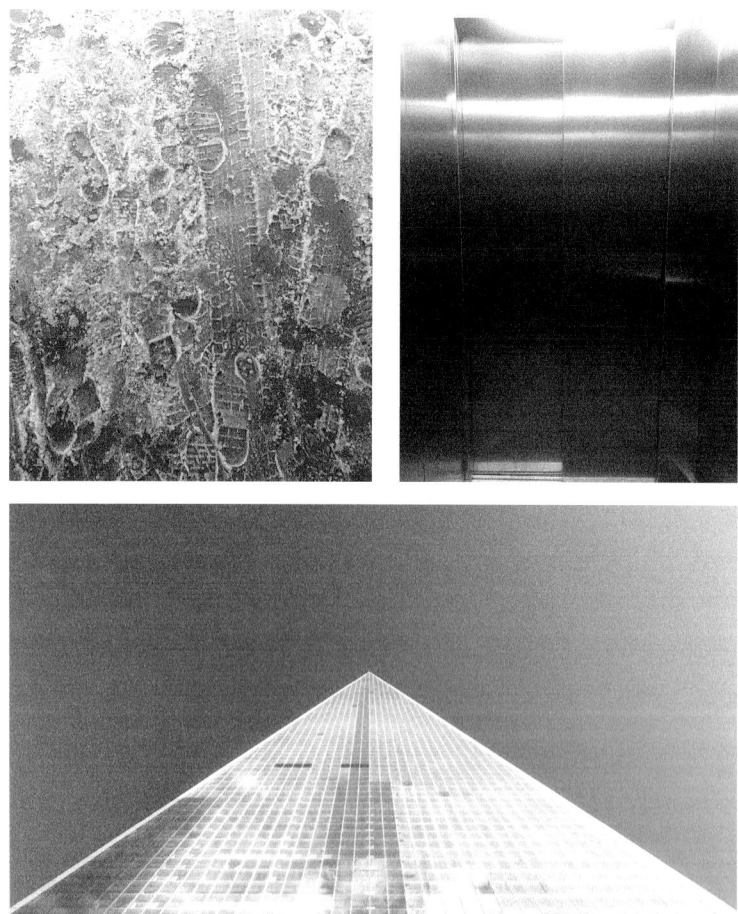

But also, a symbol of a geometrically organized and fragmented crowd separated into, levels, rooms, and cubicles. Together but separated. Maybe the elevator being a meeting point. Today an unventilated and cramped space to be used separately.

Yet for me, we who love the urban, love people. Our choice to endure the city is the choice of being with others, for better or for worse.

The news/media hardly ever talk about social distancing anymore, rather 'keep distance', in Swedish 'håll distans'. For a long time, I tried to use the phrase 'physical distancing' rather than 'social distancing' as the latter seemed too harsh for me as a social being who loves the city, the metropolis, and the urban crowd.

I follow the recommendations respectfully and meticulously as I respect the fatal consequences of this unpredictable virus, yet I have a hard time accepting that it is the social which is to blame rather than understanding that keeping a distance is a geophysical restriction to avoid a biological effect of the virus spreading. I prefer to see my restrictions as physical rather than social.

Hence, distancing as a spatial dilemma that affects us as well as the environment, which we navigate with others. Suddenly our densely populated cities and narrow pavements become a hazard.

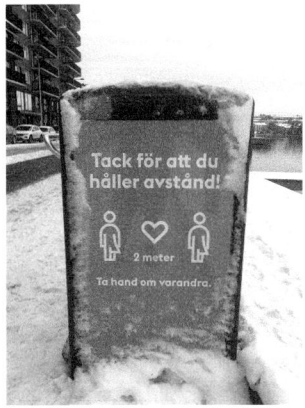 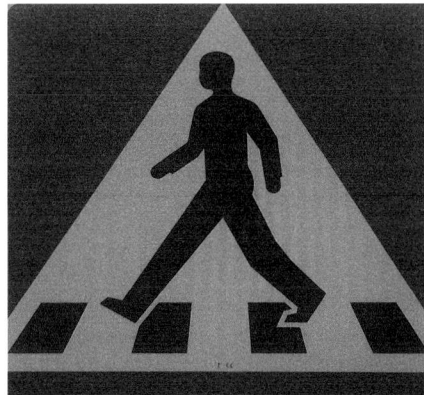

To avoid the spread of the virus we are to be distant from each other, preferably 2 meters between us. A need for space to freely/'atomly' navigate, avoiding bottlenecks and narrow tunnels. In many crowded cities, this is difficult to achieve. One-way systems for the flow of pedestrians are installed but even those can be thronged. Masks then remain the only available option.

Recently, crowded events have introduced portable, individual distance alarms to remind the participants to keep their distance from others. A phenomenon that can be easily distributed among the general population via our mobile phones.

Yet, what a symphony of penetrating sounds would these devices produce when on a crowded street.

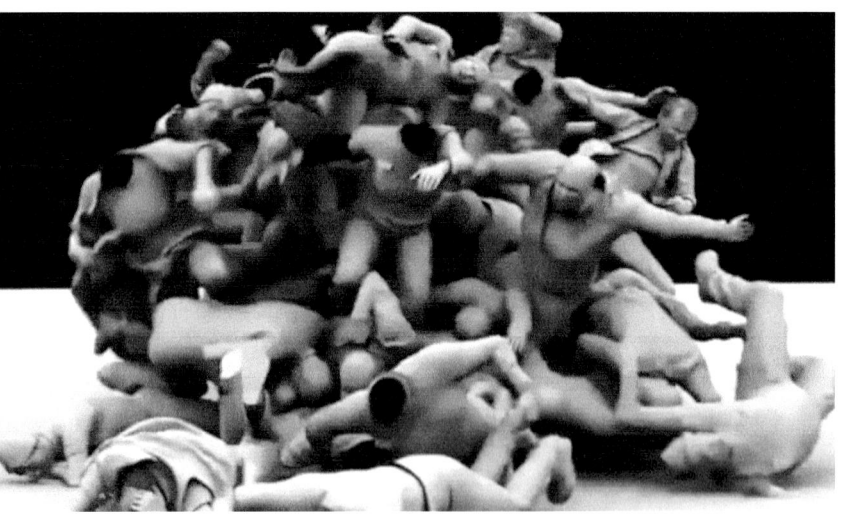

Suddenly the totalitarian architecture of broad avenues and vast squares seems oddly appealing. Architecture and urban planning which was meant to impress and suppress now becomes the means of safety and freedom for the people. Yet when looking up and away from the crowd in the street, the aesthetic of these imposing buildings, rising as ant stacks, still represents an oppressed crowd. Hence, it is rather the urban planning than the architecture which is at play.

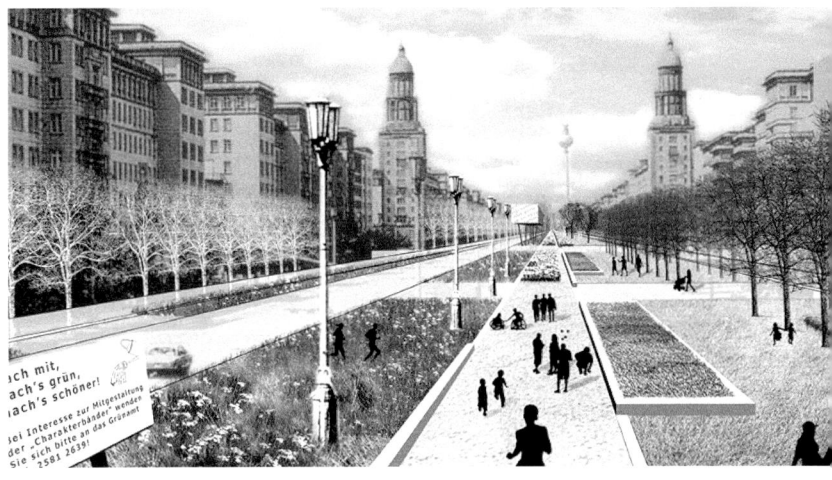

With the spread of the virus, the functional hand-operated objects in the urban landscape became contagious. Handles, knobs, and buttons (in elevators) become contaminated objects. A simple touch could infect you. Before just laced with bacteria but now the bringer of possible death. I presume that many, as I, wish there were magic glasses that would show the virus in the air and on objects. All these functional objects which are essential to navigate common spaces were now to be handled with extreme awareness.

In 2013, I made an installation titled *Public Matter* which included objects from the urban realm. Public objects such as handles, bench details, playground objects, and bollards amongst others. Functional objects touched and handled by multiple persons during the day. To sit on, play with, grip when accessing shops or go in and out of public spaces. All these objects had their shape and aesthetic altered by the repetitive use of the crowd. The trigger for this project was a metal barrier near a bus station in Italy which had become polished to a glistening and shiny gold due to people's inadvertent use. Sitting, or leaning on it while waiting for the bus.

A trigger for this project was a metal barrier I noticed in a bus station in Italy which over time had become polished to a shiny and glistening gold through people sitting or leaning on it while waiting for the bus. And a parallel here in the multiple hands that have transformed the aesthetics of the objects used or borrowed for the installation; I decided to name them 'the people's sculptures.' However, today these objects have yet a new identity: as potential spreaders of COVID-19 – not to be touched without gloves or hand sanitiser for protection. In this light, the commonality they once represented is now to be feared, and, if pandemics are to be our future, the physical effect in avoiding contact with other people in public and shared spaces will probably be reflected in more atomisation and self-regulation i.e., through automatic disinfection systems and so on.

After a year of pandemic atomisation and isolation, either online or in public spaces, we - in the recollections of my friends - long for the crowd. The crowded restaurants, cafes, museums, and streets. To be among people we do not know. We long for the strangers in the crowd. We miss the acquaintances that we spontaneously encounter in social gatherings. Spontaneity being the symbol of uncontrolled social life. We long to be close collectively. Yet, we are all living this pandemic together. It is a globally collective experience that we endure isolated from each other. The few physical crowds which have emerged during the year have been those of political urgencies, raising issues beyond life and death with an urge for solidarity and empathy. But also rioting crowds of extremists guided by hate and destruction. The fear of the other.

Canetti states that 'there is nothing man fears more than the touch of the unknown'. in that we need to know who or what is physically touching us. A behaviour that affects how we navigate the urban realm where we avoid all possible contact (to be noted that contact and distance is not necessarily the same thing) based on the fear of being touched. However, according to Canetti, when in the crowd that fear disappears, and we all become equal. This statement may not apply to the involuntarily close contact in overcrowded public transport

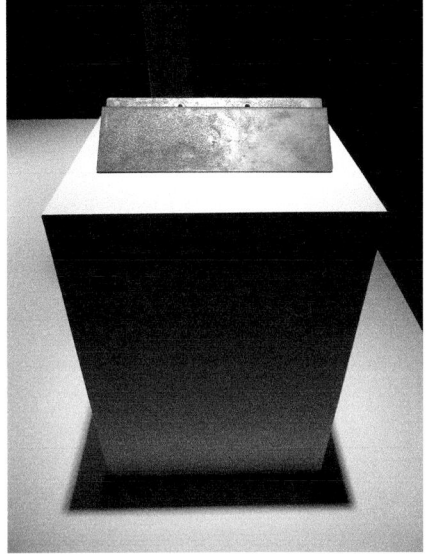

Top: Exhibition view of *Public Matter* (2013) at Botkyrka Konsthall. A handle borrowed from a shop.

Bottom: Installation view of *Public Matter* (2013) at Botkyrka Konsthall, Stockholm.

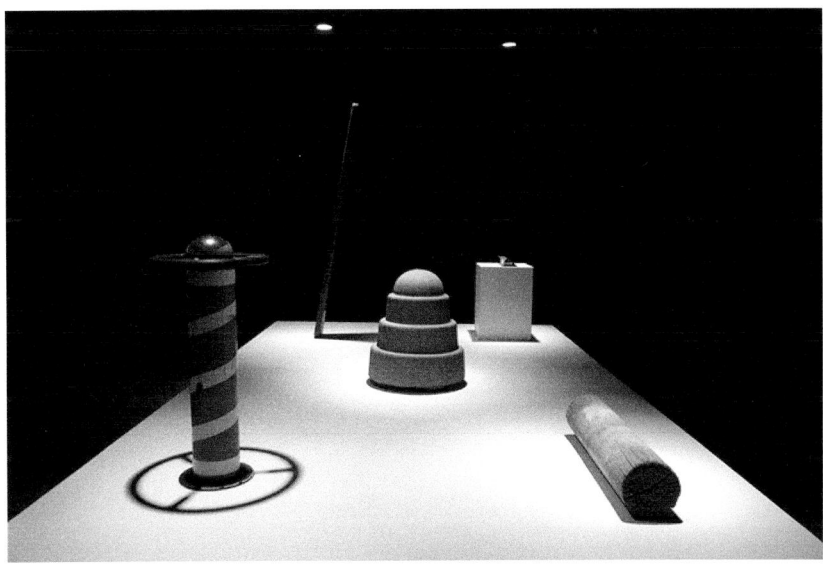

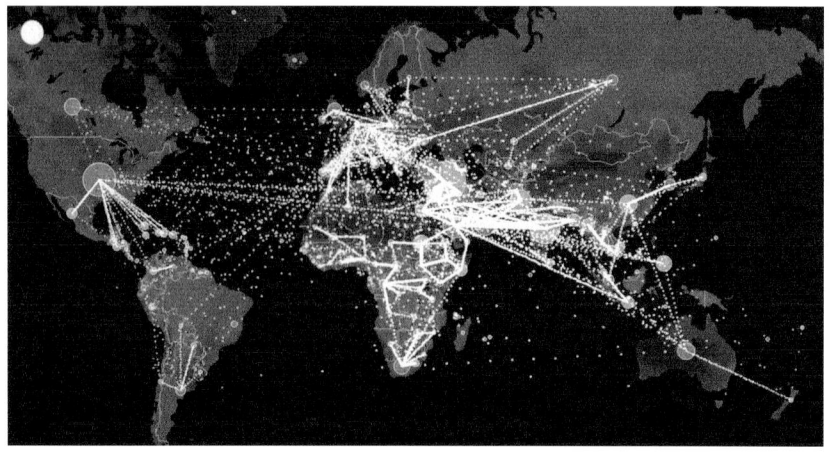

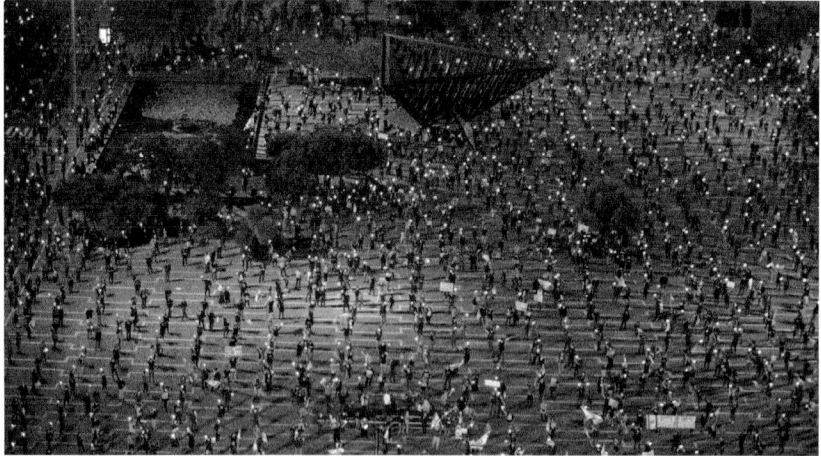

Top: Still from film *The Power of Flow.*
The Flow of Power (2020), Anna Ådahl.

Bottom: Instagram post featuring
a socially distant protest in Israel
against Benjamin Netanyahu, 2020.

during rush hour in collective traffic. At the same time, the underground and other commonly used public spaces are of great importance in gathering and making possible encounters with people who are not filtered into our lives through, family ties, social settings, or work.

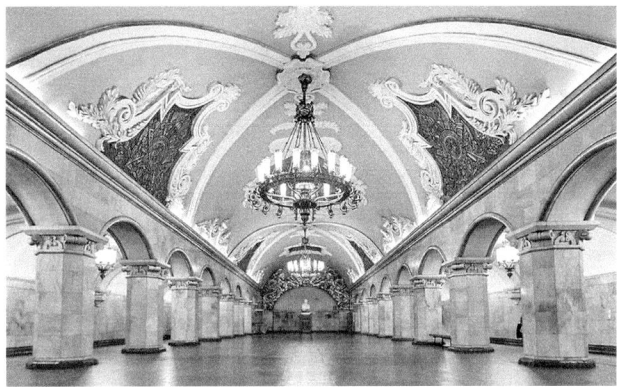

According to Canetti, the physical crowd is a potential restorer of real societal connections among people. Social gatherings of crowds that bring people together could be efficient to counterfeit polarisations if made up of people from different social and political bubbles. An evidence per se but not necessarily when thought through today's digitally operated and atomised crowds. Online, the connection would be distanced geographically and the encounter non-committal as participants can hide behind made-up identities or various filters.

As I have mentioned before, we who adhere to solidarity and empathy struggle with the contradictory feelings that social distancing and avoidance require from us during these times.

Our body language is our tool to recognise and respect the other, to be seen and to be heard, to be reckoned with. To avoid is dismissive. I experience that due to applied distance some people even avoid eye contact, as if isolated but together. As if avoiding acknowledging each other helps us to keep the distance.

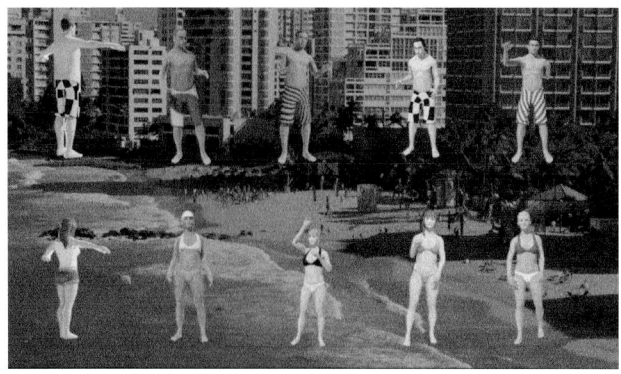

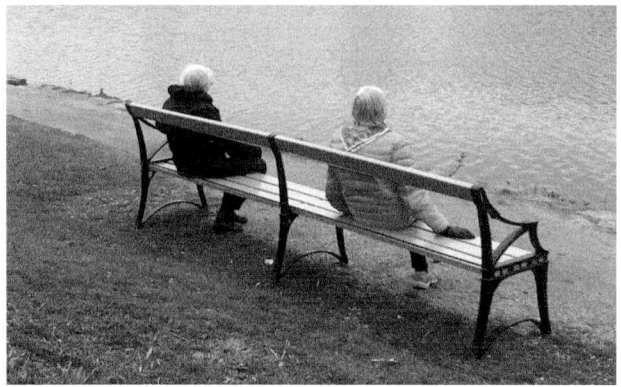

A friend of mine witnessed a traffic accident. Her first reaction was to help the wounded victim who was lying in the street. Rushing to help. At the very last split minute, she retracted remembering she could not touch or come too close with the risk to contaminate. Only the professionals from an ambulance, a doctor, or a nurse had the right to come close. A situation that brought up feelings that were disruptive and conflicting.

With the pandemic, our use of online platforms and linked technologies have intensified. Many fear an established and reinforced technocratic governance of our daily lives. Surveillance and tracking systems, as well as predictive models of our behaviour introduced by the mapping of the spread of the virus, could be used and abused in the wrong hands or simply enhance a market-oriented society.

As argued in my film *The Power of Flow. The Flow of Power* (2020), which addresses various states and notions of society, performance, production and consumption, the pandemic has halted, or paused many things in our lives. However, the internet and online communication platforms have enabled the flow to continue. Continue to work, produce, perform and consume. Continue to act within the accelerated society driven by today's economy.

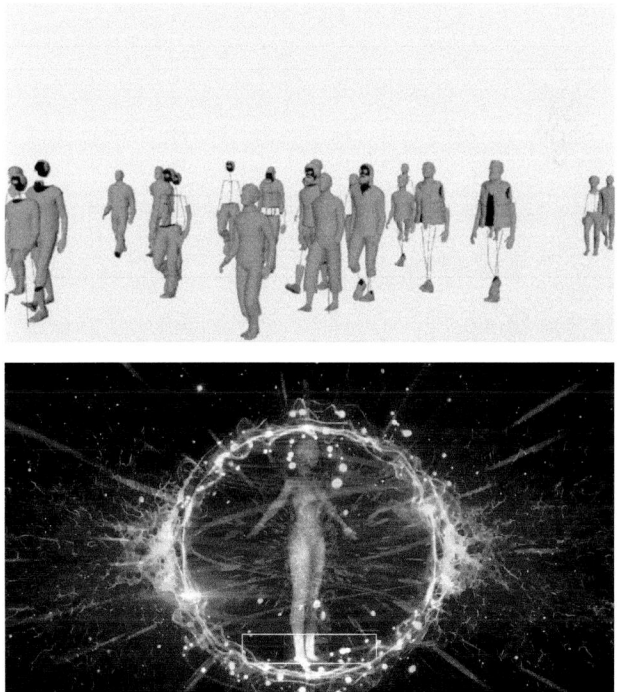

As we are atomised online so are we to be/act in the urban landscape during the pandemic. A logic of sharing a space where we do not meet. Isolated from each other.

'When the users are considered as social atoms which can then be superimposed onto a technological network, the spontaneity and innovation within the collective is given to control of the networks, which is mainly driven by intensive marketing and consumerism aimed at individuals' (Yuk Hui).

Online social atomisation is sometimes encouraged by the social networks which connect people. These online social platforms offer a simulated and edited reality presented to others. At the same time, these platforms are built mainly for economic strategies rather than that of the peer-to-peer sharing system that the internet can offer as these sites are privately owned. Our online social structures are guided by the market and not by the people. To be alone together which has been implemented by the use of our mobile devices is also social atomisation of the physical crowd.

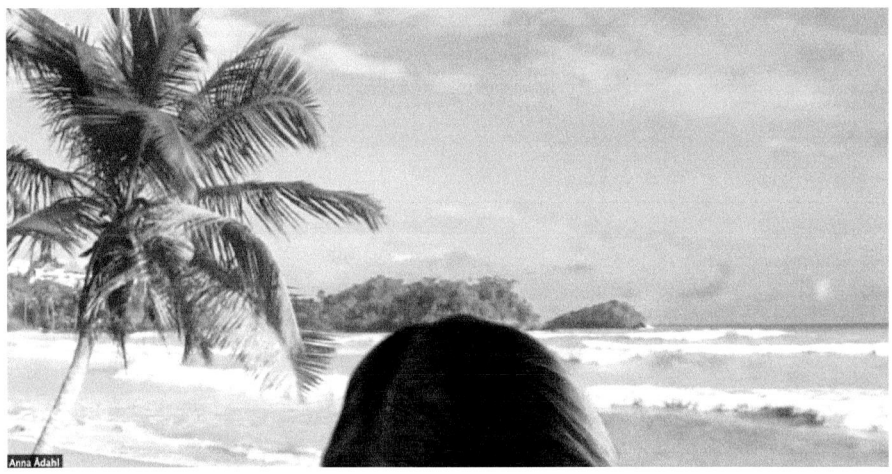

Another social platform is the chat forums which have emerged and flourished during the pandemic. Zoom just the word indicates the microcosmos it presents to us of the illusion of being together. We are not together but in connection. Yet we are thankful that we can at least talk and see each other when separated. These chat platforms enable a filtered and virtual connection of the atomised crowd. The body language abstracted reframed to details and hashed up by the digital cameras and the frame rate of the Wi-Fi connection. Our eyes looking down into the void of the gallery crowd. Many of us recognise (when computer capacity allows) the nature of this virtual meeting by using another background filter showing us in nowhere, if not disabling the camera for our name to appear in the black square obliterating our own image.

Sherry Turkle's reflections on loneliness versus solitude in *Alone Together: Why We Expect More of Technology and Less From Each Other*, written long before 2020, can be of interest in these times of self-isolation.

Loneliness is failed solitude. To experience solitude, you must be able to be yourself by yourself. The importance of feeling peace in one's own company. But trained by the net and being constantly connected/online, it is a struggle to find solitude. The net has become intrinsic to our lives, getting an education, getting the news, getting a job. And during the pandemic to stay in 'touch'. Today's second thought will require that we actively reshape our lives on the screen. Finding a new balance will be more than a matter of slowing down. The pandemic offered many of us the possibility to slow down when confined to our homes but there was no real rest.

We are not good alone together.

A study showed that the lack of social life and contact with others had the same effect on the body as to when we starve.

Yet Alone Together has been turned into a slogan and COVID hashtag in the US.

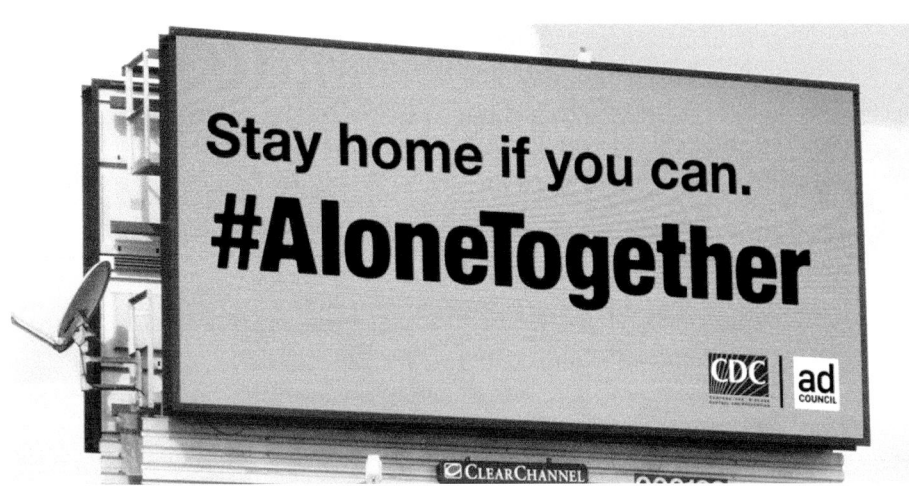

To keep people atomised and fragmented enables control. This control over people produces an enhanced power that can be abused. A phenomenon many have experienced from some leaders around the world. Yet this control is today mainly operated by a few dominant global enterprises and 'domestically' by some totalitarian regimes.

To intentionally avoid each other creates polarisations and by extent, a fragmented and divided society where people can be easily triggered by their bubbles and fear of other bubbles. Atomisatised bubbles of filtered minds of 'alikes'. Bubbles create a sense of belonging through recognisable, similar gestures and opinions.

The already segregated cities of today are developing into even more divided groupings of people controlled by their online lives. Digitally dictated formations which will help to avoid commonalities or encounters thwarting the nature and role of the city. Hopefully the weary experience of the pandemics' self-isolation may pop these divisive bubbles thanks to the longing of the social crowd.

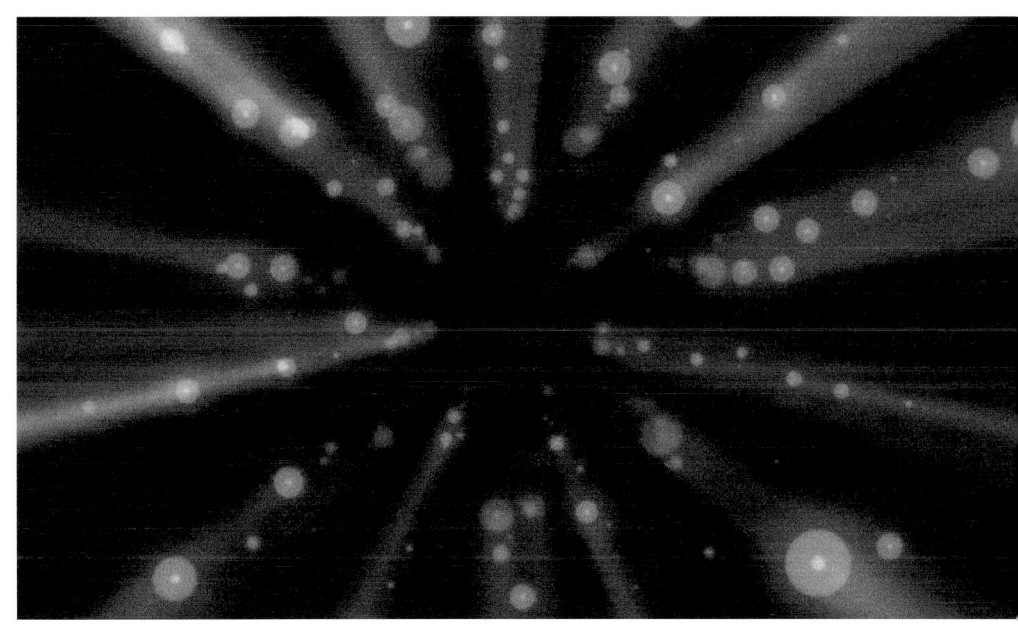

Traversing the New Byzantium:

How Los Angeles was Remade by a Changing Economy

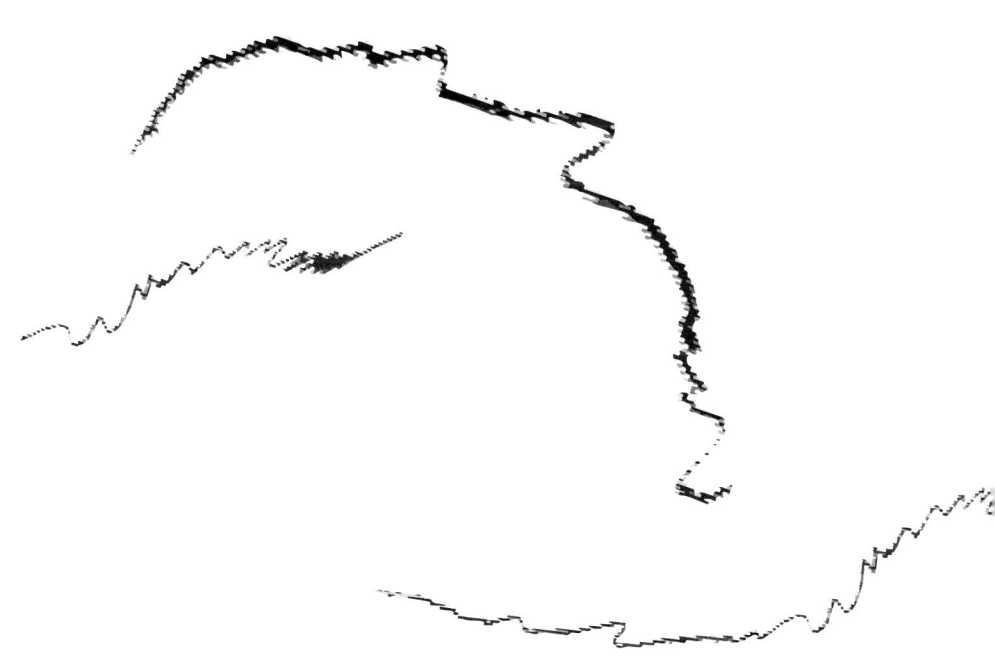

NORMAN M. KLEIN

In the fall of 2020, Americans panicked when the surges of COVID-19 came back. Trump did finally lose, and evaporated, while another 100,000 people died. The moral extremes were schizophrenic. First, there was the heroism of George Floyd protesters, frontline medical workers, and the largest voter turnout in over a century. On the other hand, there were threats by vigilante blackshirts carrying automatic weapons. Over fifty million Americans remained convinced that Biden's election was a fraud; and were ready to dismiss the constitution. The country at large was traumatized, strangely unable to move.

Nevertheless, one matter was broadly agreed upon: 2020 had accelerated problems going back forty years. This was particularly apparent in Los Angeles. Since the eighties, Southern California had been grappling with the ruins left by midcentury modernism. Movies no longer opened with overheads of LA freeways endlessly circulating. After 1980, Los Angeles essentially retrofitted its concentric multimodal plan. In its place came a more fractured mystique, about Southern California as an archipelago. Photo spreads featured tiny recovered neighborhoods, hidden canyons, lost stream beds, and isolated ecosystems.

From downtown to Venice Beach, food-truck cantinas suddenly popped up, guerrilla *loncheras* served by Asians and Latinx side by side.[1] All at once, a filigree of micro-ecologies had replaced the city of circulation. *Loncheras* are a glorified part of the vendor economy, very immigrant based, "bohemian" (a nineteenth century term for urban transients), but not simply about immigrants. They suggest the medieval caravan, a zocalo on Sunday, a farmer's market, a flea market. It's a long category nowadays. We can add online startups, *elote* street-cart vendors,[2] home-office handymen, gypsy construction crews, pop-up vintage clothing stores, itinerant auto repair shops, under-the-table carpenters who converts garages into apartments; Lyft drivers, any temp worker who never gets regularized; even adjunct professors.

All of these are responses to the swarm of short-term contract jobs replacing more stable permanent work. They indicate how fiercely labor conditions have changed in recent decades, not only in the growing service industry, but in manufacturing and construction as well; and a steep drop in work for college teachers,[3] and for "creative freelancers."[4] Food trucks (some with Zagat ratings) are the cuter, aestheticized version. The reality is more devastating, and fiercely highlighted by shutdowns during the pandemic, indicate a crisis that will only grow. Perhaps the Biden Administration rescue plan will mitigate some of this. 2021 promises to reverse some of that during the boom. But the trends are clear, related to automation, offshoring, overextended supply chains, and the growth of "logistics capitalism," so called, where gig workers deliver for Amazon or UPS, a flurry of confusion. Attempts to unionize this problem may begin in the future, but are not here today. The trucks are still waiting. Victorian travel writers imagined that vendors helped to dress up a street as "local color" or "street arabs."[5] Today, they belong to a provisional economy that keeps deepening. The lumpen precariat now includes genteel poverty in the middle class.

Back in the nineties, I called this more varied, more subaltern LA the New Byzantium. I was referring mostly to colossal waves of immigration, starting in 1965. The Immigration and Nationality Act, passed only months after the Watts Rebellion, removed immigration quotas and helped start a land rush. Within forty years, five million immigrants settled into Southern California. Los Angeles had more foreign-born residents than New York, had and become the most ethnographically diverse city in North America.[6]

Points of entry for Mexican arrivals overwhelmed the scant resources of many deeply segregated black neighborhoods. The population of Koreans and Latinx in Koreatown, just north of mostly black Crenshaw, had multiplied ten times. Soon, Jewish convenience stores in south Central—part of the story during the Watts Rebellion of 1965—were replaced by Korean owners. Here was the LA version of the Lower East Side of 1900. LA surpassed New York in its number of foreign-born residents. This flattened an urban infrastructure that already suffered from racist neglect; and inspired the hideous war on drugs by the LAPD. At the same time, this staggering immigrant diversity was also reflected in the multiple pulse points of the 1992 insurrection.

Looming over all of these, however, was an even darker omen. LA was inside a wave of growing economic turmoil worldwide. Something unstable in the global economy was driving these vast migrations into Southern California. Every underdeveloped region in the world seemed to be overwhelmed by ethnic cleansing and civil-war militias. All of this was linked to the eclipse of the Cold War. LA was connecting itself to a post-Vietnam supply chain. Immigrants were of nation states failed by globalization, in Latin America or Lebanon. They were leftovers of American stupidities abroad. The revolution in Iran ended a neurotic Cold War saga begun by the CIA in 1953. The American military tried to anxiously cauterize what European imperialism had left undone. But these clumsy efforts (often on behalf of American corporations) mostly inspired civil wars. The kleptocratic mess afterward added voids, havens for criminal warlords, blood diamond capitalists, and risky entrepreneurs of every description. Finally, the chaos was not even led by the US specifically. A new economic juggernaut was setting the world structurally on fire.

These voids had a wild-west, gangland oddness about them. In nineties Moscow, bodyguards for businessmen might cost up to $300 a day. In LA, the instabilities became quite visible during a huge recession from 1990 to 1995.[7] But the melodrama around Bloods and Crips was hiding a larger story. The perceived surge in crime was publicized while crime statistics were, in fact, dropping. The real surge was a vast economic transformation just starting off. In areas affected by the Insurrection of 1992, real estate prices dropped by two-thirds, and stayed that way for years.

In short, LA missed the boom that followed the end of the Cold War; and did not catch up until the late nineties.[8] Of course, this "boom" was a false spring anyway. The so-called "peace dividend" camouflaged disasters in the making. These finally slammed into the US with the recession of 2000–2001, again, but fiercer, with the Great Recession after 2008; and now (even larger still) in 2020.

The first cause is usually traced back to 1973, and sounds rather modest, considering the result. In January, President Nixon installed rules on how world currencies were to be priced. As a result, banks, stock trading—oil prices, tech, broadcast entertainment, the speed of investments, the explosive growth of tax havens—all had to adjust. A worship of deregulation took over, and transmogrified the structure of world trade. LA was forced to respond in the eighties, but even more so in the nineties. LA's response was even more direct than New York's 'bankruptcy' after 1975. LA lay more in the cross-hairs of the Pacific economy. By the nineties, the vectors changing globalization were centered around the Pacific. Southern California was closer to China and the Four Tigers (Hong Kong, Singapore, South Korea and Taiwan), and was forced to structurally adapt. The new immigrants came from East Asia, or from parts of Latin America that were overwhelmed by globalization, like Mexico's maquiladora. Both capital and immigrants were transmigrating from many of the same places.

Unlike the Cold War, help for LA from the federal government was not forthcoming. This was, in great measure, because too many in the federal government had already joined this globalized reality. It was a post-Cold War opposed to government programs, against master planning altogether. The neoliberal agenda in Washington D.C. preferred deregulation to new infrastructure, or human services.

This suicidal transfiguration even has roots, I hesitate to add, in the Carter Administration, but was a cult in the Reagan years. It radically empowered global banking. That amounted to a shift toward investment—and shipping—above manufacturing. Fast turnover was the answer, not the question. Everything and everyone was a portfolio, especially real estate. Los Angeles finally gussied up like Tribeca in Manhattan—a flipper's paradise that skyrocketed real estate prices. Campaigns to add affordable housing near trolley stations hardly materialized. This was a feudalistic widening in the class structure, a Baroque unaffordability.

This was promoted to stop the collapse of revenue, that one sees in many American cities.[9] Simply put, as inequality increased, the cities showed it (both high and low)—no matter how rosy the GNP looked (and still does). This fiscal juggernaut had ushered in a gilded age for tax-free oligarchs.

By 2020, the dent left by underdevelopment on public services was brutally evident. But this was already an eighties phenomenon. The public sector was treated like a casino investment that didn't pay off. In fact, one of the early names for this withering syndrome was Casino Capitalism (1986).[10] In 1978, California, underdevelopment struck like the hand of God, when Prop 13 crippled public education throughout the state. After all, the credo of Reaganism originated in Southern California.

American underdevelopment has its subtleties. It works like fifty butterfly effects at once. Its overweening cause, however—the ultimate Cold War—was the end of the Western colonization. As colonies gained their independence, the US and its NATO allies struggled to invade their economies, through the World Bank, and multinational corporations.

But in the US, that gambit backfired. It sparked a phenomenon that essentially colonized the United States itself. It was an emergent, urban industrial feudalism. This is clearly linked to the early stages of globalization and deindustrialization—both keywords from 1982, when the problem was widely noticed. They pointed toward the victory of deregulation in the Reagan/Thatcher era, that also launched digital capitalism, as an intergalactic mode of deregulation. Both Republicans and Democrats wanted deregulation, For cities, however, it was about a shrinking public sector, that reinforced inequality.

Legacy manufacturing (heavy industry) had severely declined. Factory workers in LA were savagely displaced, almost singled out. In 1971, Chrysler closed its key assembly plant in the City of Commerce. Chrysler, along with General Motors (GM) and Ford, was trying to out-Japan Japan, and failed. As early as 1971, foreign cars already accounted for 41% of sales in LA (the highest percentage in the US at the time).[11] That misery index worsened year by year. LA's eclipse was in synch with closures in steel and aluminum production in Youngstown, Ohio after 1977; marking the birth of the Rust Belt.

By 1991, heavy manufacturing was almost treated as a lost cause. So much had been offshored, so many union jobs transferred to the American south, or lost when big plants over-automated. But for LA manufacturing, there remained one huge ace card. Aerospace had still been growing. It was concentrated in a belt of 800,000 people from Hughes Aircraft below West LA, to the San Fernando Valley. During the second World War, it was centered around the Lockheed factory in Glendale/Burbank). By 1945, two thirds of all airplane manufacturing came from LA county. Southern California was suddenly the larges industrial hub in the US. The Korean War added even more—exotic missile and electronics contracts.[12] Aerospace grew even further when America went into space; and when space travel was computerized with satellites during the Vietnam War. Then came B2 and Stealth bomber research ($500 million to $1 billion for each plan). LA represented a supply chain from Saigon to Berlin.

But there were danger signals. Missile contracts began to slow down in the eighties, when aerospace actually lost another 18,000 jobs (very uncharacteristic). Then the bottom dropped out, in 1991 Northrup and Lockheed, along with their subcontractors, removed over 21,000 jobs.[13] Every month, the hole deepened to about 300,000 overall. Production of B2s dropped by 90%.

The University of California lost government grants that incubated tens of thousands of white collar technical jobs, especially in engineering. In the crime melodrama, *Falling Down* (1993), 'DFens' is a psychotic unemployed aerospace engineer named DFens. He still wears a plastic pen insert in his shirt pocket. Then, in the midst of freeway traffic, he freaks out, and goes on a killing spree. From an army-navy store (in Silver Lake on Sunset), he kills a fascist Cold War salesman, then symbolically carries around a duffle bag filled with stolen anti-tank missiles and automatic weapons. Everything about DFens is a left over from the Cold War; with echoes added the 1992 Insurrection. If the movie were remade, DFens might be a psychotic software engineer who joins QAnon.

Aerospace cutbacks came right after wounds inflicted by auto manufacturers. Ford had already shut down in Pico Rivera (1980), GM in South Gate (1986: my wife taught ESL in Southgate at the time, and the shockwave was apparent in store closures, street turmoil. Firestone closed its famous plant in South Gate (1980, dating from 1927). Goodyear's even more famous plant complex (1920–79) was a chief employer on Central Avenue, in the heart of African-American LA. Tremors were felt across the region. Mike Davis writes about Kaiser Steel's polluted odyssey in southern California, before abandoning Fontana (1982). Overall, a hundred-mile supply chain around automobiles shrank precipitously, from dealerships to auto supply outlets, to trucking.

American capitalism was undergoing savage post-hegemonic redesign. The implications were right on the surface, but often went strangely unnoticed. For example, in 2010, I visited the last fishing boat docked on Terminal Island. The local Japanese fishermen were gone,[14] along with their combined fleet of 250 vessels. Sunkist Cannery had been closed since 1985. At one time, LA produced half of all canned tuna in the US. Now, mackerel replaced tuna as the main LA catch, strictly for the Asian market.[15]

I was surprised by the ocean blasts of extreme afternoon heat. A middle-aged sailor was mending a net that symbolically had seen better days. There was no one else in sight. The sailor shook his head, explained that he needed to quit. The sadness of this fadeout was overwhelming him. Five hundred feet away, giant stick insects were unloading hundreds of container ships. Each ship could hold a thousand times what small fishermen like him might catch over an entire year. The freeze trawlers hauling fish were big, but just stegosaurs. Everything seemed to be overwhelmed by the cranes (not unlike those huge conveyors that used to dominate coal mines).

LA's shipping container industry really took off in the sixties, during the Vietnam War. Ironically, the shipping routes that serviced the weapons (from Okinawa to Vietnam) were retrofitted to deliver imports back to the US. That is essentially how those Japanese subcompacts first arrived in Long Beach. Southern California's twin ports were tailor-made for containerships. The harbor depth had been originally dredged out of mudflats (by 1913). That was its edge back then over San Diego. These mudflats proved easy to trench ever deeper, once container ships mushroomed in size, to eventually hold 12,000 containers apiece, each container 40 feet long, holding about 125,000 pounds. In 2000, nine million containers (measured as TEU) passed through the ports each year. By 2020, that figure had nearly doubled. There were signs of competition, and something changing—a slump in 2005, 5% or 10% declines on certain years—even before the pandemic. Business was platforming. Something else was in play (partly Trump's trade war with China causing a fifteen percent drop). The tremors of 2020 had already begun three years before. But just when you figure out the rules, they start to change. In the fall of 2020, container deliveries to the ports recovered from massive drops to their highest levels ever. Nonetheless, it is widely assumed that global supply chains have been growing treacherously long. A new business model is coming. And it is already showing up in the LA region. Let me explain.

Due to the ports, the 1990s LA economy saved itself. The boom in techware would never have been enough. After the Cold War ended, LA transformed into the Eastern capital of the Pacific (the "gateway"). That reengineered life on the ground for a million people at least, across five counties.

The new rules were a "neo-mercantilism." A quick historical note on that term: In the seventeenth century, the Dutch and British East India (joint-stock) Companies were given charters to function as independent sovereigns on behalf of the king. They directly owned their own fleets across Asia. The king did not control their capitalist ambitions. Mercantilism was a pluralist, deregulated form of sheer greed. Now it is back. Inside the kleptocracy of the Cold War, multinational corporations were granted unregulated authority over Pacific trade. In the Pacific, Los Angeles was the freebooting major port of call.

More background on how that happened: In 1973, the financial codes for world trade were reinvented, allowing for intense deregulation of the public sector. Banking instruments were granted special perks, not unlike the British East India Company, back in the day. But now, money could move at the speed of light. This mercantilism, like its predecessor, was highly speculative, a piratical style of business—but way faster. Like pirate coves in 1700, there were tiny British colonies in the West Indies, most notably the Cayman Islands. Like Lloyds of London doing its finagles back home, like a puppet master, Swiss and London bankers invented a new way to steal abroad. Once the internet satellites were added, by the late seventies, it was possible to launder a billion dollars in thirty seconds. Then came the eighties and nineties—the first age of Trump after all, his first puberty (hopefully 2020 being his last). The eighties were dominated by punitive neoliberal budgets that crushed public spending in Los Angeles, as in so many cities. It took forever to even launch a new trolley system. There are still no bullet trains. Homeless programs ran on nickels.

At the same time, Pacific trade was exploding, partly under cover of the dying Cold War, the velvet revolutions, the Gulf War. Offstage, the harbor of Los Angeles made special arrangements with East Asian traders—and particularly with Denmark's Maersk shipping, the largest carrier in the world. By 1990, if you walked across the two ports that constitute the LA harbor, almost every ship docking was not flying American colors. At first, these flags represented a partnership, because American multinationals ran the table on globalization in the late sixties. But soon enough, the multinationals themselves became increasingly non-American, setting up headquarters in tax-free zones. And their East Asian and West European partners were more than thoroughly independent. Like the British East India Company in 1700, American privateer corporations could shave off profits, hide income, be moguls.

The prologue to this deregulated free-for-all, was fifties consumerism, also pioneered in Southern California—bringing McDonalds, Disneyland and a mature broadcast TV to America. The invasion (privatizing) of public life began under the banner of consumer fun. Hollywood had its brand of neo-mercantilism as well, through international distribution deals. The consumer package (from Nintendo to color TV) then became the designer template for the Mackintosh in 1984.[16] The Mackintosh was announced in a TV ad where the past was blown up as if it were a Hollywood trailer. How splendid and horrible the future has been. We have cheerfully gone along, allowed for new kinds of new kinds of distortion in our memory, public archiving and even intimacy itself. This economy of the senses is a hallmark of California mercantilism.

The result has been a plastic surgery of the present, without much of a past, or much of a future. Along with medication, this frozen smile was then engineered into the Arts District of Los Angeles.[17] But there are signs of downtown hitting a wall after the pandemic. To repeat, clearly, the age of globalization is ending. What does that mean? Global consumerati are still around. As I pointed out a few pages back, the fall of 2020 was a record comeback for container shipments to the LA ports, after months of heart wrenching collapse. And yet, something is ending.

At first, vastly expanded shipping lanes along the Pacific seemed a boon to Los Angeles, They offered a regime for big box capitalism, that energized the eastern end of the LA Basin. The process, of course, was overloaded with moral ironies. Globalization literally grew out of the failures of American militarism, after early successes in Asia. By 2000, the very sea lanes that were essential to the American occupation of Japan, Korea and Vietnam turned into a supply chain for Asian shipping. Instead of missiles and napalm, it delivered compact cars from Toyota (who had been headquartered in California since 1957). This globalist business regime also favored the tax-free laundering of profits. Losses in tax revenue due to tax havens easily amount to hundreds of billions of dollars every year. It is difficult, of course, to calculate the invisible.

The seventies Cold War in LA was not simply about military hardware. It allowed for a restructuring away from heavy manufacturing toward a service-oriented economy. There was already a supply chain of industrial parks along the new freeway system. Cold War manufacturing was therefore a suburban thing, then in the late nineties, it refocused on the inner cities as well and began to gentrify various slums. Meanwhile, "Gateway Cities" like Bell and Southgate continued to absorb more immigrants than they could sustain. So did early GI suburbs in the valleys. A new diffusion of races and classes has remade what we mean by segregation, but not removed it.

UNDERDEVELOPMENT

In response to neoliberal campaigns against the public sector, social programs in cities were savaged. However, the budgets for the police remained safe (even sacrosanct), and could be gradually raised. These budgets took care of human drift, because legislators in Washington presumably did not care. They did not have to confront mass wretchedness every day. Also, cities are not the Federal Reserve. They cannot print money, they must balance deficits only through bonds and loans. So, growing police budgets had to perform double duty. They had to deliver human services in a dwindling world—like mental health and emergency care. But asking cops to double as half-baked social workers is near impossible. In the case of Los Angeles, after the Rodney King horror in 1991, and the civil unrest a year later, community policing was installed. It is fair to say that the LAPD did moderately soften its abuses. That absorbed much of the nineties, but not the decades after.

I had no idea of the extent of the scandal in the Rampart police district during 1997. Police officers committed several violations of procedure during interactions with myself although this was mitigated by more community policing. However, in public hearings and through law suits, many residents complained about county sheriffs behaving badly in the outlying districts of the county.

During the Iraq War, through the 1033 Program, the Department of Defense could "transfer excess military equipment to local law enforcement."[18] Over $7.4 billion was donated to hundreds of police forces, including the LAPD—a new boondoggle for defense contractors.[19] This weaponizing of local cops, as if they were an army of occupation in Baghdad, was probably more extreme in other cities. But the impact of immigration and growing density[20] and growing inequality could not be ignored here either.

Let us take the long view again: In sync with the Reagan Tea Party, anti-government mentality of Washington

politics, Los Angeles entered a cycle of underdevelopment
that one usually associates with developing nations.
Eventually, about one third of all imports into the US
arrived through the LA harbors, but only 3% were inspected,
so the tax revenues are dubious. Was this Pinochet's Chile?
Nevertheless, the roar of capital seemed worth cheering
about. Those trillions of dollars required a bigger distribution
chain within Southern California. What used to be seen as
'corridor cities' isolated within the county, along freeways
from the ports, were national arteries that would have been
impossible in 1960. The movement of all this merchandise,
like a watershed, finally stretched a thousand miles or more.
The Inland Empire was now basic to a nationwide empire.[21]
Some trains on the Alameda Corridor[22] continue straight to
Chicago;[23] or trucks into Mexico. The shift radiating from
the ports was more than just the unloading of containers.
It sculpted a new economic reality across the West.[24]

This new supply chain is a kind of sovereignty outside
the United States as well. It pushes the nation's western
boundary into the Pacific as never before.[25] Using seventeenth
century mercantilist imagery, LA was like a freeport on
the Open Sea (*Mare Liberum*),[26] as they called the Pacific
in the seventeenth century. Losing aerospace turned LA into
a sovereign city state, like Venice in the fifteenth century;
or Singapore today. During the nineties recession, LA was
forced to self isolate.[27] Contracts from Washington diminished,
especially when gridlock overtook Congress after 1994, after
Gingrich unleashed the Contract with America. Then nothing
much was done after Clinton's Penisgate fiasco.

INTERREGNUM

Post-Trump America even resembles medieval Byzantium
in some ways. Constantinople was sacked by Trump-like
crusaders in 1204. The Byzantines lost most of their presence
in the world, while crusaders proceeded to bleed and destroy
everything Byzantine. What followed was an interregnum
where Constantinople lost its hegemonic presence in the

Mediterranean, lost colonies to Venice, and in the north, to Russia. By the time, the city of Constantinople actually fell in 1453, it had undergone a violent drift lasting 450 years. That is the mood in the US at large in 2021. But is this the end of interregnum, or simply another stage?

The American interregnum is a dialect from the early stages of European imperialism. As empires gradually fade, they produce many dialects—a subaltern overlay of leftovers. These do not simply die; they eccentrically reincarnate, as they fracture into separate regions. The period after the Cold War revived nativist hatreds within the US. That split the nation into three political sovereignties: the Atlantic kingdom, the Pacific kingdom, and the new Confederacy. In the meantime, master planning all but ceased for generations. I leave the reader to guess whether that puts us in 2021 in the second act or the third act. Biden's first two years will tell; as will future planning in quasi-sovereign kingdoms like Los Angeles.

The rerouting of LA since 1990—and not just the ports—is a product of earthshaking proportions. Clearly, nothing will be easily resolved. Our *longue durée* resembles how the Roman empires faded away. Or the Spanish and the Mediterranean empires in the sixteenth century. Or the Ottomans after 1693; or the Ming Dynasty, the Persian kingdoms in Central Asia; India in the late middle ages. Hyper-powerful empires tend to contract, lose equilibrium. Their decay incubates new civilizations. After the Western hegemony ended, the earth was terraformed again.

The Biden Administration will redirect us away from Trump's suicidal distrust of California. But the overall transition may take fifty years. The elections of 2020 nearly toppled the Constitution itself. America is being transmogrified, that much is certain. Among the possible scenarios is that Americans will take charge of this liquid moment. I vote for that.

The eighties! Where would Trump be without the decade that made him a rock star? Whatever those 1980 fissures have been—economic, racist, technological—they came of age in 2020. And yet, somehow on a micro level: As we paused, they saturated into the fine points of everyday life.

PORTABILITY

The matrix radiating from LA harbor provides a million jobs across four counties, and 2.9 million nationwide.[28] That means 73% of all cargo in the West Coast, and 30% nationwide, on average over $2 billion a day. The supply chain from China, in particular, is now so continuous, it dissolves many boundaries within the US itself. Container trade slipped badly during the Great Recession, then recovered, and has ratcheted back and forth since. There was a 15% downtown during Trump's trade war with China. But in March, incoming trade virtually stopped, then in October, broke records.[29] But there are enough warnings that something is trembling in this neo-mercantilist universe. The pandemic has sped that up. There will be a shrinking of global supply chains around the world. The era that we call globalization is ending, even if cargo holds remain full.

At the ports themselves, new waves of automation in heavy manufacturing promise to depress employment. Digital apps are steadily replacing people. The mind of software is preordained to remove jobs.

But to service the internet of things requires more fulfilment warehouses closer to home, to keep up with e-commerce, through Amazon and FedEx. The logistics sector already accounts for 20% of all new jobs (during the pandemic, higher than that). More light manufacturing goes with more logistics: spare parts, new packaging, 3D printing. Add to that reoginal factories delivering renewable energy, like batteries and solar panels. Logistics is outstripping production in this era. The origins go back to the fifties, when high consumerism took off, to finally account for 70% of the entire economy. The internet merely turned consumerism into logistics, which means light manufacturing in industrial parks and smaller shops. Who said puppet masters are not your friend (at least on Facebook)? How involuted our madness has become.

Oops. Your screen says that Amazon just delivered a package. Talk about end-to-end visibility and flexible process![30] The pandemic is turning logistics into the last friend who can walk on your front porch. In the years to come, that means shorter supply chains to stay fast; a speedup of trends since 2016. And unfortunately, at the warehouse, that 'requires' more robots (and fewer employees) to bring a smile to your face.

The age of infinite globalization has ended, in its big-box twentieth century form. Logistics will clearly bring light manufacturing back the US. Working at home is all about logistics, while at the same time, granulating more national boundaries (who has to be near work?). Work at home is easily turning into an indenture, to an oligarch you never see.

The need for cute neighborhoods is greater than ever. Sandwich joints in office towers are in trouble. With more work at home, neighborhood bars will expand (those that survive the pandemic). Many lost store fronts will turn into apartments. And Los Angeles will have to quasi-house 10% more poverty. Homeless camps are evolving inside city parks.[31] As I often say, your grandchildren will ask you about 2020. Historians will dedicate programs to it. At the same time, children will dress up as Americans for Halloween.

ENDNOTES

I want to thank Christina Griggs and Max Maria for their hard work in helping with the research. We met almost every week for months, in meetings set up by Namik Makic. We particularly examined the ports and their outreach, the true history of densification, emerging labor crises (i.e. the gig economy), city planning documents, and broader architectural questions about the social history of LA 1980–2020.

1 In the sixties, food trucks evolved from the hashhouses and taco stands in LA. That accompanied the waves of Mexican and Asian immigration, often sharing the same neighborhoods. This caught on as a trend nationwide. Some trucks were even rated by Zagat, and their cooks opened trendy indoor restaurants during the nineties. The craze shifted toward fusion, like Korean-Mexican Kogi BBQ, until after 2008, then, after 2018, it began again. Jean Trinh, "LA's Food Truck Boom Happened 10 Years Ago. Where Are They Now," *Eater Los Angeles*, September 13, 2018. Jonathan Gold, "How America Became a Food Truck Nation (tracing the food truck revolution back to its Los Angeles roots)," *Smithsonian Magazine*, March 2012: "In LA (food rucks) can be as thick on the freeway as taxicabs on New York's Sixth Avenue." Jonathan Gold was the dean of LA food critics, he helped make LA street food a journey into vernacular neighborhood life. That helped commodify the rise of the New Byzantium. Also: Ross Resnick, "When Foodie Met Truckie: The Story of Food Trucks in LA," Thrillist, January, 16, 2016.

2 Fazila Bhimji, "Struggles, Urban Citizenship, And Belonging: The Experience of Undocumented Street Vendors and Food Truck Owners" in *Los Angeles, Urban Anthropology and Studies of Cultural Systems and World Economic Development*, Vol. 39, No. 4, Informal Economies in North America, Winter, 2010, pp. 455–492. The harassment of Mexican immigrant women vendors by the LAPD finally became citywide news in the summer of 1993: Robert Lopez, 'Vendors Demand a Hearing at City Hall,' Los Angeles Times, August 1, 1993.Robert Lopez, "Vendors Protest against LAPD," *Los Angeles Times*, Aug. 2, 1994.

3 Adrianna Kezar, Tom DePaola, Daniel T. Scott, *The Gig Academy: Mapping Labor* in the Neoliberal University (Baltimore: Johns Hopkins University Press, 2019).

4 Timothy Puko, 'In Los Angeles, an Economy Built on Freelancers Crumbles: Creative workers with multiple gigs are among the worst hit by the recession and face long roads to recovery,' *Wall Street Journal*, June 20, 2020.

5 Among the most reprinted Victorian travel guides was Gustave Doré and Blanchard Jerrold's *London: A Pilgrimage* (London: Grant and Company, 1872). Doré's black-line chiaroscuro wood engravings were adapted by David Lean for set designs in *Oliver Twist* and have

been considered classics of social realism (with a touch of local color). Jerrold's text is very purple, late Romanticist in its fascination with local poverty as colorful; with street gypsies. He advises those strolling through London to enjoy local color only from a distance, because up close, one was forced to notice the tatters in people's clothing. For a brief comparison of LA local color, see Raymond Chandler's *Farewell My Lovely* (1940): Early in the novel, Marlowe is coaxes by Moose Molloy to visit a black saloon on changing Central Avenue. There, "a big thick-necked black with a flattened face, slowly stood up straight near the bar, getting ready to throw us out." Over the thirties, the black population around Central Avenue had doubled. Local color often hides vast sociological transitions (i.e. loncheria trucks in the eighties, black street life on Central Avenue, circa 1939, when Chandler wrote *Farewell my Lovely*, based on short stories from three years before.

[6] Roger Waldinger and Mehdi Bozorgmehr, *Ethnic Los Angeles* (New York: Russell Sage Foundation, 1996), p. 13ff.

[7] James Sterngold, "A Changing California Emerges from Recession," *Los Angeles Times*, March 29, 1995. The aerospace recession essentially began in June, 1990 and was over by March, 1995. From Martha Grove, "California Still Reeling from Recession Blow," *Los Angeles Times*, June 28, 1992: "California, dazed and bloodied from its longest and deepest downturn since World War II, is acting like a punch-drunk boxer in a grueling bout with no end in sight." "Estimates vary, but California appears to have lost between 500,000 and 700,000 non-farm jobs in the downturn, which started in mid-1990. As much as 85% of that decline was in Southern California, according to Pauline Sweezey, chief economist for the state Department of Finance in Sacramento. Los Angeles County alone accounted for 63% of the state's job loss, with layoffs coming primarily in defense and aerospace, construction and financial services." Patrick Lee, "In California, Jobless Rate Soars to 9.8%," Los Angeles Times, September 5, 1992: "The state job figures also illustrate the disturbing trend toward 'de-employment," workers losing higher-paying jobs in manufacturing and goods-producing industries—hurt by defense cutbacks and the collapse of the real estate market—and working at far lower wages in service industries.'

[8] For a sense of the Mayor and City Council trying to confront the crisis, just as the recession was ending, see LA's General Plan Framework for 1996: https://planning.lacity.org/cwd/framwk/chapters/01/01. While the tone was often promotional, many clues lie close to the surface, for example: 'the deteriorating industrial area with limited future industrial potential, which market forces could recycle into more viable land uses.' This 'market-forces' policy may have inspired construction of a fiber optic matrix underneath downtown. That speedier signal may have led to MCA moving into

One Wilshire. Then other telecommunications outlets followed. Gradually, two square blocks were transmogrified into the central hub for telecommunications from Asia, in part due to the paranoia about the recession post-1995.

9 Jesus Sanchez, "High and Dry: Downtown Struggles to Recover From 1980s Building Boom That Went Bust," Los Angeles Times, October 15, 1995.

10 Susan Strange, *Casino Capitalism* (Manchester: Manchester University Press, 1997; orig. 1986), pp. 38, 52–55.

11 Bob Baker, "LA's Booming Auto Industry Now a Memory," Bob Baker, LA Times Labor Writer (a category that seems to have disappeared nationally), July 20, 1991. "Developers built almost enough new space—about 8 million square feet between 1988 and 1992—to fill Century City."

12 Allen J. Scott, "The aerospace-electronics industrial complex of Southern California: The formative years, 1940–1960," *Research Policy*, Vol. 20, No. 5, October 1991, pp. 439–456.

13 Ralph Vartabedian, "Northrup to Cut 3,000 from Work Force," *Los Angeles Time*s, March 25, 1994. The closures around aerospace continued into 1997.

14 Martin Macias Jr., "Furusato: The Lost Japanese Fishing Village Between LA's Ports,' *Courthouse News Service*, June 12, 2018. A memorial site was set up in 2002, by the children of former residents who were interned in 1942. One descendant explained: 'If something like that happened again, I would be taken;' 'Bulldozing this life, this entire community in a non-negotiable way, it's scary. It cannot be undone."

15 Tim Waters, "San Pedro Fishermen, Hurt by Closing of Canneries, Want to Buy One of Their Own : Boat Owners Seek Deal With Star-Kist," *Los Angeles Times*, March 9, 1987. The canneries died from 1918, included Chicken of the Sea (closed in 2001)) and Starkist. The canneries built a company town of 300 houses, for a community of fishermen that ranged between two and three thousand, most of them Japanese. There was still beach alongside the cement. A writer columnist for the *LA Times* wrote: "As the sun rises higher and higher, the smell of fish becomes almost a tangible cloud" (Hadley Meares, 'Off the coast of San Pedro, a Japanese community erased: Isolated from the mainland of Los Angeles, Fish Harbor was a "dreamland" until 1942,' la.curbed, March 30, 2018). The entire community was given two days to move, by presidential order. A plaque honoring their ordeal was commemorated in 2002.

16 Stephen Levy, Insanely Great: *The Life and Times of Macintosh, the Computer that Changed Everything*, (London: Penguin Books, 2000), John Webster, "Home Sweet PC," *Computerworld*, April 1, 1991.

17 Jon Regardie, "After COVID-19, Can Downtown L.A. Get Back Up?" *Los Angeles Magazine*, March 24, 2021. Since 2000,

"spectacular growth… (boosted) downtown's residential population from about 18,000 to 85,000." Also 500,000 now work downtown, or use downtown (from nearby areas). All of that was frozen during the pandemic. The November 2020 Downtown Los Angeles Community Plan Update, projected another 150,000 residents added to downtown by 2040. But these magic statistics sometimes involve magical thinking as well. The pandemic has clearly stifled the future growth of downtown for a few years. The future of many districts in the city depends on five vectors at least: the shrinking of globalization supply chains; the crises in Hollywood (exhibitors especially, like Pacific Arclight going bankrupt in April 2021); the changing logistics from the ports; the future of Silicon Beach. There will be a relative boom, but booms are always selective as well.

18 Nathaniel Lee, "How police militarization became an over $5 billion business coveted by the defense industry," *CNBC*, July 10, 2020. A scandal that was reported throughout the national media after the murder.

19 Ibid.

20 Arguments about how to densify Los Angeles, and where to densify, have come and gone over the past fifty years (mostly not amounted to very significant changes in the ratio of single-family homes to rentals): Elijah Chiland, "Single-family homes cover almost half of Los Angeles—here's how that happened," *Curbed*, Los Angeles, Jan. 15, 2020. See also under General Plan Framework (op. cit.), chapter 4 (on how the number of rentals. did not keep up with population growth from 1980 to 1990). Today, one out of three renters in LA spends more than half their income on rent. Jill Cowan and Robert Gebeloff, "As Rents Outrun Pay, California Families Live on a Knife's Edge," *New York Times*, Nov. 21, 2019, updated Feb. 12, 2021. This problem was long foreseen. However, the 1970 Centers Concept Plan—arguing for densification of rental housing—had almost no impact by 2007; and only minimally since. It was almost impossible to shift from R1 homes to a rental-first strategy. Christian Peralta, "Back To The Future: The 1970 Los Angeles 'Centers' Concept Plan," Planetizen, April 5, 2007

21 Juan De Lara, *Inland Shift: Race, Space and Capital in Southern California* (Berkeley: University of California Press, 2018). Traces the Inland Empire's rise underneath the canopy of expanding trade through the ports. It also documents the signs of the boom in new business construction in Rancho Cucamonga, and other depot sites in the Inland Empire, even during the 2020 pandemic. As global supply chains presumably tighten after 2020, the globalized Inland Empire will double more as a revitalized network for American-made inventories as well. "US Industrial Market Flash: Distribution Hubs Will Benefit from Increased Business Inventories and Supply Chain Restructuring," CBRE, May 14, 2020. CBRE is a leading corporate real estate company.

22 "Completed Projects," Acta (Alameda Corridor Transportation Authority). https://www.acta.org/about/projects/completed-projects/; Nora Zamicho, "Wilson OKs Use of Eminent Domain to Create Railway Corridor : Transit: Governor urges that condemnation be used only as a last resort in talks with Southern Pacific, which wants $260 million for its route between Downtown and the Harbor area," *Los Angeles Times*, Sept. 9, 1993. Another recession infrastructure plan. See also: *The Alameda Corridor Project: Its Successes and Challenges, Subcommittee Hearings by the United States Congress, April, 2001* (CreateSpace Independent Publishing Platform, 2018); Lane Barden, "The Trench: The Alameda Corridor Picturing Los Angeles," in Kazys Varnelis, ed., *The Infrastructural City: Networked Ecologies in Los Angeles* (Barcelona: Actar, 2009). Huge growth midway through the recovery from 2008, after the Inland Empire was among the hardest hit in California by the Great Recession: Chris Kirham, "Growth in Inland Empire soars; The region is forecast to lead the Southland in the rate of job and business creation," *Los Angeles Times*, October 23, 2014: "Overall, the Inland Empire accounted for two-thirds of the new businesses created statewide from 2012 to 2013... Over the last year, Inland Empire jobs have increased 2.7%, a faster rate than any part of California except the Bay Area. That's more than double the rate of Los Angeles County and nearly triple the pace of Orange County. Thursday's report predicts the Inland Empire will add jobs at an even faster clip—about 3.4% annually—over the next five years."

23 "Walmart's warehouse in Elwood, Illinois, operated by 3PL (third part logistics subcontractor) Schneider, is a block away... where the containers are first opened after having been closed at the factory in China"—transported from the LA ports. There was a strike at this Illinois warehouse in November, 2012. In Los Angeles, seventy workers from ILWU 663—Pier 400 at the Port of Los Angeles—also struck in sympathy, indicating two-thousand mile echoes made by this Pacific distribution chain. Global Supply Chains Research Group, "China supply chain inquiry report-back," December 5, 2015.

24 The American artist most involved in recording this maritime transition into Los Angeles, from 1972 onward, was probably Allan Sekula. One of many articles covering his work: Bill Roberts, "Production in View: Allan Sekula's Fish Story and the Thawing of Postmodernism," Tate (Museum) Papers, No. 18, Autumn 2012. "Bill Roberts argues that Fish Story 1989–95 by the photographer and theorist Allan Sekula expresses a shift from a culture of postmodernism to one of globalism and reflects the artist's effort to renew realist art in the wake of the postmodern culture of the 1980s." Also, Sekula's films *The Lottery of the Sea* (2006) and *The Forgotten Space* (2010). He grew up near the port of San Pedro but came out of a family linked to industrial labor in Erie, Pennsylvania.

[25] Port of Los Angeles annual reports, 2006 forward. Port of Los Angeles Facts and Figures, 2000 forward. Bill Sharpsteen, *The Docks*, (Berkeley: University of California Press, 2011); Among many articles tracing the growth of Pacific trade since the sixties, but especially after 2000—James Flanigan, "Keep on Trucking at the Ports," *LA Times*, October 22, 2003; Ronald White, "Soaring Port Traffic Delivers More Jobs; A boom in trade and cargo volume has turned the docks in L.A. and Long Beach into an employment engine, *Los Angeles Times*, July 19, 2004; Robert Gottlieb, "Port of Call: On Becoming China's Entrepôt," *Boom: A Journal of California*, Vol. 5, No. 1, Spring 2015, pp. 29–37. During the pandemic, the ports suffered a decline, but recovered briskly over the late summer, 2020, indicating renewed momentum, even expansion in the future. An incentive program to speed up truck turns, in order to handle the "clogged gateway' was set up in February, 2021 ($7.5 in incentive rewards): Bill Mongelluzzo, "LA port taps $7.5 million to reward productive terminals, *JOC* (*Journal of Commerce* online), January 21, 2021. This came in response to renewed fears of another logistics "meltdown" at the ports, already container ship waits at crisis levels (Ja. 13, 2021). All this was a sign of a boom confronting uneven planning and infrastructure: "Solution elusive to avoid next LA–LB port backup, *JOC* (*Journal of Commerce* online), March 19, 2021. The congestion was expected to clear up by late spring "seeing glimpses of improved productivity" (February 5, 2021). Clearly, the post pandemic trade patterns were somehow different than earlier, not simply a return to anxious normal. I would suggest that new logistics were forced by the pandemic, and that these changes suggest a more permanent shift—differences in the Pacific supply chain, a new era about to begin; probably more about shift in consumer tastes, and certain areas of manufacturing growing, with different needs, a new stage in globalization. Another shift will certainly be toward more infrastructure to support data capitalism at the ports; from *JOC*, March 2, 2020 (before the pandemic): "Container gateways evolving from cargo ports to data portals: "Initiatives aimed at turning container ports from conduits of physical freight activity into hubs for the digital information surrounding those cargo movements are underway in virtually every major global gateway."

[26] *Mare Liberum*, or The Open Sea, was a concept developed by the Dutch jurist Hugo Grotius, beginning in 1607. But it was also reframed in defense of the nation state—and strangely enough, also in defense of destroying the nation. Upon the Open Sea— the Pacific today (and the wide open Internet)—non-national carriers hemorrhage the American state. They are updates of pirates and privateers—or joint stock companies who were legally vassals of the king, but saw vassalage more as a license to steal (circa 1600–1780). The most exalted of these thieves were the Dutch East India

Company, and the British East India Company. Many historians consider globalization today a freewheeling return to Baroque mercantilist anarchy. Upon the Open Pacific in 2021, multinational entities do what they please; and prefer "freeports" rich enough to cater to their every whim; like the ports of LA. Another historical strategy, mostly after 2010, has to been to examine urban zones as freeports, then and now (i.e. mercantilist concessions to foreign traders); and the blurred meaning of sovereign urban territory then and now. This runs parallel to post-structural concepts of deterritorialization. It imagines cities reshaped by neo-mercantilism. For example: Keller Easterling, Extrastatecraft: *The Power of Infrastructure Space* (London: Verso, 2014); and Stuart Eldon, *The Birth of Territory* (Chicago: University of Chicago Press, 2013)

[27] Robert Leiter and Elissa Barbour, "Regional Planning in Southern California," in David. C. Sloane, ed., *Planning Los Angeles* (Chicago: Planners Press, 2012), pp. 162–170. How the drift between the federal government and LA's regional needs grew much wider after 1980; and especially in the nineties. I do remember FEMA being very helpful after the Northridge Earthquake (1994). But that was also the year of Gingrich's *Contract With America*, which began a defunding cycle that did not stop until 2021.

[28] James Flanigan "Keep on Trucking at the Ports," *Los Angeles Times*, October 22, 2013.

[29] Lisa Baertlein, "Ships wait to unload at Port of Los Angeles as imports boom," *Reuters*, October 18, 2020.

[30] "Impact of COVID-19 on the World's Logistics Market: Post-Pandemic Growth Opportunity Assessment Report 2020," *Research and Markets* (Global Newswire), June 29, 2020.

[31] The crisis surrounding the closure of a homeless encampment in Echo Park in late March, 2021. 174 tents were removed, and 180 protesters arrested. There is clearly more to come across the LA area. But the future for the unhoused must not be envisioned strictly as a tent. For every homeless person, imagine fifty who are nearly homeless. Then imagine millions of people a paycheck away from being on the street. How will they organize their lives? Sleep in closets, in cars, on trains? Over the next few years surely, rents will skyrocket. Over the next twenty years, the percentage of gig jobs within the labor market will also skyrocket. How many directions will bare survival require? Benjamin Oreskes, 'City plans to close Echo Park Lake and clear homeless encampment,' *Los Angeles Times*, March 23, 2021. Benjamin Oreskes, Doug Smith, "How a commune-like encampment in Echo Park became flashpoint in LA's homelessness crisis,'" *Los Angeles Times*, March 13, 2021. A program for housing the homeless has accelerated slightly in LA, due to the pandemic (another 6,500 units added in early 2021, with 62,000 already on the waiting list). However, the larger problem

must be solved nationally. That is: how to give more people a job and a future, not just a temporary roof over their heads. Since 1974, the precarious economy has been made infinitely worse by a shrunken public sector, As of 2021, the housing shockwave is so far gone, it can only be addressed by Washington first. But that alone could never be enough. The federal response must be coordinated with local bond issues as well; and with cultural reforms across the entire educational sector. And finally, corporations must offer genuine support, as a sound investment. A jobs engine of this kind, both legal and structural, can save perhaps a hundred million Americans from being '"nearly homeless'" in the future. This is not an impossibly high statistic. As FDR said at his second inaugural address in 1937 (after substantial improvement in the economy), "I see one third of a nation ill-housed, ill-clad, ill-nourished."

We Will All
Only Be Here

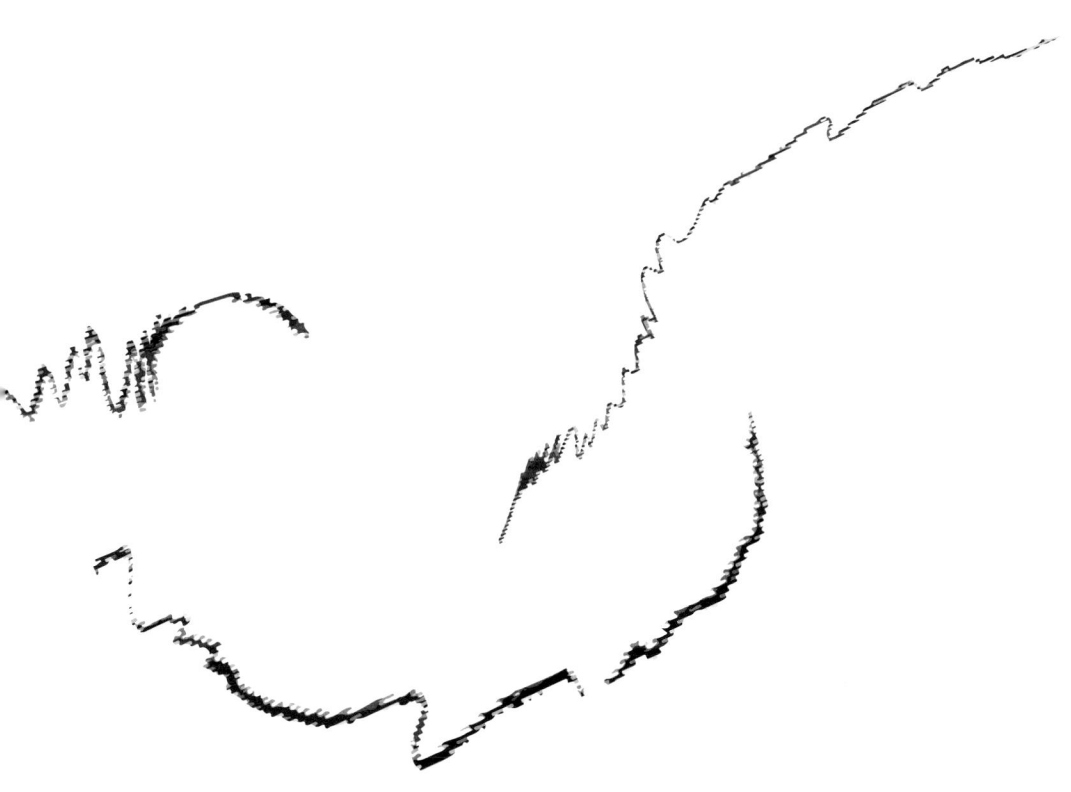

RYAN BISHOP AND ABDOUMALIQ SIMONE

The hyena is the crest of mathematics;
It knows that no leftovers can remain.
Zero is its god.
      Heiner Müller

In a temporal arc that runs from the mid-nineteenth century to the present, an arc that constitutes our current condition of mixed spatial realities in urban settings, the early 1990s appear rather late in the trajectory. At that moment, though, MCI (Microwave Communications Inc., now subsumed as part of Verizon) ran a series of television ads in the US touting the wonders of digital data and the increasing affordances provided by the Internet. The ads featured a young Anna Paquin, looking as if she'd wandered off the set of *The Piano*, clothed in a neo-Victorian outfit that evoked educational institutions and Bohemian artistry in the same material folds. In one specific ad, Paquin as narrator/guide moves in playfully precocious rapidity about a landscape empty of human or urban markers.

Our plucky futural visionary stares into the camera and says: "There will be a road that will not connect two points. It will connect all points." Sounding quizzical as if imaginatively conjuring this magical motorway on the spot, she continues, "Its speed limit will be…? [pause], the speed of light" and nods in approval of her own decision.

"It will not go from here to there" she exclaims before figure and ground flip, and she is seen in a long shot necessitating she shout, thus emphasizing the distance between speaker and audience in the next line: "There will be no more there." An echo punctuates the final word. The effect emphasizes the spatial "there" in the sentence over the existential "there' that initiates it. The emphasis is reversed, though, in the next line when the narrator returns (like a Greek epode) to her original close-up and repeats the line: "There be no more there".

She concludes sagely and enigmatically, "We will all only be here".

The line echoing across an Outback vacuity and repeated in the returned close-up anticipates the erasure of one half of a spatial dyad tethered to metaphysics: "There will be no there". While time and space manipulations have long been at the heart of various tele-technologies, this line possesses all manner of weird linguistic moves, such as the existential "there' jockeying with the spatial "there" for primacy but also creating a closed loop at the syntactic level. The play of presence and absence essential to tele-technologies, and indeed representation generally, can be traced in that tension between the existential there and the spatial there. The loss of one half of that metaphysical binarism is the triumph of the other: "We will only be here".[1]

The capacity for us all to only be here articulated in the ad's terminal line marks the metaphysics of transmission or broadcast technologies, a telepresence which allows for multiple copies of a live or recorded event to exist in real-time relations to each other. The ad's narrator performs this metaphysical maneuver in the utterance of the line itself, a speech act that whistles down the wires and proves its tautological point in the process. The "there" obliterated by the yet-to-be revealed at that moment but all too-present in our current one, results from an exoskeletal ring of telecommunications satellites in conjunction with numerous fiber optics and submarine cables carrying data in the complex infrastructure hidden by the seamless performance of our whizzbang hand-held devices and tablets. The wired/wireless cable and satellite ring configuration creates a different sense of "there" rendered present but still very much constitutive of the "here' we all occupy in a grand locality within the technosphere.

The ad offers a snappy snippet of technophilic boosterism metonymic of the breathless enthusiasm found in the public discourse of the early 1990s as the Internet entered the consumer telecoms domain. As such, the ad proleptically gestures to the condition of multi-sited realities, mixed or blended spatial relations and visual regimes operative with devices pressed into even greater usage as tools for connecting during the isolation of the COVID-19 pandemic. Already a means to be absent and present in one's corporeal space simultaneously and alternately with the shift of a gaze—a t/here in which we flit between here and there— these varied devices, as is our mixed-spatial realities, are both unprecedented and pre-scripted.[2] This material and imaginative condition is not the result of sci-fi speculative fiction, but generated by scenario planners at the RAND corporation and by the many "Wizards of Armageddon" that populated anonymous cubicles during the Cold War.

So, when we think of "walking in cities during lockdown" in the cathode-ray light of the MCI ad, we can wonder about the spatial and noetic status of the preposition "in" as well as those that pertain to the terms "here" and "there". Do these technologies mediate between spaces or do they create a new kind of space through their virtuality? And if the latter case accurately describes our condition, what kind of space is that?

Playing with the metaphysics of eliminating space (with the internet as articulated in the ad) and duration (with real-time tele-technologies), we can also loop back to the 1990s and then to the Cold War (and even back to the nineteenth century) to place the present in a kind of historically contextualized moment primarily prefigured from the middle part of the twentieth century—and indeed earlier with both wireless and wired technologies and their attendant imaginaries. As a history of keeping the past in the present, this temporal arc frames infrastructures and logistics of urbanism across planetary space, as well as the varieties of technological sensing that define such space.

We will no longer be there; we all only be here. If that is our status now—in the eternal now of real-time teletechnologies communication systems—we could churlishly create a portmanteau of metaphysics collapsing time (now) into space (here) as now-here, or nowhere. That is the one perpetual time-space moment, or "in", we paradoxically occupy.

IN, AND ITS MANIFOLD RECONSTITUTION

> The sonic charge is strangely uneven when it comes to common prepositions and other nuts and bolts. 'With', 'to', 'of' – these are almost totally forgotten by the inner ear. But 'up' (perhaps flexing its status as an adverb) has real staying power. It takes two or three hundred words before the mind forgets an 'up'.
> Martin Amis, 2020 *Inside Story*, p. 395

"In" packs the sonic charge that Martin Amis claims prepositions lack. Operating as a metaphysical bridge between time and space, as well as metaphorizing spatially temporal measurements, it also pertains to duration (e.g. in a matter of seconds), parts of things (e.g. in the chapter), modes of expression (e.g. argued in stark opposition), how things are arranged (e.g. the books stood in a pyramid), forms of dress (e.g. in a red coat), or expression of emotion (e.g. they watched in joy). It also has adjectival and adverbial wattage in its syntactic light. So thinking through the means by which the spatiality and noetic transformations of this highly operative preposition leads us to new perspectives of the technologies and data shaping the grammar of human and non-human perspectives of emergent and inchoate urban processes.

A consideration of the preposition "in" with regard to walking in cities during lockdown and engaging with teletechnologies reliant upon our collective exoskeletal planetary ring of telecomms satellites, modes of data generation and sensing the earth as planet prompts the question: where and what is "in" spatially, experientially and noetically in such a situation? In order to discuss infrastructures and logistics of urbanism across a planetary space, and thus arrive at some senses of the spatial and noetic status of "in" for our collective current moment, also entails considering the varieties of technological sensing that define such space. In addition to the pandemic, an increasing awareness around climate crises has helped underscore this point. "Planetarity itself comes into focus through orbiting imagining and terrestrial modeling technologies (satellites, sensors, servers in sync)," as Benjamin Bratton points out, "that have made it possible to measure climate change with any confidence" (Bratton 2019: 9). The convergence of disease and environmental unease intersecting with over a century of increased at-a-distance communication technologies used to track trauma and profit provide the volumetrics of the "in" of our dwelling.

These same teletechnologies that generate our multi-sited "in" with handheld devices in urban spaces also generate data for operational images, machine training to read images and machine-to-machine image making—thus images with data but without visual content for humans—information instead of representation: an "in" we can access but not experience. A good amount of operational imaging is surveillance of the earth's surface, which tethers it to military concerns as well as economic futures speculation and environmental monitoring. Machinic imaging can, and often does, bypass the human in its generation and reception while operating through human-programmed algorithms of sovereign desire: to control space as rapidly and completely as possible by turning it into data for rapid financial and/or political gain—gambling on environmental change and human erasure.

The axonometric divisions of various, multiple wireless forces sculpt the invisible "in" around and within which we shift across t/here and walk. Rather as nations generate sovereign air space in a conical formation from ground to aether, city boundaries move from underground infrastructure to surface level before beaming the city limits into space through axonometric projection. Is that the "in" we traverse? Or is that "in" further traversed at various planes, riddled with tensions and interrelationships between proprietary airwaves, information and geography, territory and control, through which sovereignties and imaginaries move across protean urban-planetary continua? (Bishop 2020, Parikka 2021). The city limits, its *limnes*, like that of the nation-state in which it exists, have become dynamic extensions of cartographic space interacting with our own corporeal boundaries. The volumetrics at play speak to the current (non-)urban conditions that indicate an urban yet-to-come that is also already reaching its limits in terms of geological, atmospheric, environmental and human existential implications (Bishop and Simone 2020), boundaries expanded and erased at the speed of falling bodies at the speed of light. This offers no stable volumetric spatiality or interior, but only the porous shell of the same with dynamic systems riven with strata and substrata at levels, including that of the ground: our "in" ever at stake that seemingly cannot hold nonetheless does and holds us in its spatial and noetic grip, through which we slip like so much sand.

Relinquishing static models of this interiority admits that any nominalization is but of an instant—a false axonometric projection as from a floor plan to projected walls and building—and one that demands we ignore the flux from which it was detached. The multi-scaled perspectives of duration, temporality, change and processual systems writ both macro and micro proffer a different means of articulating positionality and subjectivity, ones inextricably intertwined with the conditions of their possibility without erasing their necessity and readily articulated now by our handheld devices. If the Internet had intended to invoke an awe of technological capacity, it did so fully within the noetic domain of human agency and control, a domain still circulating in the consumer discourse of the present multi-sited and nested interiorities. It is a tale of comfort and mastery precariously poised in various willed lacunae—a tale of tele-surveillance and control resultant from Cold War strategies to have real-time dominance of the globe converted into consumer cultural products that reinforce agency within the subject (individual, collective or state). If we need new grammars to conceptualize, visualize and come to grips with this "in" we now have t/here, we can re-examine the prepositional, adverbial and adjectival potentials latent in "in" already on our tongues. These potentialities would include the prefix "in-" and its myriad related incarnations to its prepositional form, such as the untimeliness of "invention" and its attachment as negation of a condition or action, thus rendering operable terms inoperable. We are always and unavoidably filled with such inscriptions and their many varied potentialities.

MUZAK AND THE MULTIPLEXED MAKING OF MIXED REALITY TERRITORY

> Those of us who use the telephone today, the telegraph, the phonography, the train, bicycle or automobile, the ocean liner, dirigible or airplane, the cinema or a great daily newspaper (the synthesis of a day in the whole world) do not dream of how these diverse forms of communication, transportation and information exert such a decisive influence on our psyche.
> F. T. Marinetti (1913) "Destruction of Syntax – Wireless Imagination – Word in Freedom'

Major George Owen Squier coined the term "Muzak" while inventing many of the technological developments that allowed for telephony to be piped into homes, factories, and those great palaces of consumer culture known as department stores. He also invented telephone carrier multiplexing that after World War II led to microwave frequency multiplexing and its most recent incarnation as optical wavelength multiplexing. The process of multiple signals over a single medium—initially telephone wire—was a long standing goal of early experimenters in teletechnologies, including Alexander Graham Bell in the 1870s in his work on telegraphy. Squier developed in the first decade of the twentieth century for the US Army Signal Corps applications of wireless technological processes to wires, thus allowing up to five simultaneous conversations on one line. The inextricable intertwining of engineering innovations in wired and wireless technologies find long-lasting form in Squier's theoretical developments, leading to AT&T consumer applications in 1918, and their continued underpinning of microwave and optical fibre transmission systems for military and commercial application—and for Muzak, of course, the initial instantiation of ubiquitous ambient music.

When Squier was unduly turfed out of the Army in 1922 after one of his many dust-ups with his superiors, he turned to recalibrating his developments in multiplexing to a music service for the consumer market. In this manner he continued a rather long tradition of exchange between the military, communications technologies and music, but with the rise of engineering influences in US industrial production from Fordism to Taylorism, he found a good moment to push his ideas in both labor and recreational spheres (Lanza 26-27). Following Squier's pitch to several phone utility companies, soon the general public had offers of a variety of music and news channels on their phone lines at both work and at home, allowing for a perceived gold mine delivering entertainment, advertising and public service announcements. Nipping at their heels, though, were new developments in wireless delivery capacities, ones that allowed for greater quality of sound and ease of access, all of which eventually became FM bands that offered excellent audio fidelity.

Squier's wired world of communications transmission exists now in the submarine cables that carry about 90% of internet traffic. The wireless imagination of transmission possibilities that supplanted his innovation and that the internet provides is primarily delivered through the submarine network of cables initially laid in the 1850s.

Our urban multi-sited/mixed tele-technologies reality is layered between aqueous distributed internet data flows and the exoskeletal surveillance and transmission of satellite technologies developed for the Cold War strategy known as C3I: communications, command, control and information. No part of the world went untouched by C3I. And it delineates the organizational, economic, technological and spatial systems that derive from, rely on, and perpetuate military strategy and indeed consumer telecoms and quotidian consumerism of the same (Bishop 61)

Military R&D and consumer/business applications of telecommunications capacities and computational potentialities find a fulsome fusing in a pivotal moment in 1968 with what has been called "the mother of all demos".[3] At the Fall Joint Computer Conference in San Francisco, Douglas Englebart displayed the research he and his team at the Augmented Research Center at Stanford University had pioneered. Launched as oNLine Systems (NLS), the demo, which lasted more than an hour and a half (and which can be viewed on YouTube with your own handheld device or tablet), used tech from NASA and ARPA (the Advanced Research Projects Agency, related to the defense version DARPA) to display text editing on a word processor cathode-ray monitor, a computer mouse, hyperlinked documents and other components of the personal computing workstation. Englebart not only demonstrated these technologies to the attendees but did so "live' through a large screen projection that cut between video images of Englebart explaining the gear and images of his screen, creating a real-time transmission performance of screens projecting screens in an auditorium housing the mixed-space reality of our current daily existence.

ARPA, of course, built Arpanet as a communications system to survive nuclear attack. The design brief required a system that could survive the removal of "the head' of the system, or the central core, hence its distributed and redundant packet-switching capacities. Arpanet then becomes an important communications tool between researchers for Pentagon projects, primarily those housed in academic facilities, and provides the basic structure and technologies for the Internet, which eventually becomes the World Wide Web. Englebart's NLS became one of the first nodes on Arpanet, and "the mother of demos" introduces many of the infrastructures and logistics of urbanism across planetary space, and thus also the varieties of technological sensing that define such space. From Squier to wireless imaginaries to C3I satellites to Englebart's t/here demo of computing technologies and back to mid-nineteenth century telegraphy, we have but a few of many possible key points in the long arc that inscribes our uniquely predicted current "in".

NOW AND NOW(HERE)

Past, present and future – that old tripartite division
of the time continuum... cedes primacy
to the immediacy of a tele-presence... in which
the fourth dimension (that of time) suddenly
substitutes for the third: the material volume loses its
geometrical value as an 'effective presence'
and yields to an audiovisual volume whose self-
evident 'tele-presence' easily wins out over the
nature of the facts.
  Paul Virilio *Negative Horizon* p. 118

Doug Kahn argues, in relation to sound (re-)production technologies and the avant-garde, that three abstractions relate to the unfolding understanding of sound through and due to these technologies, abstractions that can be applied to audiovisual materials in the present: vibration, inscription and transmission (14). These abstractions, he contends, explain how "sounds are located or dislocated, contained or released, recorded or generated" (14). From the nineteenth century and research into waves and speculations around wireless technologies, vibration linked the visible world to the mystical and spiritual world of the invisible, a division of organic human visual capacities key to early modernist experimentation in technology and art. Central features of vibration, such as relationality, held important information for analyzing bodies and objects in space, emerging in sound experiments but also with synaesthetic technologies such as radar. Inscriptive technologies (such as the phonograph) empirically documented in a keenly technological fashion sound events in the world, not ones necessarily intended to convey meaning or emotion but any and all sounds, and were the products of nineteenth century mechanical experimentation. For Kahn, the two merge in transmission, which is the essence of the wireless imagination, "fusing the spatial features of vibration with the objecthood and corporeality of inscription" (20) while deepening the complexity of each. Transmission provides the projection of an object over space as a replication of itself, allowing it to be in multiple sites at the same time: the source of transmission, the medium through which it travels, and various points of reception. This technological capability shapes our multi-sited now that consumes our t/here, a configuration familiar to us in the MCI ad as well as through nearly a century and a half of tele-technological proliferation. These constitute our material and noetic companions and parameters as we walk now: "in" and here.

Walking on while standing still. This seems to have been the conundrum that Benjamin often wrestled with in his "dialectics of the standstill." That somehow the continuous unfolding of possibilities could only come together in the interruption of temporalities speeding ahead, fading behind, circling back, and veering off. Where they all converged in "the now"—something extracted from a background of both endless possibilities and deterministic constraints. For the history of that moment is unprecedented and cannot be reduced to a repetition. Whatever has constituted that

moment is fully within it, in way not dissimilar to being
"in the groove"—something that requires a "router" to
demarcate and materialize a specific territory, but which
remains fundamentally unsettled, loose, where booty is shaken
and not collected as property. To be in the now is a long
way from being "in-the-know", as things are coming at you
from all directions.

Even with all the decanting purportedly attained through
COVID procedures—all of the rules and regulations to filter
out the virus—to be inside whatever bubble was possible
to conceptualize, registered a tacit acknowledgement that
differentials of historical speeds and vectors of transmission
were relentlessly bearing down upon any strategic maneuvers
of evasion. You can't run, you can't hide, and things come
to a standstill: a position compensated for by modalities
of online social transactions that seemed to obscure original
positions, even genealogies, although at the same time
compelling interactions to amplify an original position.
However global the pandemic, it instigated the constant
questioning, "how is it there"? As if searching for such
differentiations provided the necessary surfeit of understanding
that would appropriately calibrate the registers of alarm
and relief, while also encouragingly evoking a "there' distinct
from, outside of and somehow constitutive of here.

To be "in the groove" means to be stuck in a continuous
"call-response" mode whose repetition means that there isn't
any sense of discernible forward progress—i.e. the interaction
is not proceeding to some consensual or even contested
destination—but rather that time stands still as undulating
and fluid. It can get feet moving even as there is nowhere
in particular to go. So when a convener of a Zoom workshop
of 300 attendees instructs people to "get into the groove"
by turning their cameras on, it is possible to think of such
an invocation as defeating the purpose of being in the
groove, whereas the simple registration or faintest trace
of those participants being present allowed anyone to

speculate as to what was taking place behind the scenes—all of the domestic, banal, frivolous activities concealed by the mark of a name on the black box; all of the illicit backdoor conversations taking place between strangers, sometimes using fake accounts to proposition each other with outlandish requests; all of those mixed up times and places not formally defined that could either assure any participant that their most secret desires might find a way "home" or that everyone simply now dwelled in a common oblivion. And then the occasional "zoom-bomb" that articulated everyone's perhaps deep-seated desire to subvert this and all proceedings; to indeed zoom in and unnerve the host, pointing to the parasitic nature of all social participation—one first and foremost comes to any gathering in order to "eat" (or be eaten).

At the same time, "the now" seems to have disappeared in this protracted moment of an incessant present. In the constant references to when the pandemic is over, when there is a return to normal, or to the substantially revised future that is necessary in order to redeem this moment, the now seems to be on hold, boxed in by the simultaneity of nostalgia, anticipation, dread and simply "getting through this time." Dependency on the "router", as in Wi-Fi networks, rather than the "router' as a configurer of grooves, acts to engineer a smooth surface of transactions, of sociality not prone to interruptions or interdictions, seemingly instrumental and opportunistic; the narcotizing affect entailed in traversing urban landscape of hypermodernity now empty but not ruined—the joys of ruination without the empirical evidence. While gazes in public did assume both disciplinary and transgressive functions, that messiness of everyday sociality—the awkward gestures, inappropriate comments, incessant disappointments, and sporadic convulsions of pleasure—were largely effaced, or at least smoothed over in the interest of economy and speed. Few leaps into the unknown; few flashes of febrile awareness; few risks for new combinations. Getting in the groove proves to be hard work.

As Sunil Manghani posits, there is "an ethics of rhythm" to which we become attuned when we become out of sync. As with technology, ideology, or the body, rhythm seems to work best when it appears not to be working at all. Manghani quotes Barthes on this point, "told with an acuity that persists: "From my window... I see a mother pushing an empty stroller, holding her child by the hand. She walks at her own pace, imperturbably; the child, meanwhile, is being pulled, dragged along, is forced to keep running, like an animal, or one of Sade's victims being whipped. She walks at her own pace, unaware of the fact that her son's rhythm is different. And she's his mother! Power – the subtlety of power – is effected through disrhythmy, heterorhythmy'" (Manghani: p. 157).

Nevertheless, that groove has proved essential to some as the key to survival, even as the groove was never interested in prolonging any particular disposition. But in the scramble for hospital beds, oxygen cylinders and medicine, India's elite and middle class had to operate in the middle of things, which in many respects is the time of "the now". All of the social capital that one might have accumulated, all of the connections and privileges that could be mobilized in order to facilitate access largely proved irrelevant to the actual ability to get hold of these things. In an intersection of memory, faint impressions, WhatsApp messages, dogged circulations, chasing down reports and rumours, and the most blatant of seductions, opportunities for access could suddenly present themselves for a brief moment, where things were available "now", and then no longer. Nothing could prepare one for occupying, being in, that now; there were no maps about how to get there, no privileged algorithms. Things appeared in a flash; a sudden convergence of the fortuitous, accidental, and logistical; a "now" that could not be held or sustained, but zoomed in on.

A now put on hold; the ability to get hold of in the now—both senses act to destabilize the very notion of the "hold." For all of the George Floyds held down, for all of the lives put on hold; for all of those desperate callers wanting medical treatment put on hold, and for all of those epidemiological procedures unable to really hold the virus at bay, the sense of being "in" anything, dependent as it is on a demarcation or bordering, increasingly does not hold. If a large volume of everyday transactions seem to obscure geography, where anyone can seem to reach anywhere, and if the configuration of supposedly safe operational spaces or spaces of domestication prove increasingly to be traps overrun with indebtedness, toxic intimacies, contagion, and excessive obligation, it becomes increasingly difficult to imagine an arrangement capable of holding things together, aside larger measures of coercion. For the hold is a locus of *shared affection*—both the story of individuals with their own desires and histories that come to hold on to each other for dear life, to make life endearing, and the intersection of disparate *ways of "taking"* (extracting). Just as the disciplinary injunction of the pandemic was for individuals to "get a hold on themselves" coupled with a reliance on the household as the locus for holding things in place, the predominant mode of sociality is signaled by email messages and reminder receivers of "events happening *now*", which even if they are identified as taking place somewhere, are operationalized as occurring nowhere, and often in a way, by availing themselves to a larger "public"—anyone can register—that forego attempts to steer their potential impact across specific sectors or geographies, again in a situation where the everywhere becomes the nowhere, and "the now", a speeded up zone of crashing and cascading fragments, which do not so much take Benjamian "leaps" into new flashes of unprecedented possibility, but mimic a constant profusion of memes and GIF's. This can translate into a pleasure associated with the "now you have it, now you don't", where attainment and loss collapse into each other. Just as the most watched YouTtube videos in Indonesia entail a person suddenly and inexplicably acquiring a luxury item and destroying it minutes after its acquisition (sort of an updated visual Zen koan or individualized potlatch).

The question may be the extent to which the time of "the now" is weaponized, deployed to constantly stun, deliver shocks without punctuation, thus anaesthetizing the recipient of constant disruption. When one walks "in" the urban—now at a planetary scale also bringing uncertain punctuation—we know that there remains something about it that "hits you in the face," an aesthetics of appearance where things can be anything whatsoever. A single force does not drive these aesthetics. They do not match up in a point-by-point correspondence to empirical conditions. Rather, these "remains" exist as an underlying reverberation, an impulsion to continuously "move on" that overrides the very registers of value that are "negotiated" at the intersection of capital and local vernacular processes. This is not about the assemblage of hybrid urbanizations, mutant forms, or cyborg worlding. Rather, it is a continuous proliferation of non-subsumable details incapable of being made *inter-operable* in the intersection of a generalizable, planetary scalable urban form and its instantiation within specific fields. But this "now" easily is protracted into a series of "thens", or "nowheres", where the dissipation of frames and the constant immediacy of access acculturates "users" to the theft of orientation and the twilight of place.

A PARAMETRIC VARIATION ON THE THEME OF "IN"

The ways in which the profusion of parametric devices (and thus parameters) both (in)habit spaces and constitute specific modalities and sensibilities of the inside convey further implications for urbanization and living "inside" the urban. Force, impact, and movement are registered according to parameters that track the composites of action, the ways in which different circulations, behaviours, and operations affect each other or are calculated as doing such (for all parameters entail choices). The range of modulated impacts to be registered can be built into the tracking system. But there are gradients of determination—that is the ways in which, for example, the interactions of different material flows, human uses, and environmental conditions in a city generate an incalculable number of possible actualities. As such any parameter, any established frame of attunement, registration and tracking is potentially affected by a multiplicity of inclinations, qualities, senses, and intensities— as Luciana Parisi delineates. A parameter not only is a device for translating movements, circulations, flows, vibrations, illuminations, frictions, and frequencies into counts, measures, and decisions, but is also a thing in itself, a thing with its own potentials. As such, "novel configurations of space are not derived from continual variations of form, but from a universe of discontinuous potentialities abducting the actual relations of data and thus exposing parametric aesthetics to the infinite quantities accompanying any set of possibilities" (Parisi: p. 186). Thus the sequential running of algorithms generates incomputable quantities and patternless data that have no application to existent realities, and thus introduce new forms of contingency within computational design that then give rise to events outside of any conceivable control. The long temporal arc we have delineated here is just such a case. It constitutes the conditions of possibility without which our current mixed-reality of time-space configurations of prosthetic teletechnological enhancement would not be possible, but our specific configurations of now(here) is not reducible to these conditions of possibility. This makes it, as noted, wholly prescribed and completely unprecedented.

To further these points, consider the ways in which the movement of people, energy, water, traffic, services, goods, and information in cities is increasingly shaped and regulated by parametric design. This brings together different data sets related to these phenomena, modulates the variable relationships among them, and alters their properties as a result. For example, they make water and energy and sanitation and transport and municipal finance and economic development all impact on each other through recursive feedback loops—some mutual influence is intentional, others not. New unpredictable, unfixable realities are produced in the very act of trying to better control things, to generate precise definitions of the operations of urban interiorities (and thus control them, our own updated C3I). That they elude such control, which in turn leads to intensifications of algorithmic calculations that similarly generate additional failures, is what Heidegger referred to as "technicity": the momentum of applications resident within technologies.

This uncertain positioning, even disorientation, is something that many residents of Global South cities have known all along. That by taking materials out of their usual contexts, uses, and meanings and then piecing them together, they could produce unforeseen and not readily controllable outcomes—specific ways of existing, thinking, seeing, claiming, affecting, informing, and making that do not belong to specific actors, subject forms, or modes of organizing. They derail predictive calculations. What inhabitants came up with in their outcomes is not always what they wanted or could conceive of; not always or even often fair and just, but a position from which they could move. They move with the volatilities of the city; volatilities which their efforts also help bring about.

And so in the planetary effacing of clear coordinates— and here and there—on what it means to operate "in" the city, many of these urban inhabitants know that the real action is always elsewhere, away from where they "find' themselves, where they are apprehended, tracked or targeted—much as global cities were made "global" as such during the Cold War by their status for nuclear targeting and destruction.[4] They are impelled toward the action but also deterred from fully reaching it. What they pay attention to and are inclined to do may traverse along well-worn grooves and sediments, which are only sustained through unexpected veering, as well as inexplicable starts and stops, as each avoidance or deterrence of threat or discomfort exposes the person to new uncertainties.

The combinatory agencies of things, materials, and bodies exert pushes and pulls as consciousness seeks to insist upon its own impertinence as a counter-intuitive maneuver in face of all the slips and falls through the cracks of seamless experience. Efforts are made to turn up the volume—not as sound—but as dimensionality; to register reverberations and resonance in the intersection of things, to spin off and on different axes, fold into and out of sightlines. The oscillations of soundscapes, the various qualities of the roar and murmur, distant whisperings and harsh declarations, all are the products of particular interactional intensities, including with sensors and their variously scaled data generation.

So the landscapes of inhabitation are full of sensors, and it is this status of gestures, looks, sentiment, and touch which itself is censored. Rather than behaviors reflecting a sound or wounded mind, or states of psychological attainment, they are also the avant-garde, "posses" sent ahead, instruments for stirring up the waters as well as detecting the duration and scope of currents and eddies. The long lulls ahead of incipient breaks in routine and the sudden and irreversible irruptions of bewilderment or anger can install a constant restlessness that simply reproduces itself, as if ordinary dwelling took place on a smooth surface always suspected of harboring a precipice here and there, or t/here. And with these teletechnologically and computationally metaphysical shifts, we stand and walk t/here "in" cities, all the while figuratively and literally "beside ourselves".

ENDNOTES

[1] How might one think of the price of this attainment, which is the conundrum of any framing: that the confidence of emplacement always must face the prospect that things are always already moving out the frame. Although "tracking" may seem to obviate this problem, it raises another question as to whether the entity being tracks remains the same—in terms of probabilities—that "left" the frame. Whether all "theres" folded into any position render any framing, itself, obsolete in an incessantly topological prefiguration of the disappearance of the emergent is then a matter of "butterfly wings" perhaps?

[2] Literacy and print were earlier communications technologies that allowed for shifts between corporeal presence and mental absence

150

or presence depending on attention. Reading a book, just as scrolling through a social media platform, allows readers to shift between physical presence and tele-presence.

[3] This event is wonderfully described in the introduction to Kris Paulsen's book on art and telepresence (*1-8*) and at length in John Markoff's *What the Doormouse Said: How the Sixties Counterculture Shaped the Personal Computer Industry.*

[4] See Ryan Bishop and Greg Clancey (2023), 'The City as Target, or Perpetuation and Death' in *Postcolonial Urbanism.*

REFERENCES

Amis, Martin (2020) *Inside Story: a novel.* London: Jonathan Cape.

Bishop, Ryan (2020) "Frictionless Sovereignty: An Introduction" in the special issue "Frictionless Sovereignty" (ed. Ryan Bishop) boundary 2 online, 5:2, August 2020.

Bishop, Ryan and Simone, AbdouMaliq (2020) "Extending Sovereignty in the Light of Black Urbanity," in the special issue "Frictionless Sovereignty" (ed. Ryan Bishop) boundary 2 online, 5:2, August 2020.

Bratton, Benjamin (2019) *The Terraforming.* Moscow: Strelka Press. Kahn, Douglas (1992) "Introduction: Histories of Sound Once Removed," in (eds. Douglas Kahn and Gregory Whitehead) *Wireless Imagination: Sound, Radio and the Avant-Garde.* Cambridge MA and London: MIT Press.

Lanza, Joseph (1994) *Elevator Music: A Surreal History of Muzak, Easy-Listening and other Moodsong.* London: Quartet Books.

Manghani, Sunil (2020) "Idiorrhythmy" in (eds. Paola Crespi and Sunil Manghani) *Rhythm and Critique: Technics, Modalities, Practices.* Edinburgh: Edinburgh University Press.

Markoff, John (2006) What the Dormouse Said: *How the Sixties Counterculture Shaped the Persona Computer Industry,* Harmondsworth: Penguin.

Parikka, Jussi (forthcoming) *A Natural History of Logistics and Other Studio Briefs: Problem Spaces for Planetary Design.*

Parisi, Luciana (2013) Contagious Architecture: *Computation, Aesthetics and Space.* Cambridge MA and London: MIT Press.

Paulsen, Kris (2017) Here/There: *Telepresence, Touch, and Art at the Interface.* Cambridge MA and London: MIT Press.

London Experienced
at a Safe Distance

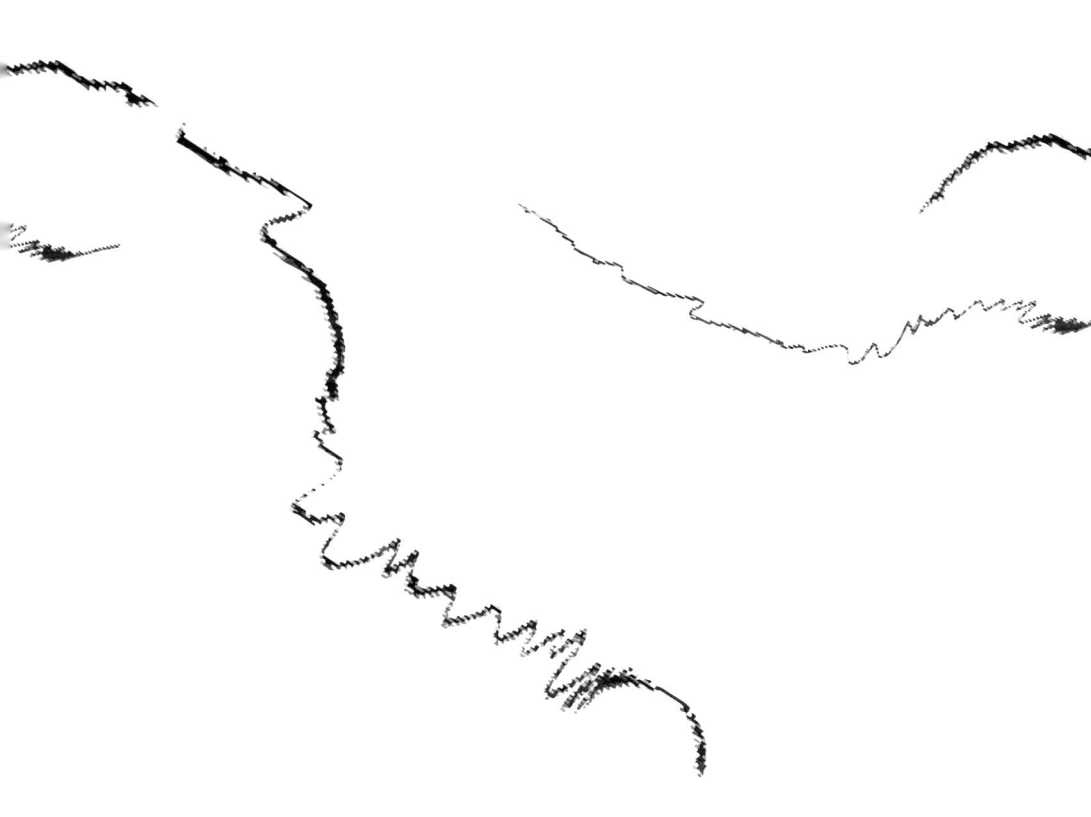

DUNCAN HAY

In his hybrid cultural history/memoir *New Model Island*, Alex Niven describes the effect of the continuing economic dominance of the South East of England on the United Kingdom on those who came of age in the 1990s and early 2000s:

> Typically, people born in London and the south-east can, if they wish (and if they are of the right class and race), remain close to their friends and family pretty easily for the entirety of their lives, from school and higher education, through to the early, middle and later stages of their professional careers. People born in, say, Liverpool, Newport or Belfast can look forward to a radically different experience if they want to "follow their dreams", one full of migration from place to place in search of employment and domestic security. [...] They will have to cope with the continual need to reinvent their sense of self and find new circles of friends and support networks, ending most often in long interludes of isolation and loneliness.[1]

Though Niven was writing before the ongoing COVID-19 pandemic, this insight seemed particularly acute to me as I read it under the conditions of the first lockdown in March 2020. I had recently undergone a displacement. Having lived in London for much of the previous decade, priced out, my partner and I had recently moved to a small city in the North West of England, close to where I had studied and where she has family. Our first child arrived within six months of moving, and, stretched between two relatively precarious academic positions, the first year had been a blur of commuting to and from the capital, sleepless nights with the baby, and acclimatising to parenthood, a new home, and a new job. I was so busy, and so frequently in London, that though I was tired, I didn't really feel the move. The depressing venality of contemporary politics had driven me to stop following the news with any great closeness, and, in common with the British Government, I was somewhat taken by surprise by the arrival of coronavirus in February 2020. I was even more surprised to find myself confined to the place to which I had moved, and from which I have not travelled more than 20 miles from in the subsequent 18 months.

Niven's insight speaks to my own experience. Though I was born in London, I spent most of my formative years in rural Yorkshire, studied in Manchester, and worked for a time in Hull, before moving to London during my PhD. But it resonates also with a structure of feeling that goes some way to explain the appeal of the (first) subject of my serious academic research: contemporary British 'place writing', as typified by the 'psychogeographic' practices of an author like Iain Sinclair. Though this isn't the place to rehearse what seem now to be well-worn arguments, psychogeography was, in 1990s Britain, a form of writing which, through a sustained engagement with the history of place, sought to bring meaning to a present which it found bleak. In its terminology, it borrowed some of the outsiderness and radicalism of the European libertarian Marxism of the 1960s. Though if earlier avant-garde artists had looked to remake the city, to revolutionise a whole way of life, then British psychogeography seemed to desire something much more modest. The filmmaker Patrick Keiller perhaps got to the heart of it best: it is 'as if the power of the financial sector is such that subjective re-imagination offered the only possibility for change that had become unattainable in other ways.'[2]

Yet to a young man living in the North, reading a text like Iain Sinclair's *Lights Out for the Territory* (1996) or later, *White Chappell, Scarlet Tracings* (1987), was almost unbearably romantic. Though tightly-focussed on London, Sinclair's work explicitly engages with subcultural currents which were definitionally at the edges of the British mainstream, and as such conjures a particular image of the capital which is more interested (both literally and figuratively) in its peripheries and margins. A London of outsiders, of occulted patterns and irrepressible cultural energies which, for all that Sinclair rages against the forces of gentrification and financialisation that were, for him, ruining the city; is a London which nevertheless could be lived in, and which could be a home to a form of dissenting bohemianism. These things seemed very desirable, and desperately unavailable, from the perspective of semi-rural Yorkshire. Though Sinclair's writing abounds with sophisticated metafictional devices and adopts fractured, non-narrative structures, what his texts present, in the enveloping insistence of his distinctive prose, is a promise of wholeness. Moreover, the cultural archaeology of psychogeographic practice offered the prospect of healing the displacements inflicted by contemporary ways of living. It was these factors which led me to study these works at length, and what brought me (eventually) to London. What has been so strange about the coronavirus crisis is that I have found myself isolated from London once again, and thinking once more about what drew me there and to those writers in the first place.

***

After finishing my PhD, I eventually found employment in the academy, though not, as I expected and had trained for, as a literary critic, but as a software developer. Self-funded through my studies, I had taught myself how to build websites, and, quite by coincidence become involved in a series of projects which involved creating interactive maps. It was this eccentric combination of research interests and digital skills which brought me employment at University College London, where, as a researcher at the Bartlett I have worked on a number of interactive maps which document the history of place. The first of these was for the architectural history research group the Survey of London, and consisted of a map of every building in Whitechapel through which the Survey's research into the parish could be published, and further materials from the public gathered. Subsequent maps built upon this project, including the Memory Map of the Jewish East End, a collaboration with one of the early pioneers of British psychogeography, Rachel Lichtenstein, to create a resource documenting the history of the Jewish community in Whitechapel. Further maps have followed with local history groups, historians, geographers, social scientists, artists, and writers.

These projects, though largely tangential to what I considered my primary research interests, are connected to it in that they are concerned with the history of place and how that history is mediated. Yet grappling with the digital form opened uncomfortable questions: quandaries raised by the psychogeographers which were amplified (and left unresolved) by digital media. At the heart of the British psychogeographic revival were a series of questions related to time and history. In short, what does the present owe to the past? And what moral hold does it have over the contemporary moment? In a novel such as Iain Sinclair's *Downriver* these questions can be felt in the ghosts that stalk its pages: Pocahontas, the victims of the 1878 Princess Alice disaster, or Franz Müller, the first person to commit murder on a British train. In *Lud Heat* and *White Chappell, Scarlet Tracings*, they're there in those works' preoccupation with the Whitechapel murders of the 1880s. In *London Orbital*, which documents a series of walks around the M25, they're felt as London itself, which becomes a glaring absence in view of the text's suburban focus. (A spectral, Derridean reading of Sinclair's work always remains plausible.)

These questions are felt also through these works in their form. Though well aware of the failures of the revolutionary ambitions of the twentieth century European avant-garde movements, British psychogeography held a commitment to the transformative power of the authentic, socially engaged artwork. In dealing with the past, the point of psychogeographic writing wasn't, in the manner of a historical novel, to create a believable image of the city 'as it was', but to bring that history into critical dialogue with the present. In so doing, history can be encountered in the text as *difference*, and a critical view on the now opened. The paucity (for a dissenting writer such as Sinclair) of the present revealed, and pathways to personal and cultural renewal opened.

In working on the digital mapping projects referred to above, I have always felt that the speed of digital media sits uncomfortably with the questions of temporality raised by the work of Sinclair and other writers of the British psychogeographic revival. On the one hand, they bring the voices of the past (literally in the case of the Memory Map of the Jewish East End) to public consciousness, and to a far wider audience than they would ever otherwise have reached. They offer unprecedented access, through digital versions of historic maps which were previously only available in reference libraries, to the history of place. In short, they make the past active in the present in a hugely compelling form, and (I hope) foster precisely the sort of critical thinking about the relationship between the past and the present that British psychogeograpy is concerned with. Yet digital projects have short memories. Though launched only in 2018, the Survey of London Whitechapel website is already, from a technical perspective, outdated. It is unlikely that in 10 years' time (unless further funding is found for its redevelopment) that it will still be accessible, and it is no small irony that the material gathered through the project will be published as a printed book to ensure that it lives on.

As the sketch above intimates, British psychogeography was a resolutely literary movement. Whilst other forms fall into its orbit (the films of Patrick Keiller; Alan Moore's graphic novel *From Hell*; radio series such as John Rogers and Nick Papadimitriou's *Ventures and Adventures in Topography*; at a stretch, music such as John Foxx's *London*

Overgrown or Burial's first album), it had a deep commitment to the printed book. Pre-internet culture, by virtue of the fact that you could only experience what was available to you where you were, tended to follow a hereditary model of cultural transmission. A generation of artists would build upon, respond to (or reject) the previous one; cultural currents, birthed in one place, would reappear, in mis-translated or mutated forms. So Surrealism responds to Dada; the Situationists to Surrealism. Psychogeography, born in Paris in the late 1950s, gets picked up again in 1990s London, and, displaced from the revolutionary milieu in which it was first incubated, becomes a literary genre.

The physical book represents a tangible link between the present and the past, and in this sense has an archaeological quality. As a former dealer of rare books, Sinclair was deeply aware of this. In the words of the narrator of *White Chappell, Scarlet Tracings* on the discovery of a first edition of Arthur Conan Doyle's *A Study in Scarlet*: 'he had, once again, uncovered a piece of history, a true splinter of the 1880s'.[3] Online digital media, by contrast, by giving at least the *appearance* that all of culture is available to anyone, anytime, anywhere, tend to collapse different temporal strata into an undifferentiated plane. In the late 1990s and early 2000s, many theorists characterised digital media by their formal characteristics (Lev Manovich, in *The Language of New Media* writes of copying, pasting, juxtaposition; the database or the timeline as aesthetic forms.)[4] Though these points still hold salience, the difference between digital media and their analogue forebears might be also understood by the rhythms of behaviour that they elicit. For Walter Benjamin, this rhythm was characterised by the jolts and shocks of the encounter with knowledge (akin to those experienced by the urban pedestrian) and the slower process of writing and reading: 'in the fields with which we are concerned, knowledge comes only in lightning flashes.

The text is the roll of thunder that follows.'[5] These marks of slowness, so characteristic of print culture, are difficult to preserve in a medium which emphasises speed of information retrieval, simultaneity, and continual revision.

***

On first coming to London I tried to recreate something of the psychogeographic experience I had read so much about, and, many times, succeeded. Whilst the genre of psychogeography is, in a sense, always retrospective (by the time one finds a glimpse whatever numinous quality one was expecting to find, the 'true' seekers will already have moved on to the next thing), it is nevertheless the case that the juxtapositions afforded by city living offer, if not transcendence, then at least moments in which one's sense of self is tested against otherness. The city's density, in terms of both people and the overwhelming traces of their material and cultural histories, provides ample opportunity for the chance encounter, the 'shocks' or jolts which for Simmel were experienced with discomfort and for Benjamin were experienced with pleasure.

I took great pride in walking and cycling in London, of coming to know its geography and atmospheres under my own motive power. On one such excursion, I found myself in Spitalfields, the setting of several of Sinclair's works. In the period that Sinclair was writing about it in his novels, the whole area was still dominated by an active fruit and vegetable market and was far from desirable real estate. By the time I got there, the redevelopment of the market was complete, the wholesalers displaced to Leyton and replaced by upmarket shops, restaurants and offices.

Walking through the Bishops Square development, I noticed at the slightly less crowded end of the shopping precinct a glass-covered trench. This contains the remains of a twelfth century Charnel House.

The Charnel House, a remnant of St Mary Spital, the priory and hospital which gives Spitalfields its name, was formerly used to house the bones of the dead who could no longer be accommodated in the burial grounds surrounding the priory. When it was excavated in 1999, the remains of 10,000 bodies were removed.

There is something quite telling about the way in which Foster + Partners have chosen to incorporate the site into the Bishops Square development. Whilst the decision to place the building behind glass has been taken for the practical purpose of protecting the ancient monument, it also serves as a distancing device, sealing the historic off from the contemporary. Reading the Foster + Partners catalogue serves only to reinforce this impression, the text on the historic building reading: 'the Charnel House, a twelfth-century chapel discovered during archaeological excavations on the site [of Bishops Square], has been preserved and exhibited with other artifacts [sic] in a sunken courtyard, sheltered beneath a glass pavement'. The text here tactfully refrains from noting the actual purpose of the building, merely noting its age and the fact that it has been preserved.

Following the outbreak of the pandemic, my perimeter, having previously encompassed (on foot or by bicycle) the orbit of London (from Woolwich to Richmond, the Alexandra Palace to Crystal Palace), was suddenly restricted to what could be reached on foot from my house, bordering estuarine marshland to the south and the outskirts of a provincial town to the North. Inadvertently, I found myself re-living the estrangement that had led me to Sinclair's work in the first place, and I found myself yearning for a London that I'd not been entirely sorry to leave. Yet now, those digital projects I have worked on allow me, vicariously and virtually, to re-walk the streets of the capital. In so doing, it strikes me that to account for the moral hold that the past has over the present, then it's probably not going to be possible if we continue to keep that past under glass.

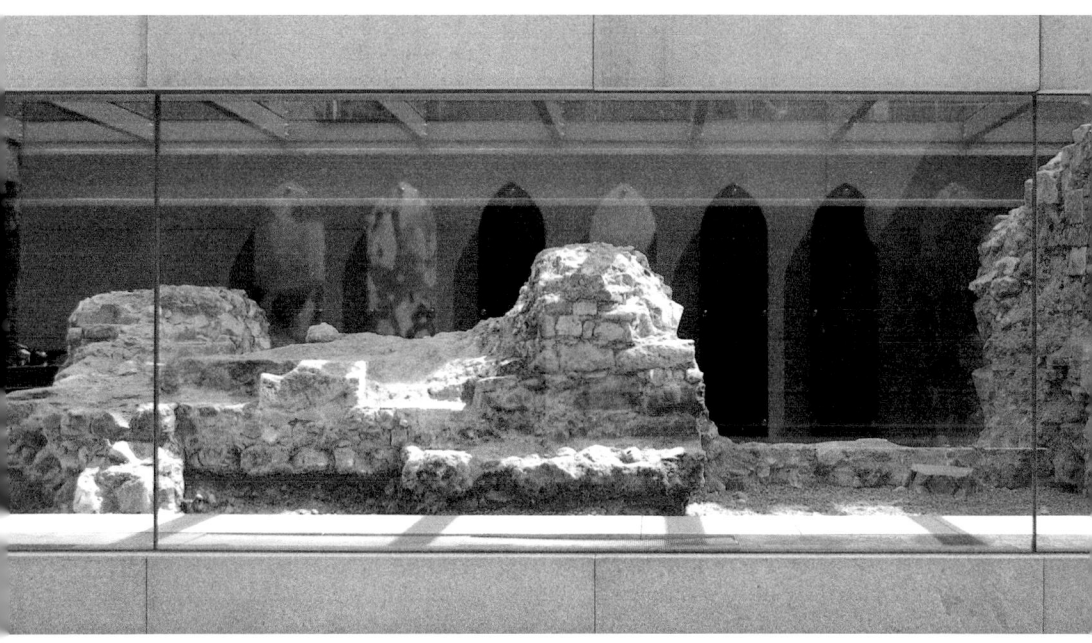

ENDNOTES

[1] Alex Niven, *New Model Island: How to Build a Radical Culture Beyond the Idea of England* (London: Repeater, 2019), pp. 79-80.

[2] Patrick Keiller, *The View from the Train: Cities and Other Landscapes* (London: Verso, 2014), p. 186.

[3] Iain Sinclair, *White Chappell, Scarlet Tracings* (London: Granta, 1998), p. 26. Parenthetically, it is surely significant that for Guy Debord, who holds at least partial responsibility for the coining of the term psychogeography in the first place, held that the printed book was one of the few places where the spectacle, at least in part, did not obtain. 'Thus it is hardly surprising that children should enthusiastically start their education at an early age with the Absolute Knowledge of computer science; while they are still unable to read, for reading demands making judgements at every line; and is the only access to the wealth of pre-spectacular human experience.' Guy Debord, *Comments on the Society of the Spectacle* (London: Verso, 1998), p. 21.

[4] Lev Manovich, *The Language of New Media* (Cambridge, MA: The MIT Press, 2001).

[5] Walter Benjamin, *The Arcades Project* (Cambridge, MA: Harvard University Press, 1999), p. 456.

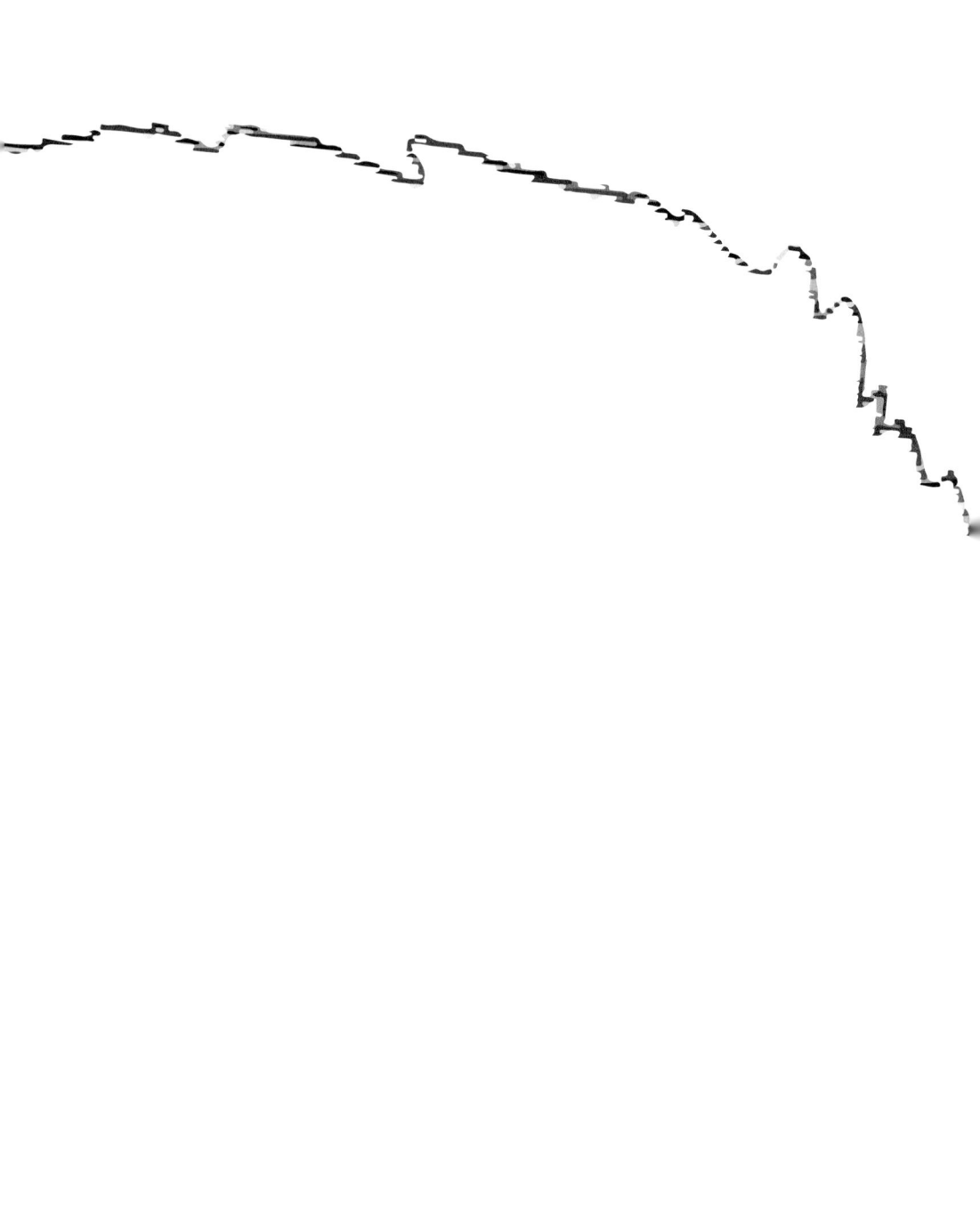

Art and
the Urban

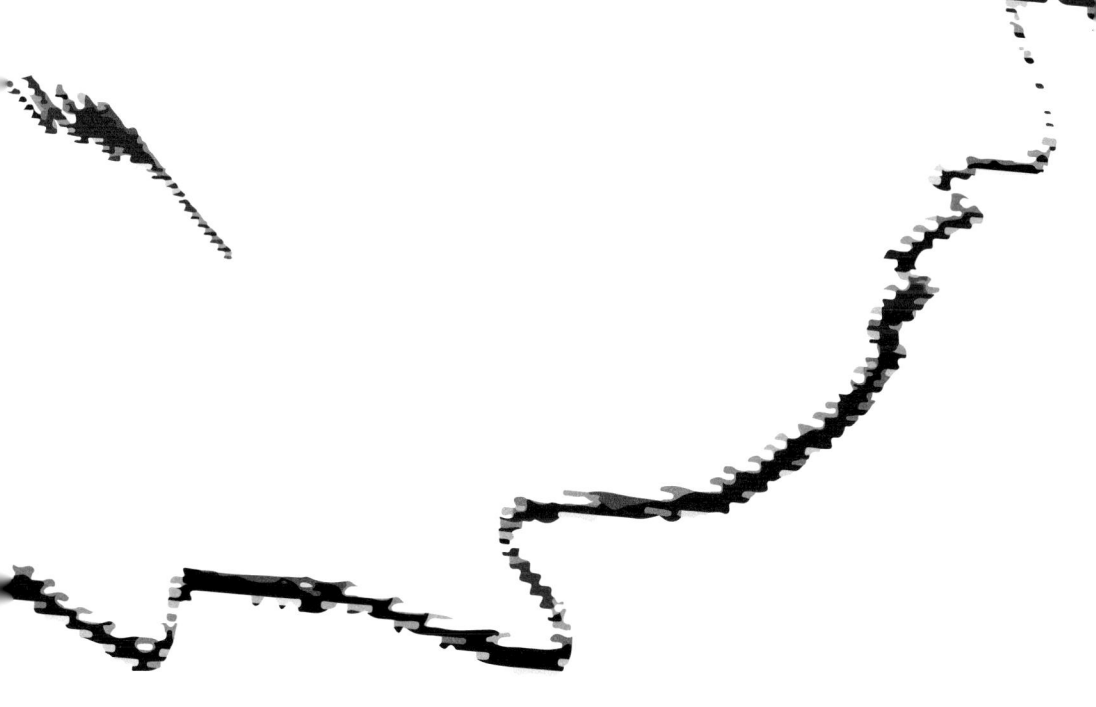

Lockdown Art Practice: Twelve Months in Berlin

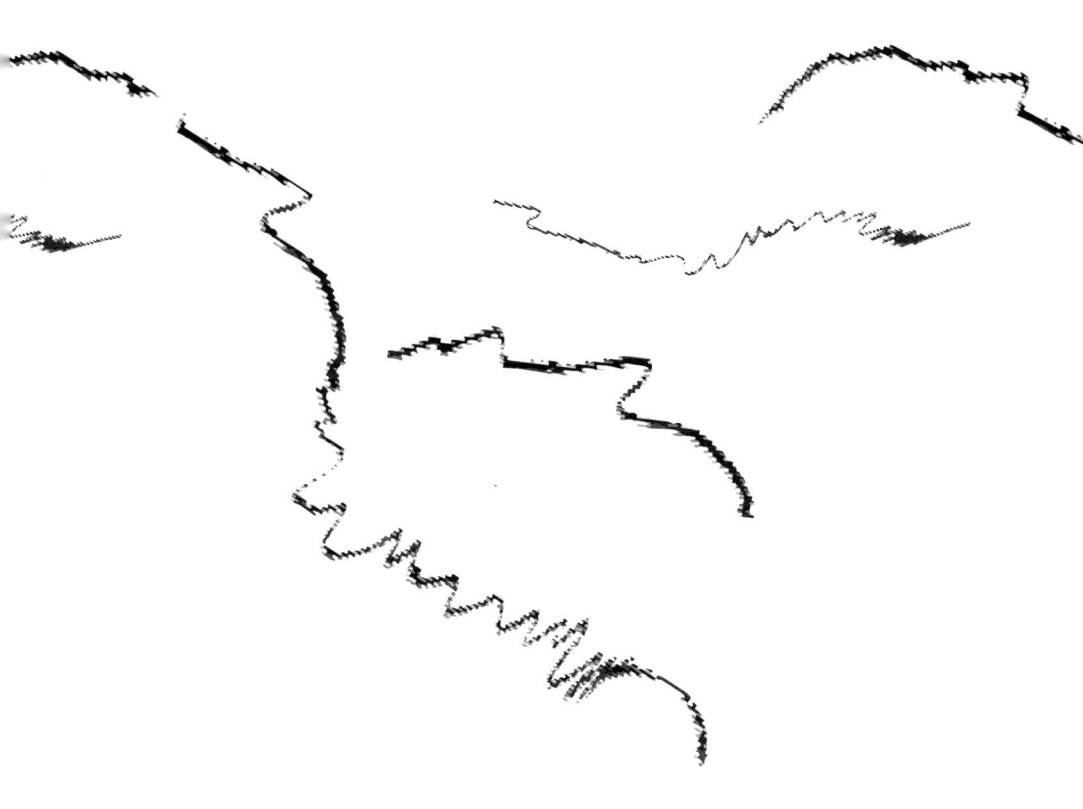

ANTONIA LOW

MARCH 2020

A short, yet awkward trip to London: the halls of the National Gallery and the National Portrait Gallery almost deserted and hardly any tourists in Trafalgar Square or Piccadilly Circus. An atmosphere of uneasiness amongst friends – no hugs, no kisses, help yourself to drinks, don't use any door handles, wash your hands for 20 seconds humming 'Happy Birthday' twice. We joke it might be the last time to meet for some time. In the airport I see a few Italians wearing masks. I think about buying hand sanitiser, but decide not to. However, back in Berlin, I find neither disinfection spray, hand sanitiser, nor regular hand soap in the drug stores, only empty shelves. From the window I see the same neighbour on the street coming home with toilet paper three times in a row. Then the streets turn dead.

Due to a slight cough I cancel my next trip to Stuttgart. A show in LA and another two in Berlin are postponed. I stay in bed until noon listening to the news. A sudden halt in our accelerated lives and we have so much new time. Instead, time slots are arranged to fetch last learning materials from schools before they close; we start organising contact avoidance. You are meant to drop off things in front of doors and call once you have left.

APRIL 2020

It's three weeks into the lockdown and I am invited to
a spontaneous neighbourhood show in Prenzlauer Berg.
Out of the direct need to reconnect, *Die Balkone* is initiated
by the curators Övül Ö. Durmusoglu and Joanna Warsza :

> Life, art, pandemic and proximity invites members
> of the artistic community living in Prenzlauer Berg
> to activate/inhabit their windows and balconies
> on Easter Sunday and Monday. We are at the very
> beginning of a new cycle that we cannot yet situate
> ourselves in. Its first palpable experiences are shifts
> in the relationship between inside and outside; in
> the distance between one day and another; between
> what is private, public, and political. Balconies serve
> as the public apertures of the private. They seem to
> be where the house ends, and yet not. In their political
> history, they have both been terraces of openness
> and hope, as well as platforms for authoritarianism
> and supremacy. (...) When some of us are cut off
> from our plans and our loved ones, we reach out
> to the balconies of the world, against isolation and
> individualization, not leaving everything in the hands
> of the virus and the fear it generates.

After having been alone at home for almost a month,
it feels very natural to set up a work in the window of our
living room: A printed curtain of a neglected house in Italy,
its window covered with a sign 'Vende'. Olevano Romano,
a medieval village that inspired a whole generation of
German painters in the Romantic Era, has been sold out
in recent years, as the young generation of today have moved
away for the cities. In comparison to this phenomenon in
rural Italy, artists in Berlin face gentrification as one effect
of urban population increase. Presented in a window of a
Berlin house with similar grey facade and covered in graffiti

the visual juxtaposition of the two buildings manifests their coexistence.

As I walk along the streets looking at the works of the other artists, I am quite surprised how many artists have managed to remain living in the renovated pastel-coloured houses of Prenzlauer Berg – with SUVs parked in front and cafés below instead of the long-gone rotten bars we used to meet in.

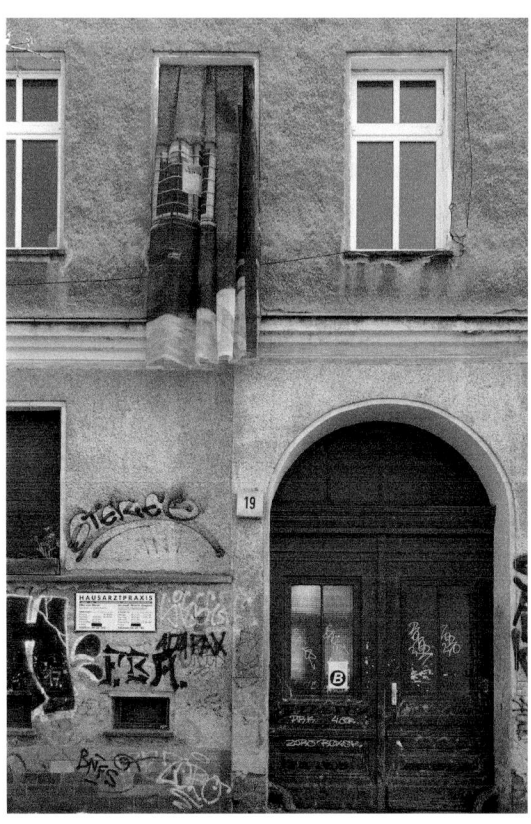

MAY 2020

Walking in Berlin I am cautious about my body's presence in public, my pace, my breath. With this awareness I try to keep a safe distance from elderly, fragile-looking people. An equal distance I keep to heavy sweating joggers and gathering groups in the parks. I imagine clouds of sweat and saliva drops surrounding such hyperactive individuals as aerosols unfolding from their bodies and unmasked mouths.

I am in a constant mood for stepping far away from all and walk in pure solitude. The smell and feel of clean, fresh air from trees, bushes and lawns have become a tangible pleasure. But in the parks I meet many more people than in the streets of Berlin. Everyone seems to have a similar longing for fresh unpolluted oxygen.

It is the first of May and people have started demonstrating against the lockdown measures in front of the "Volksbühne" theatre. They have initiated a weekly demonstration called "Hygienedemo". Because of the restrictions to the number of participants, numerous demonstrations are registered in different locations. I cycle around looking for angry shouting groups to get a picture of the people. However, I only see a few scattered around, mostly journalists with cameras and police setting up fences. Everyone seems adrift, lost and uncertain what to do. This reminds me of a description by Richard Sennett in '*Flesh and Stone*' of the festivals to celebrate Liberty after the French Revolution:

> ...The participating group almost immediately disintegrated, not knowing what to do or to say to one another. Quatremère de Quincy had thought the sheer volume of the open space would arouse the public's sense of the majesty of law. And the public had watched listlessly this show of unity and strength on the field."(...) "these festivals made clear a disturbing lesson about freedom. Freedom which seeks to overcome resistance, to abolish

obstacles, to start afresh with a blank slate–freedom
conceived like a pure, transparent volume – dulls
the body. It is anaesthetic. Freedom which arouses
the body does so by accepting impurity, difficulty,
and obstruction as part of the very experience
of liberty.

In this sense, the "Hygienedemo" seems rather about
creating bodily friction than a struggle for freedom – people
miss each other's smell, touch and body warmth. They want
to get together.

JUNE 2020

It's my second exhibition in Berlin under COVID-19. Drinks
outside on the lawn, upstairs in the exhibition space, Scharaun,
not more than 5 people are let in. I am unsure whether
to wear a mask or not. We make jokes about wearing them.
Outside we quickly take off the masks and adjust to the new
given distance. A Korean artist friend wears her masks with
pure elegance and confidence. She tells me that she prefers
to wear a mask, but is hesitant about wearing one in public,
She tells me that she is hesitant about wearing a mask in public
on her own, because she gets hostile looks for being an Asian
with a mask. People keep a deliberate distance to her.

When I wear a mask no one takes notice. I have started
to wear self-tailored cloth masks, because I am haunted by
the thought of a person coughing into my face while passing
by and their germs entering my nostrils, creeping deep down
into my lungs. I cannot get enough distance to other people.
I have started getting a sort of claustrophobia when I am
surrounded by others, especially on public transport. I feel
I am trapped in an enclosed capsule with no air and only
infectious aerosols for me to breath. It is also a growing worry
that you will end up standing next to a person who might
refuse to wear a mask and who possibly wants to start an
argument about it.

On the way home I pass groups of people sitting with their own drinks along the canal. They play music and seem to be having a great time. Apparently, outdoor parties have started taking place in parks all over Berlin.

JULY 2020

We are driving in Southeast China, from Shantou towards three small villages near Chenghai. It is 2018 and I am searching for the house of my grandfather, from whom I have nothing more than a photograph and an address dating back to the 1980s. My friend, Shiyun in Beijing, has found through WeChat a translator, Baqi, and he can help with communicating in the local dialect, teochew. He has borrowed his mother's car and we drive to the three villages, all called "Dongli." In Chinese the address is "house in front of the West temple of Dongli," so the starting points are those few remaining temples in the area. Baqi works as a curator in Shenzhen and his family is from the same region, so he pays his family a visit at the same time as helping me find the house. I cannot stop staring out of the window and filming what is unfolding in front of me: women doing the laundry in a lake, men repairing their bicycles and families overtaking us on scooters. The everyday life of this Saturday morning appears very calm and casual compared to Saturdays in Berlin.

I was planning to go back and do more research on the house. But because we are not able to travel in 2020 the research project of my grandfather's house goes on a virtual journey, in three different parts.

As a new decade has just begun, the curator Maria Lind initiated a project on Instagram for which she invites artists to inhabit the instagram account '52proposalsforthe20s' to make weekly proposals for the coming decade.

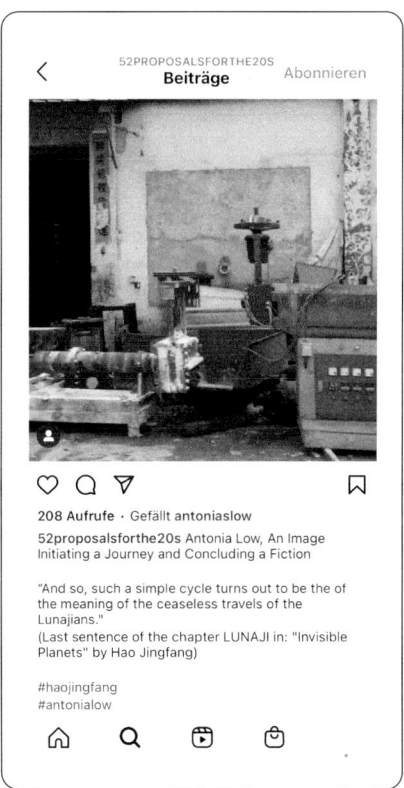

The film footage of the first car drive to one of the villages called Dongli is divided into seven parts and posted daily. The short sequences show passing variations of house facades, fences, building openings and shutters. I combine the loops with the final sentences of seven chapters in *Invisible Planets* by the Chinese science fiction writer, Hao Jingfang. The sentences conclude the descriptions of seven fictional planets.

AUGUST 2020

The COVID-19 numbers are low and we drive out of Berlin
to a lake. We buy a small inflatable boat with which we go far
out onto the lake, away from the crowds of young people and
families at the shore. We are safe as we watch them swim, laugh
and shout. The noise of their voices travels over the water
towards us. Solitude, sun and cooling water around us.
No masks needed.

Wearing a mask has become a statement about attitudes
and beliefs. On some weekends, I purposely put on a mask
to distinguish myself from demonstrating groups in public
places and on the streets of Berlin. A growing number of
people from all sorts of backgrounds and beliefs regularly
start coming to the city from all over Germany to demonstrate
as "Querdenker" against the semi-strict rules and procedures
to limit the pandemic; against vaccination; and against Angela
Merkel's supposed dictatorship – all along with alt-right, anti-
democratic "Reichsbürger." Public places in Berlin have turned
into sites for negotiation of all attitudes and beliefs triggered
and generated online on social media.

But this seems all so far away, sitting on a lake, in an
inflatable boat, 20 metres away from the roaring crowd. What
actually makes me want to escape into nature – virus or humans?

SEPTEMBER 2020

Close artist friends have become very dear to me after this
first lockdown. I am longing to reconnect with them so
I invite a few friends to meet in person and to go on a half-day
walk together through Lichtenberg, a suburb of Berlin, as
a type of collaboration. We exchange our personal experience
of the past months while also reflecting on the redefinition
of closeness and exchange as we walk down shabby streets
and through small urban gardens. Pointing out details,
referring to something else, seeing through each other's eyes,
our dialogue emerges through sharing the experience of
walking together. These very natural and old methods of

being together, now seem so refreshing. It's like reaching out into the past, another reality of being human.

I meet Ingo Gerken, an artist friend, for a walk. We pass by an old bridge and hear loud rave music. This really reminds me of the 1990s and when I used to go to raves – dancing in meadows all nights. Is it possible that under COVID-19 people still party the way I did? We walk around the bushes and find an opening leading us to an overgrown valley. Five toilet huts and a shed where two girls sit behind a clear acrylic sheet with a guest list and hand sanitiser. They stop us to ask whether we have registered online. The smell of incense hangs in the air. Young people dancing. It's like sudden time travel and seems so unreal in the midst of a pandemic.

We return to the streets. A few blocks further on, pass another outdoor party in front of a student residential block. Students, many from abroad, wear masks. Some even only, watch the party going on from their windows. We are invited in for a bratwurst and beer. I watch the group from a distance, but I feel very bad about us keeping a distance to them. They must be desperate to get to know more Berliners and yet we dare not mingle.

OCTOBER 2020

I meet Astrid Busch, another artist friend in Lichtenberg. We walk along windows covered in German flags and Asian children playing on the streets. Astrid tells me that an old friend of hers has suddenly started writing unsettling emails that express far-right political views. What surprises her most is the implicitness with which he turns to her in his extreme attitude. The same has happened to me. WhatsApp messages from an old friend. Out of the blue, this friend tries to warn me about lies constructing a pandemic and urges me not to believe the news but instead read the included article by a scientist I never have heard of. In a spontaneous reaction I have asked whether she sent the text by mistake – it is far too confidential after years of non-communication.

Also my neighbour, a doctor, has had a similar experience in receiving text messages with unsubstantial content by an old colleague. He showed me the message and we could not help but laugh.

However, alternative facts seem to be spreading, seeping into old friendships. Instead, we grow close to physical neighbours, with their actual facial expressions to read and to sympathize with. But we drift apart from old friends and their attempts to reach out by sending text messages. We live in different realities with differing facts.

As Astrid and I walk through the awkward streets of Lichtenberg, beside German flags in the windows, wet laundry hanging from fences and building openings taped over with blue plastic, we realise that in this area, we must seem like aliens with our hairstyles and looks from Prenzlauer Berg. Our parallel reality is 15 minutes away, and it is not only the look of our streets and us that drive us apart. The most unsettling gaps between our appearance are the differing facts that construct our realities.

NOVEMBER 2020

In November, the second lockdown is just a few days away, I step outside my house and I realise that I have almost forgotten about a show that actually is taking place, more or less, in front of my door! Three curators, Gino Gianuizzi, Giovanna Sarti and Eva Scharrer, invite artists to Note di sguardi – an exhibition taking place in three European cities (Berlin, Bologna, Cervia). On poster stands photographs by three artists are shown simultaneously in these cities. Because of the pandemic restrictions it has been an exhibition without an opening, without the possibility of inviting artist friends and initiating any other social gathering. I realise that through this lack it has become a very abstract event to me.

Virtually, I have reposted images of the three exhibition sites on social media and have received a lot of responses in the form of likes and emojis. Yet it seems not to have entered my conscious mind properly. The exhibition remains in this abstract fuss of online meetings and shared hearts and flames.

Initially, I had considered inviting my 87-year-old father to come to Berlin. I wanted him to see the exhibited image of his father's house in Southeast China. But the pandemic had cancelled all such plans.

When the house was built, my father was a child in Malaysia and he still has memories of his parents discussing the architectural plans next to him. He remembers their considerations to build in the Chinese traditional feng shui style and choosing British steel and cement as modern building materials. He has never had the opportunity to see the resulting house because of the Cultural Revolution and his exile in Europe. I found the house in 2018, it was used as a t-shirt factory for the African market by my nephew. It has its own charm, a hybrid between Chinese and British colonial style.

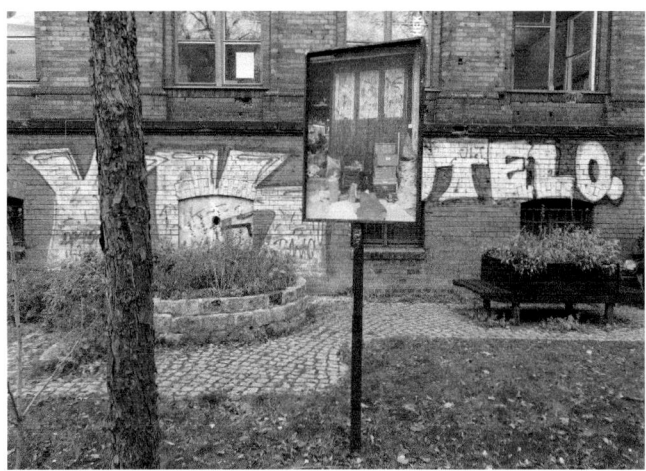

The image of the house had been presented in the courtyard outside the museum of Prenzlauer Berg for a month without me thinking about it. I might even have walked past it without noticing it, like the majority of Berliners must have done. It seems as if this house has existed in the mind of my Chinese-Malaysian family for decades, and what I had found one day in 2018 was more of a virtual idea than of an actual site. After my discovery of it, the house slipped back into the deep Southeast Chinese everyday-life, so far away from the reality here. Reduced to digital images I have shared. If I never have built a house on my own? How much is the remote and virtual space literally taking over and turning my own head into a bubble?

DECEMBER 2020

Virtually, we stand in front of a small creole cottage in New Orleans. Manon Bellet and Erik Kiesewetter have invited artist friends to contribute to their event "Voir une voie / to see a voice," in the garden of their house, during lockdown:

> Our project poses the question of the relationship between art and public space—in our present and for the future—during this public health crisis. Each Saturday evening from 8.30—11pm, texts and images are projected as a loop on the neighboring façade from our home at 701 Spain Street through the Fall. (...) Imagine yourself walking through the streets of New Orleans, discussing or contemplating the urgencies of our time. What comes to your mind? What would you like to share in public?

I had sent them an image of my grandfather's house, the view from the roof terrace overlooking the other roofs of the Chinese village. In our hybrid meeting, we reach out and virtually connect New Orleans, Berlin and Dongli, without spreading a virus – but sharing emojis.

   At the beginning of the pandemic, the family in China had written a message on WeChat asking whether we needed masks. But then the app needed an update and I lost contact with them, all of a sudden. Manon and Erik want to end their project early, their situation has become too severe in the US under COVID-19. All the attempts to stay in contact seem to have come to a halt, while above the rooftops Elon Musk's network of satellites, Mars missions and giga factories seems to continuously expand.

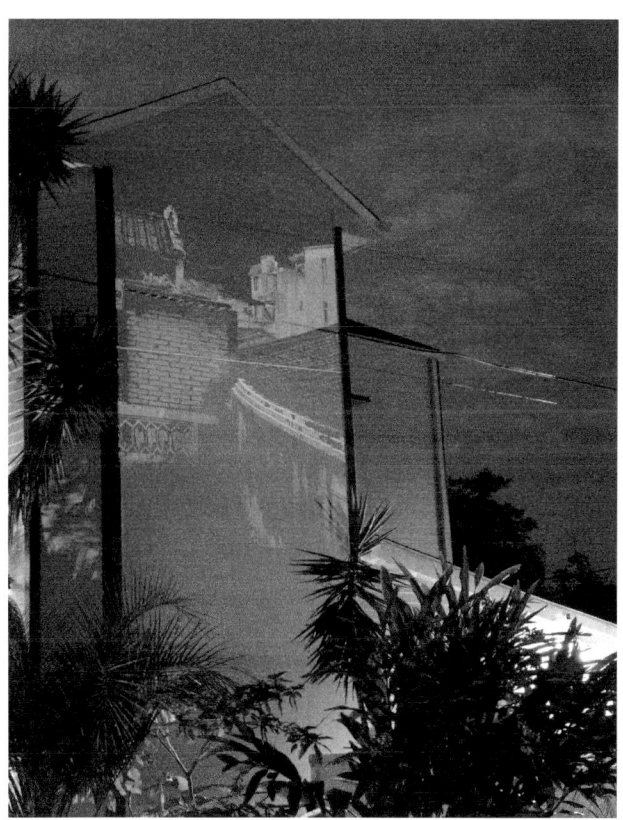

JANUARY 2021

A proxy leads me through an exhibition via Zoom. She is very chatty and even shows the back of artworks to make me understand their materiality. It's a new way of looking at art and it's much more social and entertaining than before. However, after half an hour I feel nauseous, because the visually transmitted movements of the person walking me through the space are not synchronised with my passive body in front of the screen. Three days in a row at home. At a certain moment during lockdown an image popped into my mind – the image that my head has turned into a big bubble. Constantly being at home, in front of my personal computer, zooming in and out I have produced this huge, soft flesh-coloured bubble consisting of abstract thoughts and hot air by the puffing laptop in front of me. Thoughts resulting from nothing, produced in the endless talks in daily remote meetings, triggered by transmitted voices diffused by the computer's fan. All these online discussions – pros and cons, more and more suggestions merging into endless discussions on what has to be done, what could have been done and what should have never happened, without doing anything but talking things over again and again. I sit, thinking I am doing something while actually I am only staring at or talking at a screen, pressing some plastic keys here and there below the talking screen. My body – apart from the fingertips – feels completely disconnected to what seems to be happening in front of me. At the end of each day, leaving the virtual space I feel totally remote from whom I have supposedly met, the words we were exchanging and the subjects we have discussed.

The moment a day of remote meetings is over, the computer closed, I slip back into the actual space that surrounds me I start feeling my back, I look down at my feet, realise what I have been wearing all day and feel the tiredness of a head on top of an aching body.

FEBRUARY 2021

Since I cannot do sports in a gym, I have started to play badminton with my partner in a big open area in Prenzlauer Berg. This public space consists of a playground, a deserted running track, a football field and two ping-pong tables. This area mainly seems to have served the function of a shortcut between two streets. This area mainly seems to serve the function of a shortcut between two streets. Two years ago, in China, I was very much taken by the use of such public spaces: choir gatherings, dancing groups and other sportive activities. All seemed united in group activity.

Through the pandemic the public space in Berlin seems to be likewise renegotiated. A growing group of people are desperate to meet, taking an hour off during the day to have some sports activity: students playing ping-pong, a group of young fathers playing football while their little toddlers desperately try to get a foot on the ball, too. A single man does sit-ups next to us, while we are playing badminton. We all seem to give the public space a new meaning and a few passers-by notice this change, smile, and seem to reconsider the purpose of the spot themselves. However, other individuals are just too used to the shortcut and pass through without noticing. They walk straight through the newly defined playing field, in which we are playing badminton. A *Tagesmutter* (nanny) ignores the swinging rackets and balls around her while steering a cart with three little kids. She continuously stares at her phone.

A young mother crosses with her pram – headphones on, coffee-to-go in one hand, a smartphone in the other. Many others seem similarly absent to their surroundings, absorbed into another reality. It almost seems as if they have lost a sensual connection to their surroundings, as if eyes, ears, and awareness are switched... switched entirely to a remote or virtual world. While some seem to see and explore the new potential of public space, others seem to have completely lost an awareness of their bodies moving through actual spaces.

MARCH 2021

Today, I had a very moving encounter: I was on my routine exercise, cycling through Berlin, when I saw this man. He was standing in the Tiergarten park, one hand holding his grey bicycle, the other arm stretching around a tree, hugging it. His head and his entire torso were leaning against the massive brown trunk. This human bonding with a tree, seemed full of relief and created such an intense image that it made me stop. An overwhelming aura that seemed to seal off the two creatures from the urban hustle and bustle – the hovering helicopters and howling ambulances that we had got so used to having around us. One year after the first lockdown we have adapted to so many changes: Sweatpants, long hair, no make-up. Closed shops, closed cafés, closed restaurants, closed exhibition spaces. Wearing masks indoors, not recognising friends because of their masks, not understanding them through their masks, discarded masks on pavements. Estimate 1.5 metres to another depending on trust. The idea of a handshake or even kissing someone else's cheek makes us frown: Did we really used to do this?

The Rise of
the Infinity Pool

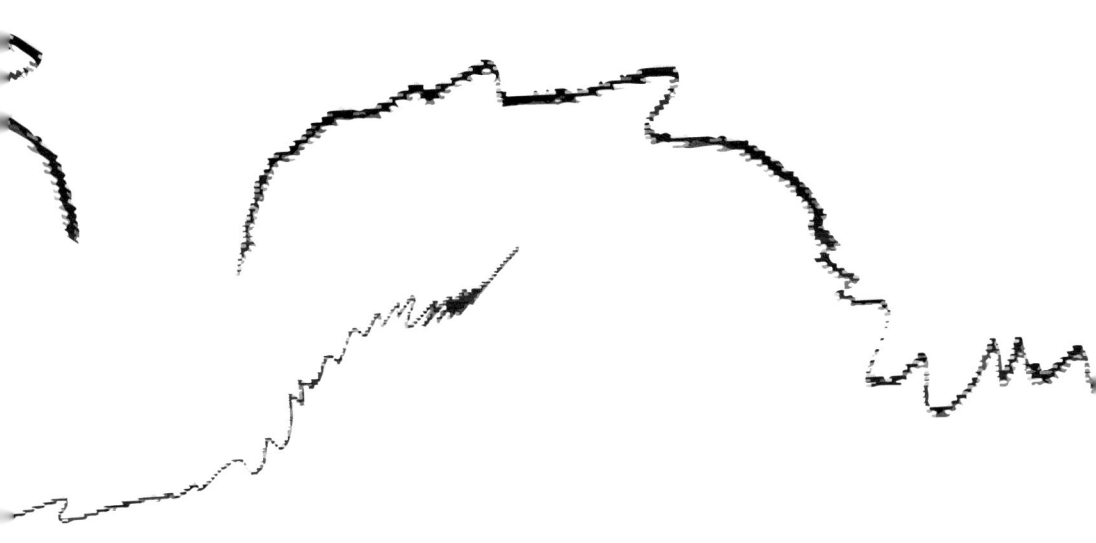

JASPAR JOSEPH-LESTER

Looking up from the ground we see a translucent container filled with water. Moving high above, a swimmer experiences the sensation of floating in space, gravity is suspended as the body glides through the air. When we encounter the sky pool the only thing that breaks the image of water joining sky is the sight of floating bodies passing overhead. The conflation of capitalism and cultural products leaves us with the ever greater question of how we situate ourselves in a city where that which should be on the ground appears to us in the sky.

The sky pool stands, in almost every respect, as the most advanced material expression of the ideological forces that constitute capitalism today.

Karl Marx argued that capitalism is built on a fundamentally unethical principle: a system of exchange where there is no limit to profit. The infinity pool was designed from its conception in 1960's California, or even before that in the 1670s with the fountains in the gardens of Versailles, to defy physical limits. The disappearance of a perceivable edge produces a sense of limitlessness and delirium. As we gaze at one expanse of water, we experience it seamlessly joining with another terrain. The pool becomes the sea, the sky and the surrounding landscape. Various tonalities of blue take us to the limits of the horizon and then further into the dreamscape of floating high above the constraints of the physical world.

The zero edge is the mechanism for creating the illusion of limitlessness.

The first generation infinity pool, which entered into our collective consciousness as a backdrop to the 1971 James Bond film *Diamonds Are Forever*, fully exploited the affects of this visual technology. This earlier iteration of the infinity pool has become a common feature of hotel marketing and lifestyle promotions. The environment that we perceive as having no boundaries speaks both of freedom and deceit. But is our experience of the infinity pool really one of deceit? We know very well that the disappearance of an edge is a mere illusion (and quite a clunky one at that). We understand that the zero edge is in fact a hair's lip of water lapping over a solid wall yet we continue to allow ourselves to be drawn in by the simulated experience of limitlessness. We wilfully deceive ourselves in order to experience a world that cannot exist. And here we have it, the world that appears to us as image stands in for the older world of physical boundaries and human relations. But this long established critique of the image is not encountered by us in the way that Guy Debord speaks of spectacle. The infinity pool is more transcendental than the intoxicating images Debord associates with the media culture of the late 1960s. We might instead argue that Ludwig Feuerbach's attack on Christianity, in his book *The Essence of Christianity* from 1841, provides a closer alignment with what can be thought of as a modern day image of the heavens.

Feuerbach identifies the collective amnesia that established itself when Christian belief was considered to be the product of divine creation—rather than an ideological construct shaped by the human brain. Other theological foundations include the churches of the High Renaissance, with the tradition of trompe l'oeil ceiling paintings depicting the heavens. When seen from a certain stand-point, the extreme perspective of Andrea Pozzo's late seventeenth century painting on the ceiling of the Church of Sant'Ignazio in Rome conjures up an image of depth that stands in for the limitations of physical architectural space. There is a playful back and forth of perception. One moment there is a clear and powerful image but from another vantage point there is only distortion. However, when the illusion mutates into media image—captured as a jpeg or on video—the perceptual

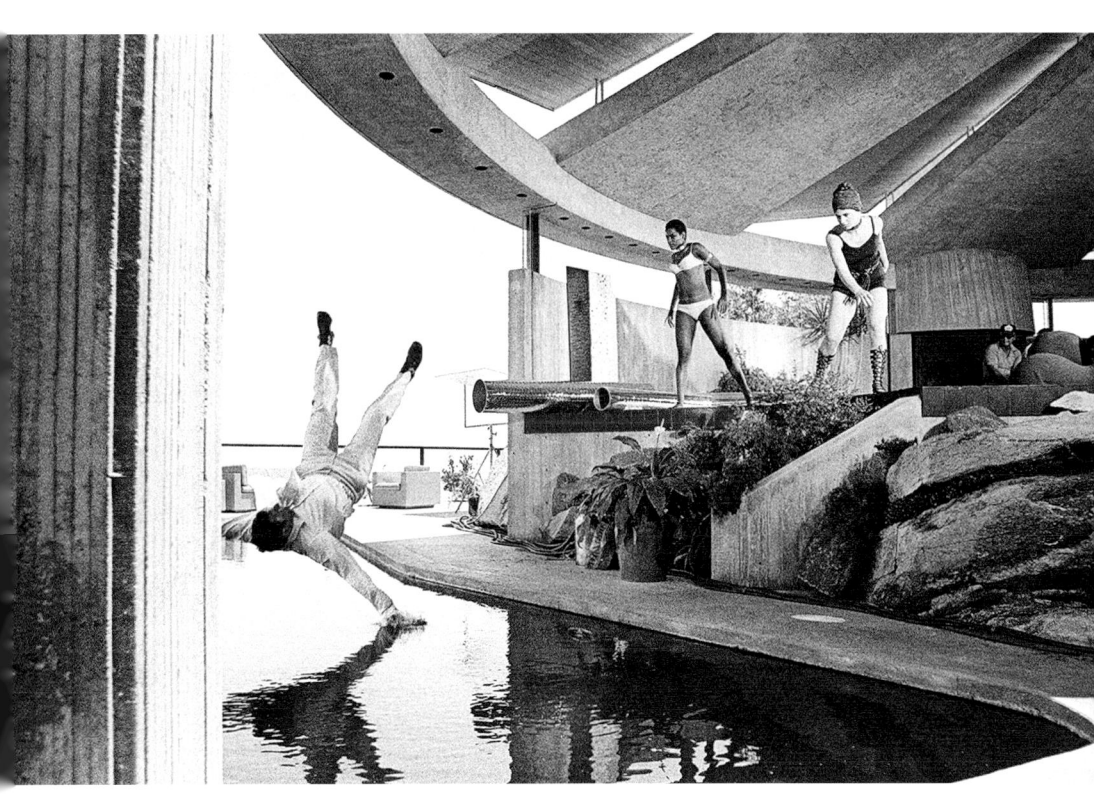

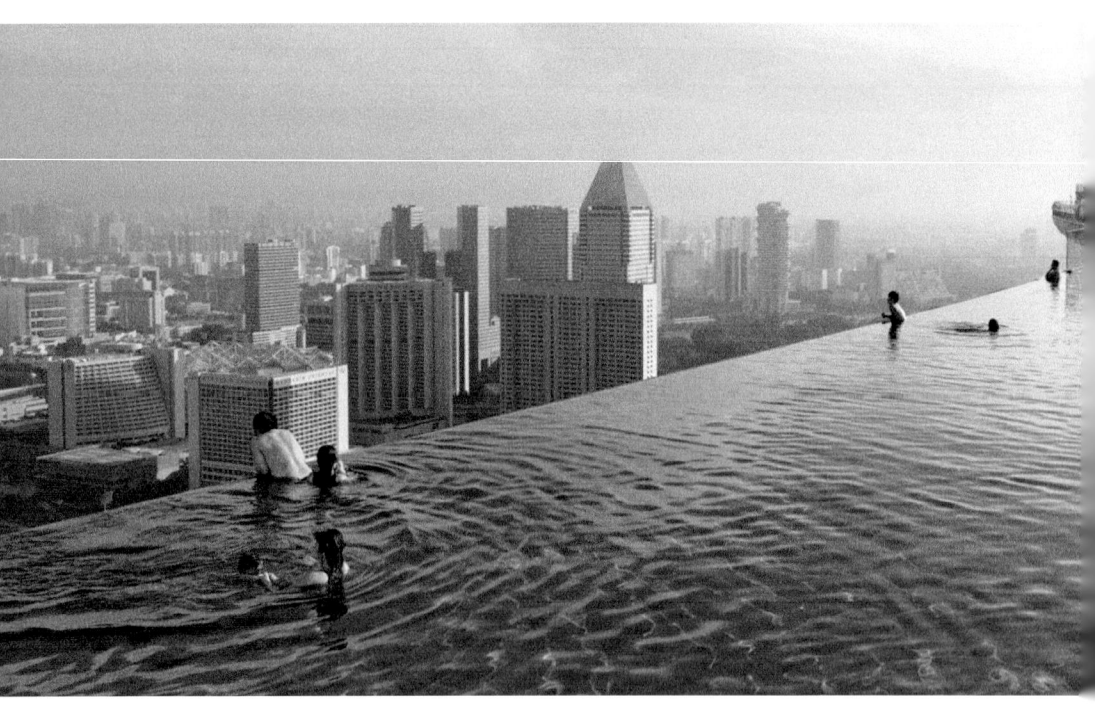

movement between alignment and distortion is tied down to a singular phantasmic encounter.

The transubstantiation of water into the dream of freedom born from the capitalist illusion of limitlessness is always best played out on the glossy pages of sales catalogues and holiday promotions or the Instagram sites of holiday-makers and influencers.

The more recent introduction of the sky pool marks an important technological, ideological and economic turn. Lifting the infinity pool high into the sky means that the catch and the trough are only seen when leaning over the zero edge—which is not allowed because of Health and Safety. The analogue glitching, the precariousness of the illusion, the falling away of the image, these are all problems associated with the first generation infinity pool. The sky pool, such as the one built in Singapore as part of Mandalay Sands Hotel in 2010, is the technological advancement of the zero edge but remains somewhere between the first generation infinity pool and the later translucent sky pool. Here we find the infinity pool quite literally in the sky. The experience of floating or even flying over the city is made possible through suspending large volumes of water across massive supporting structures. Here we are invited to float within a suspended infinity pool. Architecture and body defy gravity to form a union that enables a new experience of physical space. Yet, in the face of all this technological advancement, there remains the older technologies of the catch and trough. The concealed apparatus might be hidden by the lapping water but the hidden wall remains physically present.

The most recent iteration of the sky pool was unveiled over lockdown in May 2021. The sky pool in Nine Elms (London) has jettisoned the now outmoded technologies of concealed structures and perceptual effects of lapping water. Unlike the first generation infinity pool, the sky pool at Nine Elms does not require the hidden paraphernalia behind the scenes but simply uses acrylic panels to create the illusion of infinity. The ten-storey-high translucent container cannot be called architecture, it is instead the highest form of engineering. Everything is now made visible, the combination of elevation, water and vast acrylic panels might be thought of as the holy trinity of infinity pools. The zero edge is absolute; water, acrylic and sky merge into a single form without resistance or struggle.

As we look up at the sky we see the occasional swimmer passing overhead. Bodies floating through the air without limits, without boundaries: limitlessness and boundlessness, an image in space that speaks to the imagination while remaining unquestionably real. On the ground we experience a new level of delirium, one that is utterly confounding. That which should be on the ground now appears to us in the sky.

The text and video stills in this section are adapted from SKY POOL, commissioned by Copy Press for the Becoming Fireflies series. The 10 minute video is written and directed by Jaspar Joseph-Lester and is available for viewing at www.copypress.co.uk

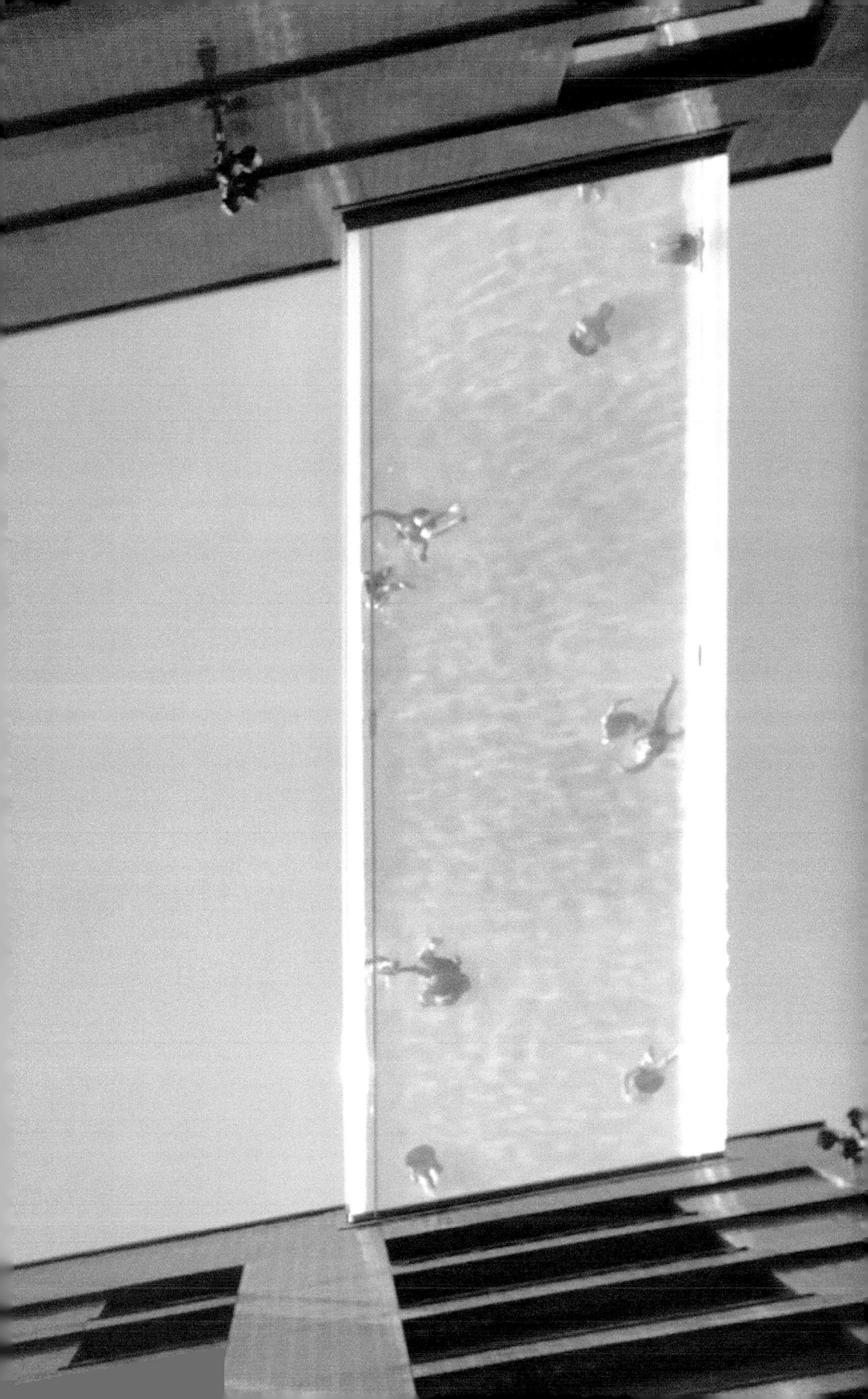

Wanderlust
Brixton

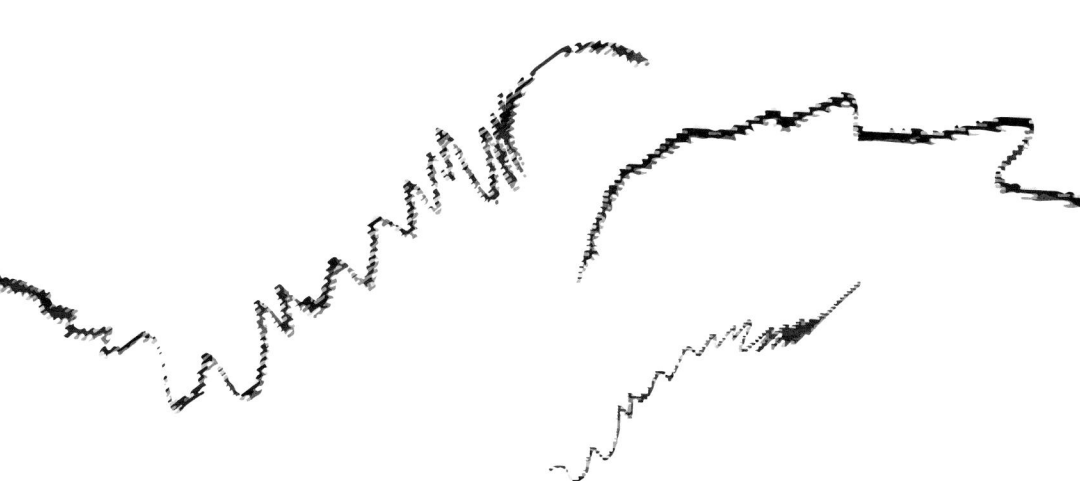

VIRGINIA NIMARKOH

A Emerging tentatively from another COVID-19 lockdown, the world feels much changed and yet still the same. Walks around my neighbourhood are taken with fresh eyes. The location is Brixton, south London – an area steeped in social activism, and the focus of sustained gentrification and civic remodelling. Every intervention into public space takes on a political dimension.

I've chosen six 'sculptural' interventions/installations in public space: public statues, street furniture, guerrilla/community gardens. Each of them highlights the big themes that have touched me most during the pandemic – concerning identity politics and the environment and where these issues intersect. Some themes offer a sense of hope for the future, others less so.

My various creative practices stem from walking alone, exploring my neighbourhood for inspiration, for connection, or just for the hell of it. During the pandemic, we've all had to reassess these freedoms because the home has become a necessary and obligatory place of safety from the virus.

For me, as a woman and person of colour, the right to walk freely in public space has become ever more contentious. Let it not be so. Ultimately, every step taken becomes a small act of defiance. Let it be so for you too.

In July 2020, monolithic concrete slabs appeared unannounced along the perimeter of Windrush Square. They are temporary safety measures designed to "protect against the threat posed by a vehicle-borne terrorist attack". Permanent "heritage" style bollards will eventually take their place.

The concrete slabs are an eyesore. Despite their ugliness, they have taken on a multi-functional purpose – impromptu and very welcome – as socially distanced seating and tables, and sites for activists' posters and street art.

Windrush Square was designed with minimal seating to discourage loitering and social gathering. The community's appropriation of these slabs has enabled the Square to become (albeit temporarily) a more informal, people-friendly space to linger rather than pass through.

Like many areas across London, certain streets in central Brixton are now newly designated Low Traffic Neighbourhoods, part of the Mayor of London's initiative to reduce carbon emissions across the capital. During lockdown, curious wooden objects have emerged on our roads – part bollard, part planter, part seating. Their purpose is to stem traffic, their aesthetics are secondary. Perhaps, as time goes by, we will find better, affordable, sustainable, design solutions. Or perhaps we will become used to the new visual vocabulary presently emerging. For sure, aesthetics is a worthwhile trade-off for cleaner air.

In the wake of the George Floyd murder in the United States and the subsequent global outcry, there has been much public debate over civic statuary – who do we commemorate and why? How do we reconcile the legacies of colonialism with the lived realities of contemporary multi-ethnic communities?

A statue of Sir Henry Tate stands in front of Brixton's Tate Library. Sugar industry magnate and philanthropist, Tate's wealth was built on the infrastructure of the slave trade. There has been little public debate over the Tate statue. Perhaps this is because of its context amid Windrush Square,

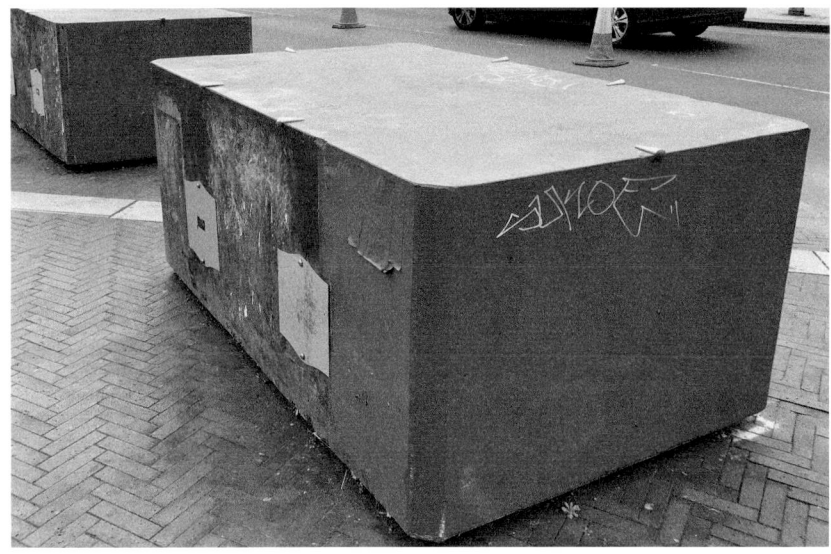

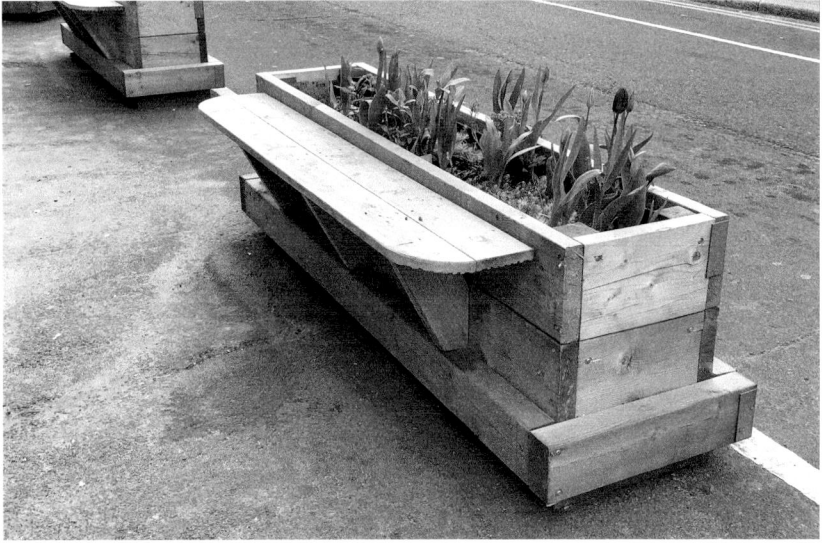

Top: Anti-terror measures,
Windrush Square, April 2021.

Bottom: Low Traffic Neighbourhood,
Atlantic Road, March 2021.

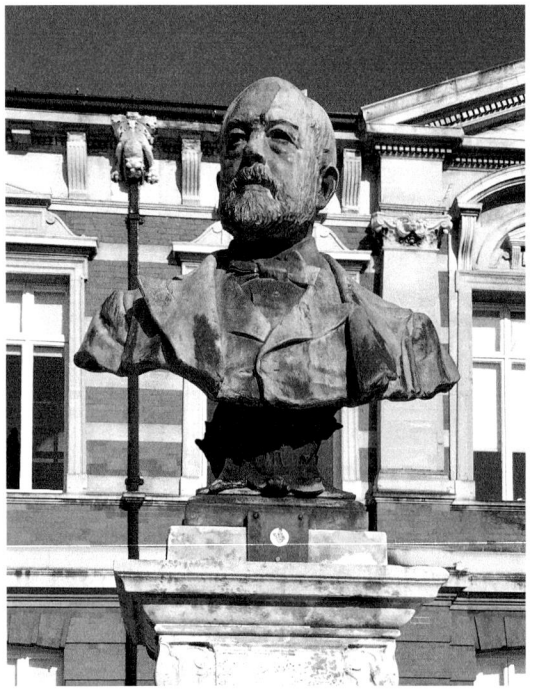

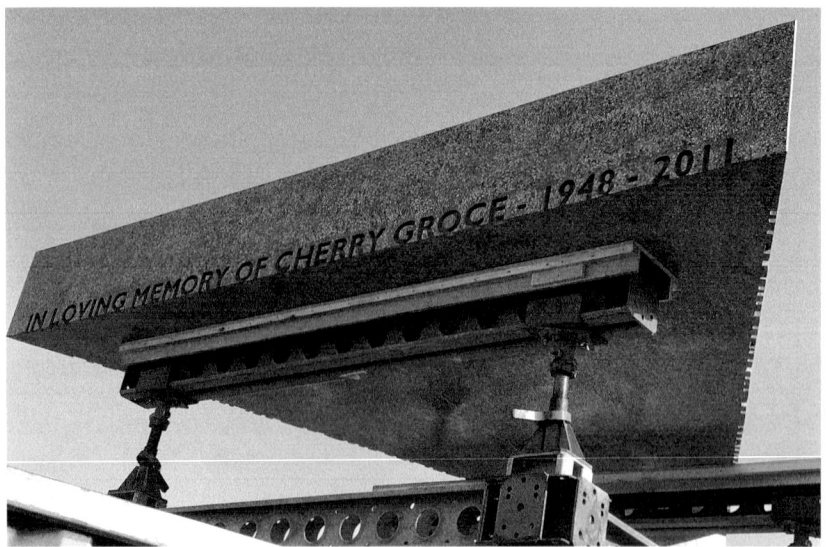

Top: Sir Henry Tate , bronze bust,
Windrush Square, Brixton, March 2021.

Bottom: Cherry Groce Memorial Pavilion,
Windrush Square, March 2021.

named after the *Empire Windrush* ship that brought the first sizeable group of Caribbean migrants to the UK in 1948. Other monuments on the Square are to the Sharpeville Massacre in apartheid South Africa in 1960; a war memorial to servicemen from Africa and the Caribbean who served alongside the British in World Wars I and II; and a plaque commemorating the Morant Bay Rebellion in Jamaica in 1865.

Without doubt, the presence of Sir Henry Tate's statue in Windrush Square is a necessary part of a painful, ever-evolving and complex dialogue around Britain's colonial past and its legacies to this day.

At the time of writing, a memorial to Cherry Groce is being installed in Windrush Square. In 1985, the Metropolitan Police shot Cherry Groce, an innocent Black mother, in her home during a bungled raid. The event sparked the Brixton riot of that year. The shooting paralysed Cherry Groce; she died in 2011 as a direct result of her injuries.

Chillingly, the installation of the Cherry Groce memorial took place in the same month as the murder of an innocent white woman, Sarah Everard. A serving Metropolitan Police Officer has been convicted with her killing, in the same borough of Lambeth, 36 years after the Cherry Groce shooting. Public horror led to national protests following police violence at a peaceful vigil to commemorate Sarah Everard's life. The UK government is currently debating a 'police, crime, sentencing and courts' bill that will potentially restrict public protests.

So, 36 years apart, the tragic incidents concerning these two women each reignited distinct and urgent debates around policing, race, class, gender, and our right to protest and to commemorate.

The Cherry Groce Memorial Pavilion is important and overdue. A permanent memorial is being planned for Sarah Everard. As a society, the struggle continues – towards a time when the need for such memorials no longer exists because the atrocities no longer happen.

A community-constructed 'parklet' was built on Rattray Road during the pandemic. It is a temporary intervention, complete with socially distanced seating and hand-sanitiser, but the plan is to secure planning permission and funding to build a permanent, landscape architect-designed space there. The parklet is a blueprint, a sketch, a maquette. As a gesture to the future, made in a time of global crisis and heralding a promise of people coming together, growing and tending land collectively, it is heart-melting.

A temporary garden – part of local Extinction Rebellion activism – was built on a sliver of soon-to-be-redeveloped land a couple of years ago. Part community garden, part guerrilla garden, it runs according to an 'open to all', 'help yourself' ethos. Located just metres from Brixton's (pre-pandemic) heaving cafés, bars and restaurants, it offers an alternative to prevalent notions of consumption. Activist residents regularly tended the site which boasts a greenhouse, rainwater butts, herbs, fruit trees and vegetables. During the pandemic, the site has gone untended. Reassuringly, Mother Nature does as she will, and the fruit trees continue to blossom, and the herbs grow wildly regardless.

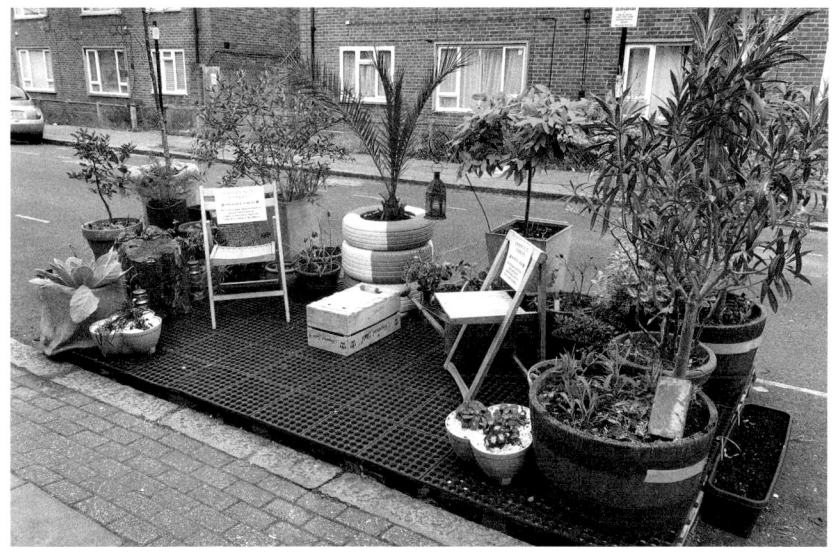

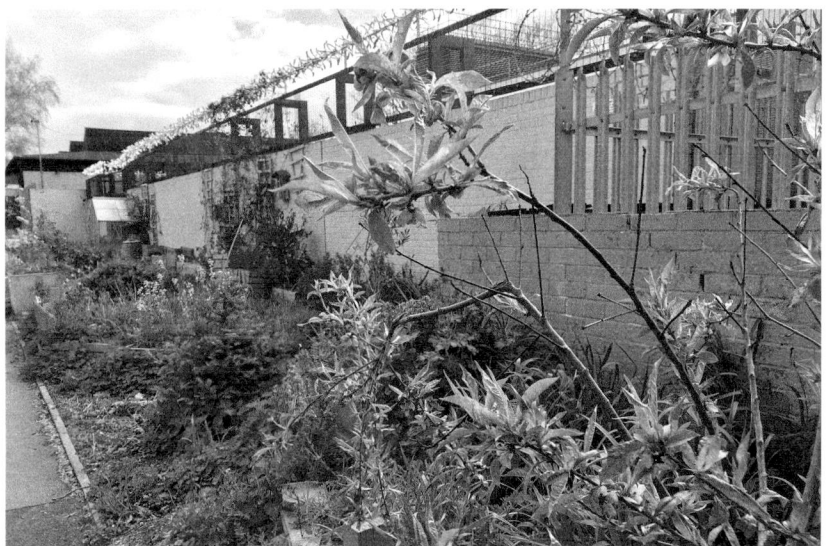

Top: Community Parklet,
Rattray Road, April 2021.

Bottom: Extinction Rebellion Garden,
Somerleyton Road, April 2021.

Pandemic Landscape: Fieldnotes from London Heathrow

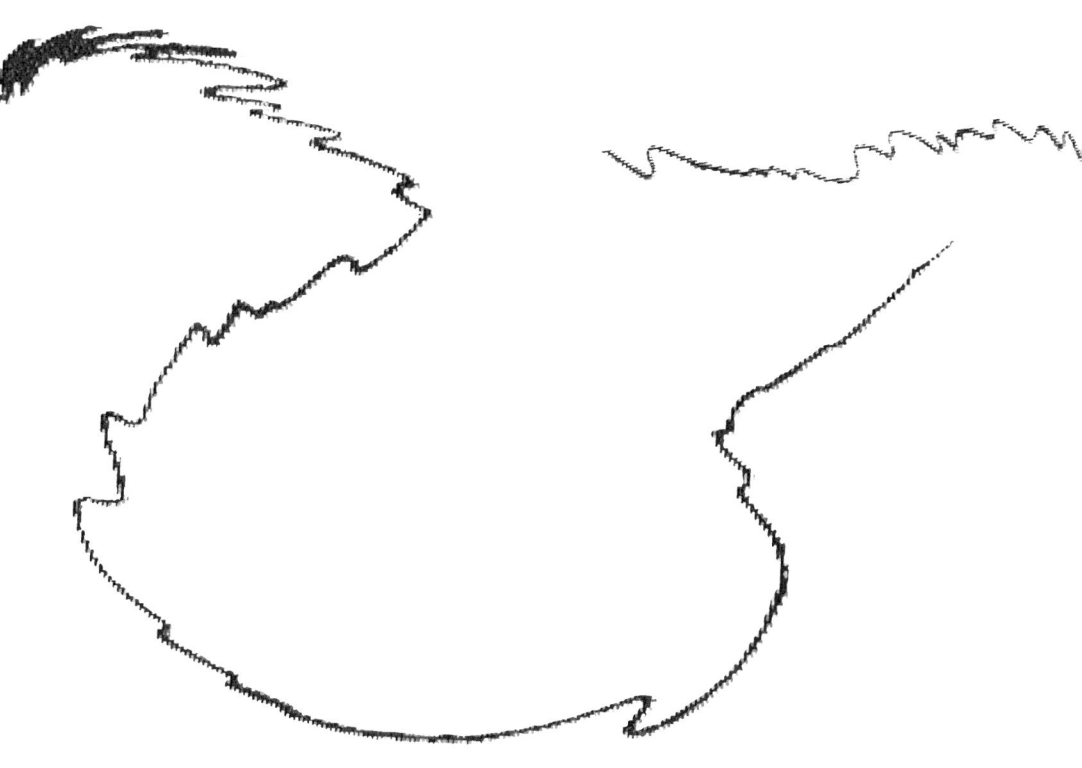

NICHOLAS FERGUSON

RUINS

It is six weeks into the first national COVID-19 lockdown, and I am at Heathrow Airport. Technically, I'm here for exercise though in truth I have come to see for myself the great pause that the pandemic has imposed on global aviation. On the northern edge of the perimeter fence there remains just one car, in Business Parking. It is a Ford Mustang and almost certainly belongs to a male who has travelled abroad as the pandemic struck and can't get home.

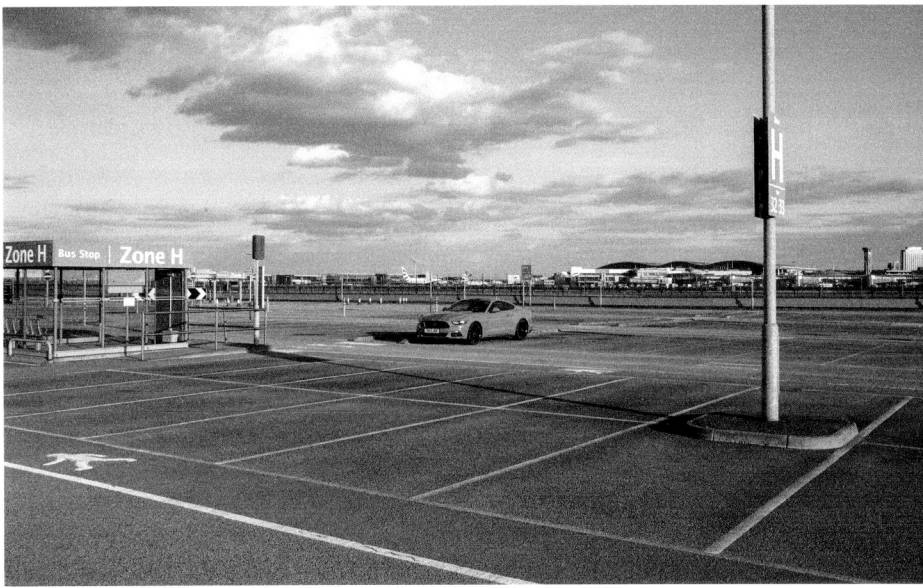

I am reminded of Pierre Dupont, the French businessman in the prologue of *Non-Places. An Anthropology of Supermodernity*.[1] Dupont's journey to work takes him through a soulless land without identity, history or social relations. He travels along an autoroute, pays a machine, parks in an alphabetically encoded row. The present for Dupont is an overwhelming stream of technology, entertainment and advertisements that is both demanding of his person but also thoroughly normalised. It is incisively figured in the centreless, nowhere land of airports.

Non-Places put a finger on a new kind of socio-spatial experience that was coming to grip upwardly mobile Europeans in the 1990s. Yet the view of the lone Mustang unsettles Augé's account. We could think of it as an image of the world describes in a state of ruin. A future present. And in the aesthetic tradition that attends to ruins, it calls on us to consider the meaning of supermodernity and the lives of those of us caught within it.

For artists, as for Dupont, the eliminated element of daily life during the pandemic was travel. While a comprehensive exploration of the reasons is beyond the scope here, it is noteworthy that the influence of travel, particularly air travel, on artists' lifestyles and creative processes has evolved significantly. Originating in the late 1960s in the United States and expanding to Europe by the 1990s, the era of affordable flights has transformed the traditional image of artists working in solitary studios.[2] This shift has given rise to a nomadic way of life in which artists traverse the globe in a cycle of international exhibitions, speaking engagements, and residencies.[3] Hence, it is apt that my contribution as an artist to collective memory should revolve around an international airport.

GROUNDED

To ascertain how the owner of the Mustang is faring, we'd need to know more about his state of mind when the pandemic struck. Augé tells us that on the day he parked in row J, "[f]or a few hours (the time it would take to fly over the Mediterranean, the Arabian Sea and the Bay of Bengal), Dupont would be alone at last"). It is clear that flight brought something of a relief to Augé's protagonist, as if it was here that, once he'd given over responsibility for his life to airspace, he was able to properly rest.

Following the closure of international borders in March 2020, this may have all changed. For it is possible he is now holed up under *le confinement* in an overseas hotel room where he will have found more respite than he will ever have dreamed of but may also have found time to read the newspaper article by compatriot Bruno Latour published in early March, and which celebrates the opportunity the global pause had provided for a reality check. Latour tells us that the virus is not an enemy that we fight, but part of our living world that is continuously mutating, and with which we will need to learn to live. The pause has granted us breathing space to think about this fact and adjust our lives as necessary. "Adjust", is the key idea here but his choice of example with respect to that which needs adjustment will surely have registered with Dupont and the English translation is worth quoting in full.

> A Dutch florist was on television the other day,
> weeping because he had to trash tonnes of tulips
> that were ready for shipping. Without customers,
> he couldn't air-freight them around the world.
> Of course, we cannot but feel for him; and it is right
> he is recompensed. But then the camera tracked
> back onto the tulips that he was growing without
> soil under artificial light before sending them
> off from Schiphol airport, on air-freighters with
> kerosene raining down, which makes one wonder:
> 'Is it really useful to prolong this way of producing
> and selling these types of flowers?[4]

Stranded abroad with his car at risk of impoundment, Dupont is unlikely to have been in the right frame of mind for an ecology lesson. The implied connections between the pandemic, ecologically irresponsible farming and global aviation will have come across as a bit of a stretch. Yet the unnaturalness of his aeromobile way of life and the question of its necessity will for sure have given him pause for thought.

Yet it is also possible that no such moment of enlightenment has presented itself for Dupont. Perhaps, quite the opposite, the pandemic has accentuated the stress of his transnational labour as he has fought to move online, and he is busier than ever. Furthermore, considering his recent plane journey, and given the notorious haven aircraft cabins offer to biological agents[5] (National Research Council in 2002), it is entirely plausible that he might have contracted the virus. He may this moment be recumbent in a hospital bed, his visage obscured by the mask of a respirator. In the vicinity of his car meanwhile, the painted demarcations of Business Parking spaces are beginning to fade and crack under the summer sun and the lone and level airport stretches into the distance. Around the periphery, groundsel and hogweed, those resilient harbingers of nature's reclamation, have begun to sprout between the kerbstones. Under the constant surveillance of CCTV, I've occasionally lingered to absorb this tableau, yet no one has come to investigate my intentions. In truth, there may be nobody to come.

AIRPORT EXPANSION

From a political standpoint, the recent history of Heathrow Airport is complex and volatile. It centres on an expansion plan, initially introduced by the New Labour Government in 2003 and since adopted into policy, that involves the controversial construction of an additional runway. This history is vividly documented in the paperback *Expansion Rebellion*, by journalist Celeste Hicks in 2022, who recounts the rise, fall, and subsequent resurgence of the plans and situates them within the context of the UK's evolving climate aspirations, and against significant milestones.[6] These include: the pivotal 2008 Climate Change Act, which set forth a goal of an 80% reduction in greenhouse gas emissions from 1990 levels by 2050, the global commitment of the Paris Agreement to limit temperature increases to 1.5 degrees Celsius above pre industrial levels; the 2019 recommendation by the Committee for Climate Change for an upgraded Climate Change Act, entailing a Net Zero commitment by 2050 and the inclusion of aviation and shipping in the nation's carbon budget.

These conditions are woven into a broader socio-political fabric, characterised by projected consumer demand on one side and a surge of media-savvy climate activism on the other. Notably, movements like Extinction Rebellion and Youth Strike for Climate have exerted substantial influence on legislative discussions. February 27, 2020, saw a significant turning point in the tide of power as the Court of Appeal ruled in favour of claimants, including Friends of the Earth, asserting that the government's policy permitting expansion breached its commitment to assess climate change impacts, as outlined in the Planning Act 2008. This landmark judgement overturned a prior High Court ruling from May 2019.

Though *Expansion Rebellion* does not draw attention to this point, the proceedings, because they were carried out during the pandemic, marks a historical convergence of three concepts: – airport infrastructure, pandemic and socio ecological justice. Hicks describes how the pandemic necessitated that proceedings were mediated through digital screens and speakers. It is conceivable that this convergence, in conjunction with the prevailing mood of the times and a yearning for novel paradigms, subtly influenced the course of the judicial process.

PARKED PLANES

At Hatton Cross interchange there is a footbridge from which opens to the north a view of parked aircraft. These and others stationed elsewhere around the airport represent a significant part of the British Airways fleet and have been brought here for storage. Nearby, in the southeast corner of the compound, some of the larger aircraft have been squeezed into a line that stretches for the best part of a kilometre between maintenance hangars and the airport perimeter fence. Standing in it is a Boeing 747 whose livery declares sponsorship of British athletes bound for the Olympic Games, Tokyo 2020. Another, as if in possession of foresight of its impending museum status, is painted up with a BOAC logo dating

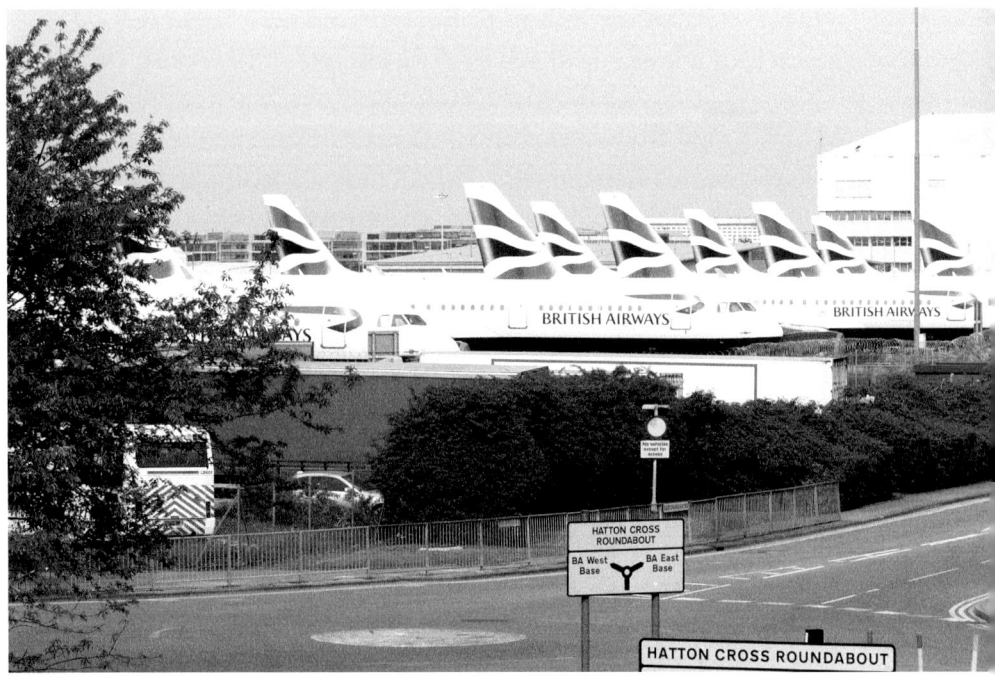

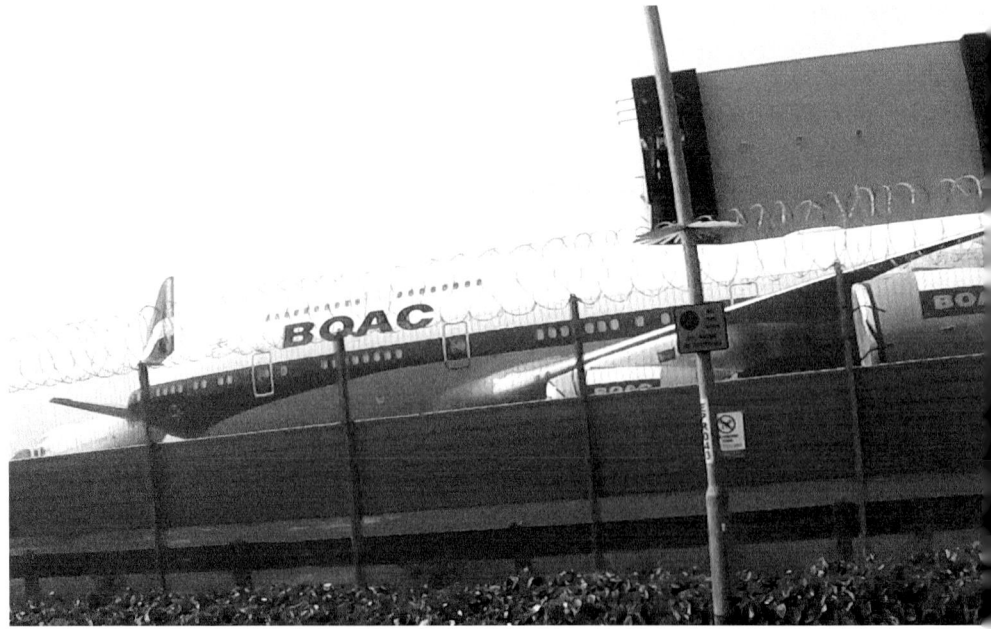

from 1940. Another boasts One World. Only months ago, these machines signified the ongoing emergence of a new global regime of connectivity, networks, information and capital flow. Today where Zoom and Microsoft Teams have come to dominate communication interfaces, they seem distinctly analogue. The unexpected need for aircraft storage has been a huge logistical puzzle for the airport authority. An aura of chaos shrouds the scene, panic even. The stowage protocol is so rigid that once the pandemic subsides, dismantling the aforementioned line will only be feasible by extracting each plane in the inverse order of its insertion, and backwards. The storage gear betrays an absence of planning. During downtime, safeguarding jet engines from foreign objects – be it the result of nesting birds or abrasive sand – entails the application of a purpose-built breathable membrane that sits over the front of the air inlet. Yet today, these engines are enveloped in polythene sheeting such as that available from a builder's merchant. The iconic Rolls Royce emblems engage in a semiotic dance with strips of adhesive tape that are, quite literally, holding everything together.

Such ad hoc arrangements unveil facets of the industry typically obscured. Foremost among them is undoubtedly magnitude. Ordinarily dispersed across the expanse of the world's airspace and terminals, the fleet, as an entity, remains perpetually out of the public's gaze. There have been instances of aircraft fleets being collectively grounded, but none on a global scale: the events of September 11, 2001, brought a two-day halt to North American airspace; the 2010 Eyjafjallajökull eruption led to the closure of European airspace, grounding 100,000 flights.[7] The pandemic marks the first incident in aviation history that necessitated the grounding of entire fleets. Thus, it ushers in the first opportunity to witness the enormity of an otherwise elusive spatial-material assemblage. The resultant effect is a process of de-abstraction. Typically, knowledge manifests quantitatively – fleet numbers, destination numbers, voyage numbers, passenger numbers, carbon emissions and so forth, each understood solely by industry experts, legal minds, and members of regulatory bodies. Yet now this knowledge has transformed into something tangible and more public: the tactile experience of fleet volume juxtaposed against a human observer. The capacity to perpetually veil an operation is exceptionally advantageous when the operation's true scale might raise concerns if exposed. Invisibility facilitates its existence and even expansion without attracting public attention. In the realm of intellect, this veil poses a dual threat, potentially stifling both analytical thought (what will be) and normative thought (what ought to be). Nevertheless, when an operation materializes before the observer, as has happened in front of me here, the mind is set free.

THE ARTIST AT THE AIRPORT

The Prologue to *Non-Places* was reprinted in *Airport, The Most Important Buildings of the Twentieth Century*, the catalogue for the eponymous photography exhibition at the Photographer's Gallery London in 1977 and curated by Jeremy Millar and Steven Bode.[8] Its inclusion indicates the importance of presentness in artistic circles at the time and also by extension, as a window onto the extent to which airports animated the world of art. Today it may be taken as a temporal marker of how these relations may have changed. The publication, much of it in full colour, and some 140 pages in length, betrays a pleasure taken in the experience of airports, even where that pleasure is granted an aestheticizing distance through a kind of counter perspective of horror that undercuts any kind of moral claim our pleasure may have on us. Augé is accompanied by several other canonical figures, including the far-right Italian artist F.T. Marinetti, who led the Futurist movement, and the English science fiction novelist J.G. Ballard, renowned for his gripping dystopian but prescient works like *Crash* and *Drowned World*. Also present is artist Martha Rosler, whose photo essay titled "In the Place of the Public: Observations of a Frequent Flyer" meticulously documented the departure lounges, walkways and aircraft interiors that define a career made feasible by air travel. Rosler's observations offer two vital perspectives for the current analysis. First, her title encapsulates the airport's eradication of the public nature of the travel experience and its supplantation by a fully encompassing industrial one, a phenomenon she traces, via Henri Lefebvre, to late capitalism. Second, she precisely identifies the historical moment at which, in the US at least, art's integration with flight reached an irreversible juncture. She writes: "By the end of the 1970s... the art world required a lot of jetting about by artists for shows, and lectures. As an artist whose fare was paid for by various institutions, I all but abandoned the buses for airplanes".[9]

That Dupont found his way into *Airports* brings into focus the attraction of presentness for artists. Presentness gave a name and theoretical framing to an otherwise esoteric subject matter, but also valorised a certain artist subject position that resisted, either by way of post structuralist semiotics or appeal to the aesthete's gaze, moral judgement of what had become a way of life.

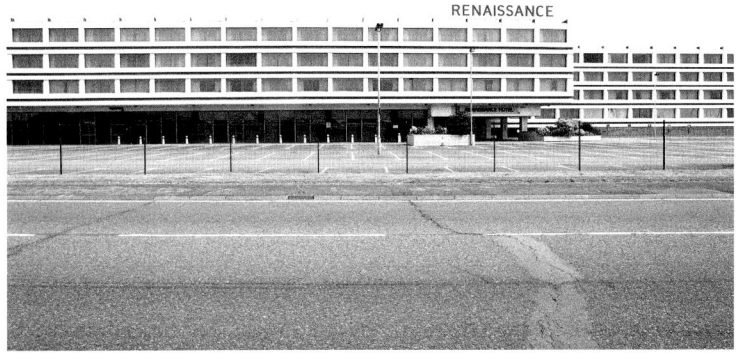

THE FUTURE

The Renaissance Hotel, completed in 1973, stands on the northern edge of the perimeter fence. Despite the name, it is thoroughly soaked in the high modern aesthetics of its time, not least the cinematic view it offers of the airport. The building ordinarily captures the thrill, glamour and romance that once characterised airport architecture. But eery and empty under lockdown, it would seem to speak less of the past than of time to come. This allegorical reading exploits the potential of a deserted place to suggest how it might look following a future catastrophe. The Jewish mystic philosopher Walter Benjamin made the point when in 1925 he wrote:

> Just as there are plants that are said to confer the power to see in the future, so there are places that possess such virtue. For the most part they are deserted places .... [where] it seems as if all that lies in store for us has become the past.[10]

Ruin commentators who came before Benjamin took interest primarily in the decay of past magnificence, noticing in them a capacity to communicate the limitations of human existence. While acknowledging this tradition, Benjamin introduced a variation where collapse and abandonment play a potentially providential role. At the core of this conceptualization was the notion that contemplating ruins could give rise to eschatological consciousness, wherein catastrophe is a prerequisite for political action and the organisation of something different.[11]

In the contemporary context, the experience of climate change, ecocide, and threat of human extinction due to our industrial lifestyle[12] imparts a specific causal dimension to Benjamin's speculations that vastly exceeds any he might have originally conceived. Especially at London Heathrow, where over a thousand polluting planes depart daily, and where there are plans to expand capacity for still more, it is difficult not to see the Renaissance Hotel under the conditions of lockdown as already in the future and seen from the viewpoint of the world without us.

BIOLOGICAL REALITY

Since late April, Purple Parking Long Stay, situated on the airport's southern periphery, has been designated a COVID-19 testing hub. One of numerous government run drive-through centres within the metropolis, it is used to identify among symptom bearers genetic material belonging to the virus through the employment of the polymerase chain reaction technique (PCR). The choice of location capitalises on a surplus pool of labour coupled with well-developed road infrastructure and extensive expanses of otherwise redundant tarmac. I pay a visit with my unwell son.

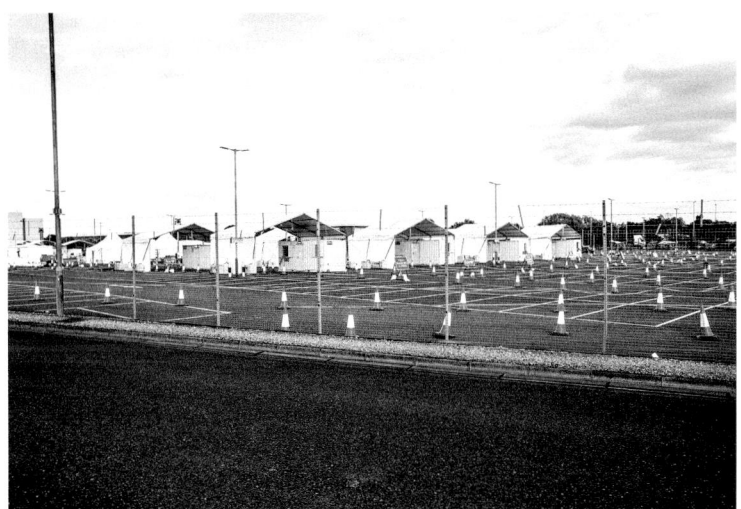

We are greeted at the entrance by multiple signs. Behind them masked staff beckon us through traffic cones. We loop around the edges on a route seemingly designed to slow and space vehicles arriving on mass. But it appears we are the only customers, an eventuality that only adds to the sense of foreboding. We pass a bus shelter where a few weeks earlier passengers had waited for their terminal shuttle and are brought to a stop by a man in a white all-in-one. We have arrived at a shipping container on which is printed a sunflower logo, yellow on green and the name of its owner, Sunbelt Rentals. The man holds up a sign: "Open the top part of your window".

The Gaia hypothesis, initially advanced by atmospheric chemist James Lovelock and microbiologist Theresa Margolis during the 1970s, suggests that life, encompassing the earth's crust, surface and atmosphere, forms an intricately interconnected and mutually dependent system.[13] Within the system, there are no discrete and isolated components. Despite these now-established insights, airports seem to be treated as exceptions. Among all the landscapes in Britain, Heathrow wrestles on a daily basis with vegetation, birds, pests, and all other life forms that challenge its predefined function. The intrinsic essence of space, its intricate nature, co-dependence and vulnerability, is largely overlooked. A clear separation is established between the natural and the human, the animate and the inanimate. This division is driven by the necessity for a distinct logic, one that ensures an aircraft can generate the required energy to achieve repeated take-offs, within financial constraints, and with minimal risk to passengers.

Nevertheless, the virus has offered a reality check.[14] It doesn't discriminate between spaces designated as infrastructure hubs and those marked as protected conservation areas. It doesn't distinguish between concrete runways emitting carbon and the distant peat bogs (the airport authority has recently purchased many hectares of such terrain in Lancashire, UK) absorbing it. It does not acknowledge perimeter fences or hinterlands. The virus transcends such categorizations with indifference. As long as there are hosts to facilitate its replication, it thrives. The virus leaves no room for doubt that the airport is a living entity, intricately linked with the entirety of planetary existence.

The man hands me a test kit through my car window, along with instructional booklets. Among these, the most useful advises me to activate my hazard lights if I encounter any difficulties. Upon completing the nasal swab, I realise that the vial designed to hold the cotton bud stick is too short for the stick itself. I'm left with the choice of either snapping the stick or obtaining a longer vial. After a wait of around 5 minutes, a man in a high-visibility vest approaches my blinking vehicle. He carries a sign displaying a phone number and the instruction "Call this number". Moments later, I observe through the windscreen as he retrieves his phone from his pocket to answer my call.

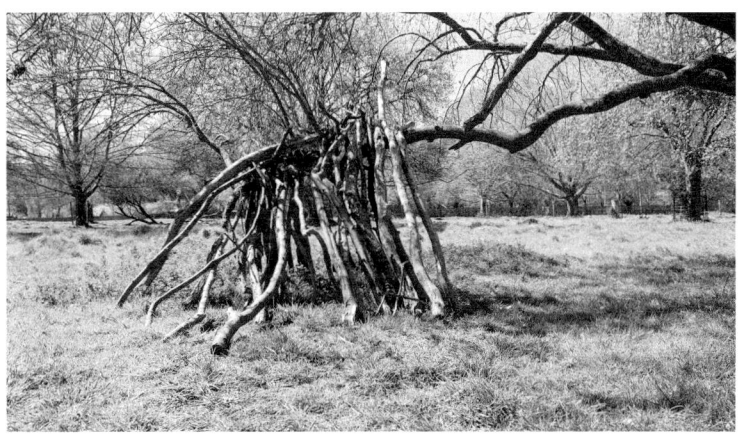

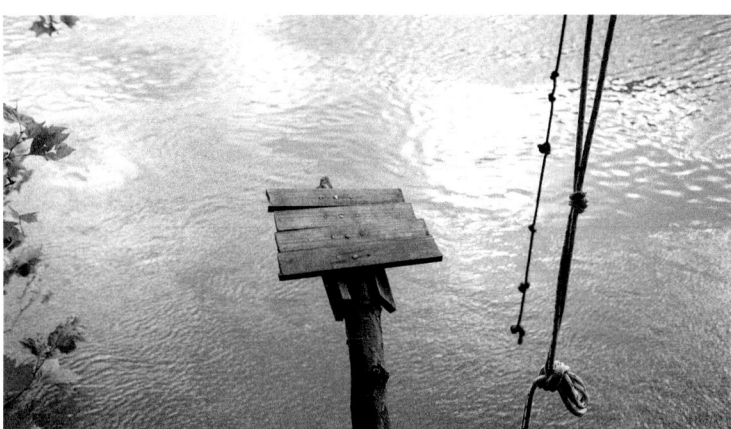

The airport in lockdown is set in relief by cultural revival in the surrounding neighbourhood. For example, Bushy Park, to the south is teeming with children's dens. Children have always made dens in this park, but I do not recall them in such numbers. Along the banks of the Thames in a neighbourhood repeatedly referred to by the aforementioned Ballard as Heathrow's suburb, are more constructions: treehouses, rope swings; diving boards. The autonomy, formal diversity, and social capabilities of these structures contrast favourably to commissions conditioned by airport patronage, pointing to a socio-cultural world of making against which official and/or administered arts are poised. Park dens rather than MoMA Heathrow, they seem to say. It is a picture flanked by others of cultural autonomy, flânerie and mutual aid. The irony is that these vernacular, bottom-up, forms of creativity embody much of the reciprocal creative labour and social engagement that much art criticism since the mid-1990s have claimed for officiated art.[15] They are also, of course, infinitely more carbon efficient.

POSTSCRIPT

On a visit to Heathrow in late summer, 2020, I find the Mustang gone. I find myself attempting to track it down digitally. Perhaps I will be reassured by the knowledge that it was still somewhere. I visit the website of the Government's Driver and Vehicle Licencing Agency (DVLA) and punch the registration plate into the vehicle enquiry page: DU17 JKY. A bold sans serif text, black on grey, reported back: Vehicle details could not be found.

That same summer the line of parked aircraft also disappeared. I knew they could not be back in service, at least not all of them: the news had reported that the Boeings were to be retired. A month or so later, while I was holidaying at Porth Mawgan, Cornwall, the incongruous view of giant aircraft on the far side of a farmer's field caught my attention. They were serene in the setting, Surreal even, a view enhanced by the fact that to see them I needed to negotiate a herd of cattle who had congregated around a gate waiting to be fed. One particular plane caught my attention. It was a 747 whose livery bore the message 'One World'.

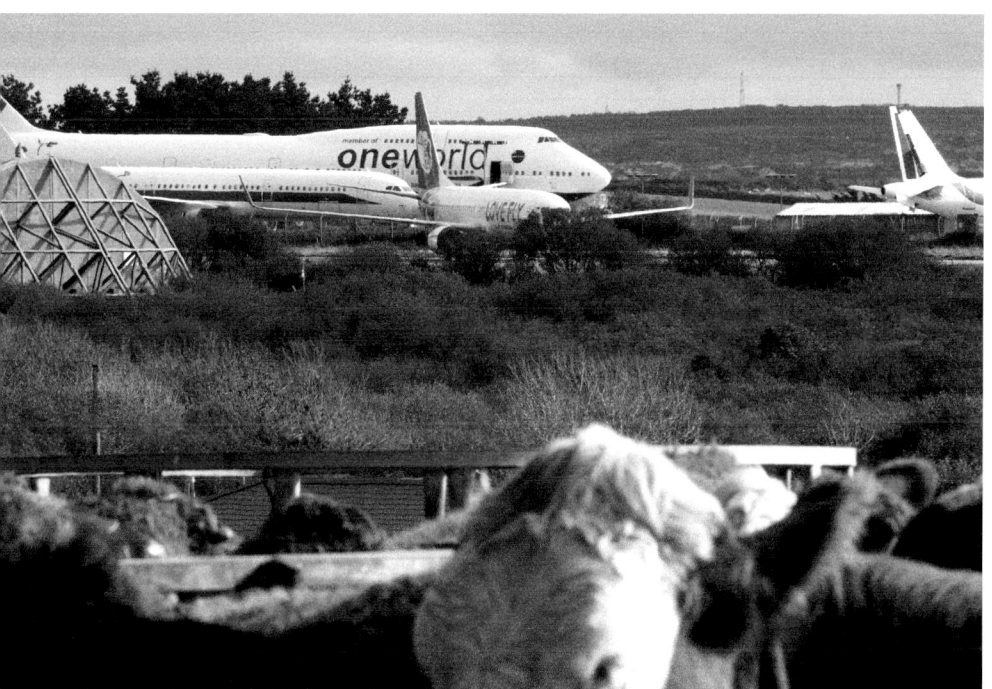

ENDNOTES

1 Marc Augé, *Non-Places: Introduction to an Anthropology of Supermodernity* (London and New York: Verso Books, 1995).

2 Charles Taylor, *Sources of the Self: The Making of the Modern Identity*, Reprint edition (Cambridge, MA: Harvard University Press, 1992). ; J. Hoffmann, *The Studio* (London and Cambridge, MA: MIT Press, 2012).

3 Marcus Verhagen, 'NOMADISM', *Art Monthly*, no. 300 (1 October 2006): 7–10.; Nicolas Bourriaud, *Altermodern: Tate Triennial 2009* (London: Tate Publishing, 2009).

4 Bruno Latour and Stephen Muecke, 'Protective Measures', *Cultural Politics* 17, no. 1 (1 March 2021): 11–16, https://doi.org/10.1215/17432197-8797459.

5 National Research Council (US) Committee on Air Quality in Passenger Cabins of Commercial Aircraft, *The Airliner Cabin Environment and the Health of Passengers and Crew* (Washington (DC): National Academies Press (US), 2002), http://www.ncbi.nlm.nih.gov/books/NBK207485/.

6 Celeste Hicks, *Expansion Rebellion: Using the Law to Fight a Runway and Save the Planet* (Manchester: Manchester University Press, 2022).

7 Volcanoes Working Group, 'Impacts & Mitigation - Impact of 2010 Eyjafjallajökull Eruption', accessed 19 October 2023, https://volcanoes.usgs.gov/volcanic_ash/ash_clouds_air_routes_eyjafjallajokull.html.

8 Jeremy Millar and Steven Bode, *Airport: Most Important New Buildings of the Twentieth Century*, First Edition (London: The Photographers' Gallery, 1997).

9 Millar and Bode, 91.

10 Walter Benjamin, *Berlin Childhood around 1900* (Cambridge, MA: Belknap Press of Harvard University Press, 2006), 79.

11 Walter Benjamin, *The Origin of German Tragic Drama* (London and New York: Verso Books, 2023).

12 Dipesh Chakrabarty, *The Climate of History in a Planetary Age* (London and Chicago, IL: University of Chicago Press, 2021).

13 James Lovelock, *Gaia: A New Look at Life on Earth*, Subsequent edition (Oxford: OUP, 2000).

14 Benjamin Bratton, *The Revenge of the Real: Politics for a Post-Pandemic World* (London and New York: Verso, 2021).

15 Grant H. Kester, *The One and the Many: Contemporary Collaborative Art in a Global Context*, Illustrated edition (Durham: Duke University Press Books, 2011).

16 The photographs in this section are by Nicholas Ferguson, Heathrow Airport, 2020.

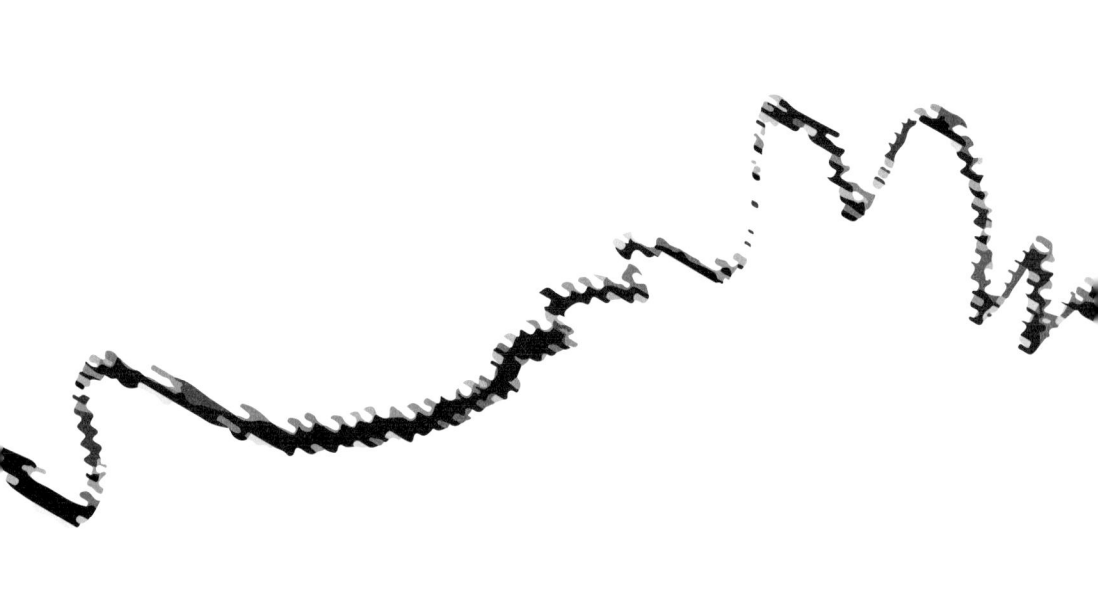

Dialogue and Collaboration

A COVID-19 Crisis:

From a Delhi perspective and a Half Way Between London and Delhi

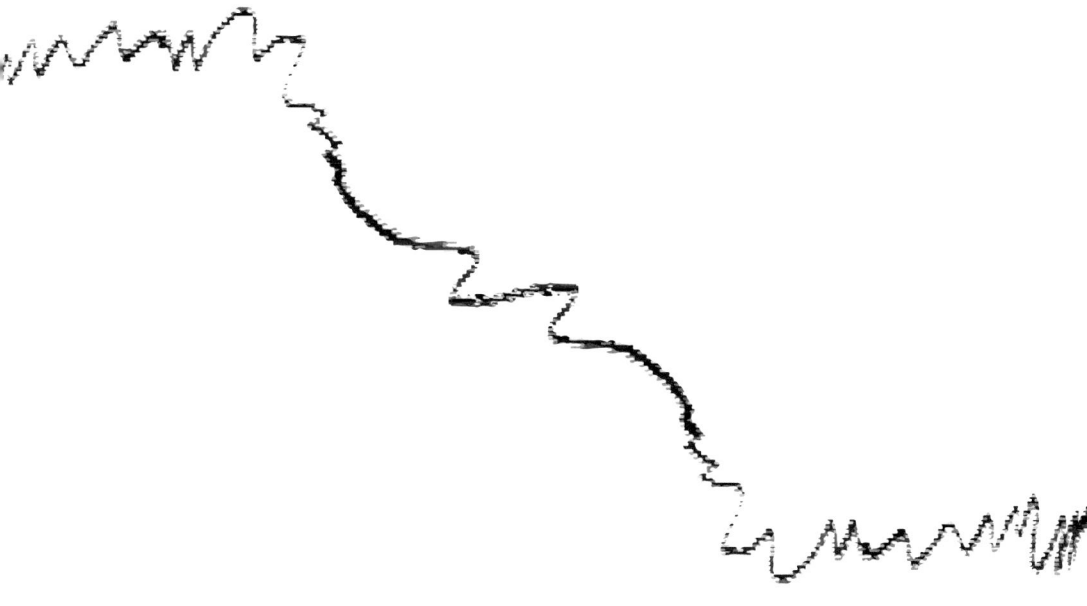

ASHISH SAHOO AND
JASONE MIRANDA-BILBAO

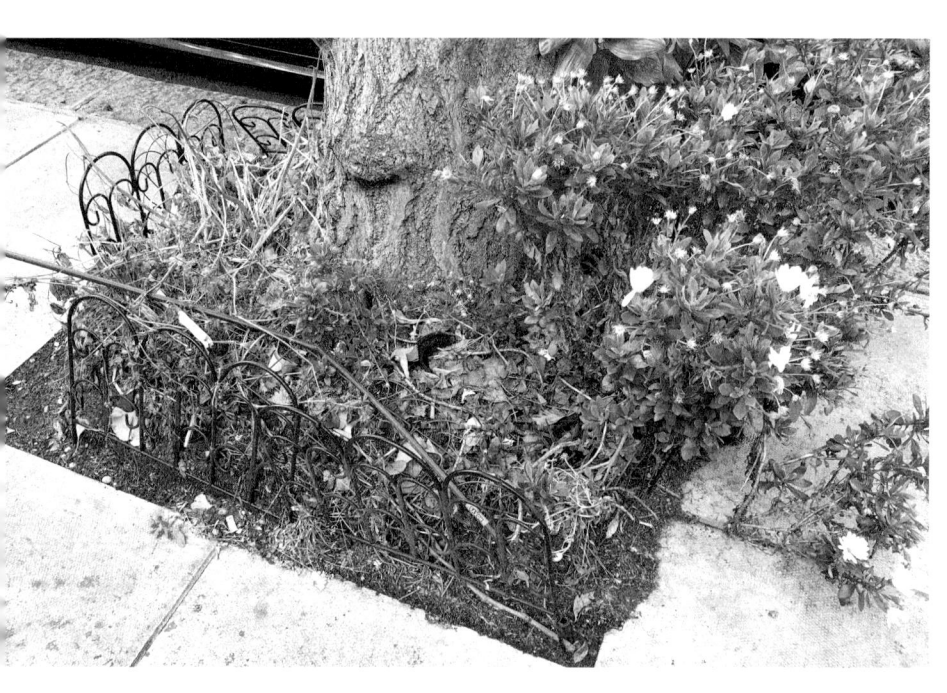

Ashish Sahoo and Jasone Miranda-Bilbao are practising artists. Ashish is based in Delhi and Jasone divides her time between London and Delhi. They have live-work studios across the road from each other in the Southern Delhi neighbourhood of Chhatarpur, where Ashish also runs the artist collective Maze Studio in collaboration with Zahara Yazdani. During the COVID-19 crisis they met regularly online as Jasone remained in London due to travel restrictions.

After a few months of conversations between London and Delhi, the four and a half hours' time difference that separates the two countries (five and a half depending on the season) began to compensate for the dislocation created by the pandemic and a third space emerged to fill the physical and temporal distance between the two artists. A space of ambiguity in which to re-imagine closeness and solidarity as well as knowledge and to plan new projects and collaborations.

At this point Delhi turned into an amalgamation of images seen, imagined and remembered. Jasone heard and watched stories sent to her by Ashish from Delhi and juxtaposed them with her own memories and images taken during previous visits. Ashish juxtaposed his first-hand experience, from his base in Chhatarpur, with Jasone's parallel experience in London. Interestingly, this overlap highlighted some of their artistic concerns over others – Ashish's passion for film and analogue photography created without the aid of digital technology and Jasone's concern for how we generate relations and notions of distance and materiality. Although these interests had already been identified by them within their own individual practices, somehow the two artists now gained a new alignment and different sense of place and isolation.

It is hard to come up with a better example of the inhumane process of construction and destruction that characterises advanced capitalism than what occurred in Delhi during the Covid-19 crisis. The city has a large population of migrants from other parts of India who come in search of work and life opportunities.

Many live on small incomes and have little savings. In March 2020, with the first announcement by the Prime Minister, Narendra Modi, of the compete closure of the country at short notice, jobs and transport came to a halt for 21 days[1] and thousands found themselves stranded in places where they could no longer maintain their own livelihoods. Without state support that would see them through this difficult time, the only alternative was the return to their families and villages where they could pull together as one. The exodus was of biblical proportions. Thousands walked hundreds of kilometres back home, sometimes with young children. Even for a country as resilient as India, this is a trauma that will take time to heal.

The average person in India is 26.7 years old. Europeans' average is 42.5 and the UK is a bit younger, an age average

16 MARCH 2020

ASHISH SAHOO. *Heiii Jasone, how is your mother? I just heard that this corona shit is hitting Spain badly and the UK is also bad, what's happening to the world?*

JASONE MIRANDA-BILBAO. *Hello Ashish! My mum is well thank you and yes the situation in London seems hopeless.*

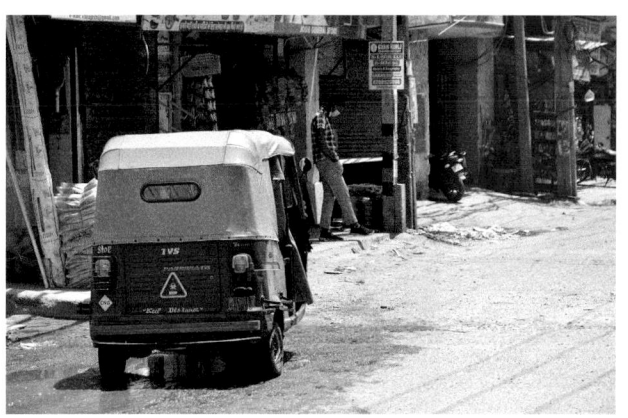

25 MARCH 2020

AS. *Jasone good morning entire India is in curfew...completely shut no one can go outside except buying groceries. How are you spending the lockdown?*

JA. *Hi Ashish! Mostly drawing and looking out the window, London is a ghost city.*

of 40.2 years.[2] The first outbreak of the virus, one that was most dangerous to older people, caused comparatively little damage but as it began to mutate and create new variants this changed. A few months after Modi's announcement to the world that COVID had brought India to its knees, a new reality set in. In May 2021 Delhi entered a second lockdown. Indians in their thousands were left gasping for air as hospitals and health services were overwhelmed by new virus variants that were as vicious with the young as with the old.

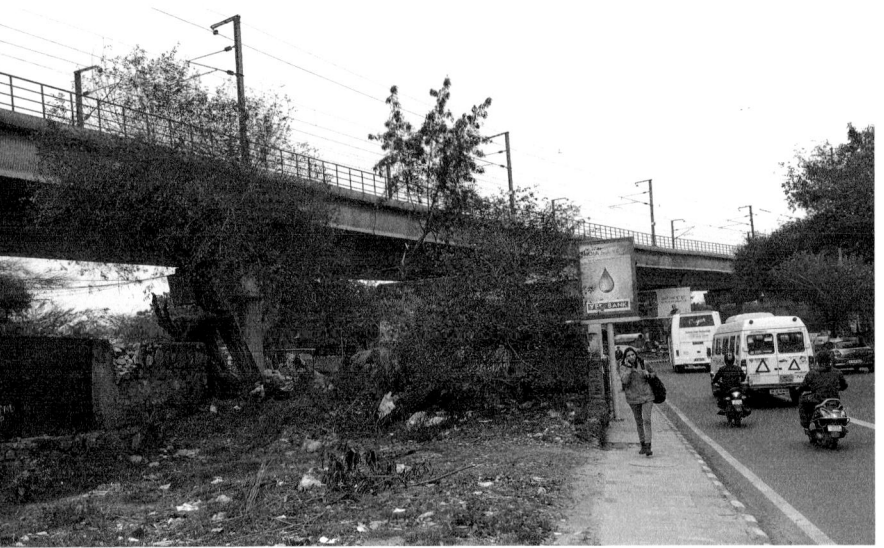

As Indian institutions began to use COVID as a convenient blanket to impose changes that were non-COVID related, such as the curtailing of the freedom of the press and the crisis became the new normal, Jasone and Ashish's project on Delhi's lockdown shifted toward a journey into their neighbourhood and surrounding areas as they perceived them and remember them from within the specifics of their situation.

Chhatarpur is a Delhi constituency that occupies an area of approximately 89 square kilometres. It is surrounded by the neighbourhoods of Sultanpur, Maidan Garhi and Kutub

AS. *Morning Jasone how are you? I have just sent you an Email about a project Zahara and I are doing at Maze. When you get time have a look and let me know what you think. I heard the UK is getting worse…*

JA. *Morning Ashish, I'm well thank you. Yes the situation here is not looking great, I will look at your stuff and get back to you.*

AS. *In India Gov is taking lot of action and by end of this month we should see if COVID is under control, I hope things get back to normal soon*

JA. *So fast you think? It sounds as if the Indian government is asking a lot from people!*

AS. *Yaaa, they have made some shelters for people that live in slum and are giving basic food stuff out but imagine, the pm requested the doctors who are fighting the virus to waive 2 months of their salary for fund…just think what a scumbag he is. What to say…can't even curse this guy.*

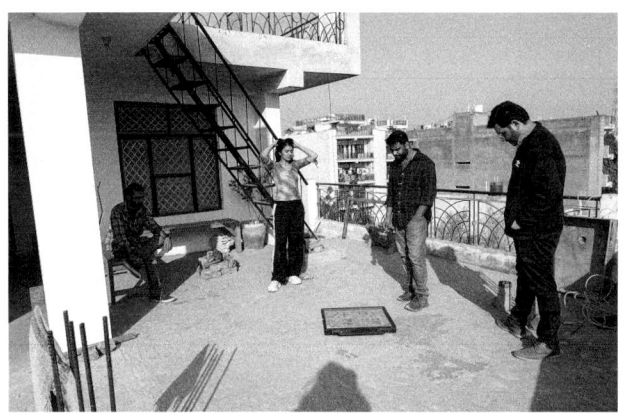

Minar. The gallery quarter of Lado Sarai and Saket's City Walk Shopping Mall that houses the Kiran Nadar Museum are only a stone's throw away. Low rents and easy access to the city centre via the Delhi Metro makes it popular amongst artists and the locality has a large concentration of artist studios. The area was not designed to be navigated by foot. A dual carriageway cuts through it dividing it into distinct areas. To the West is Chhatarpur Farms known for its "farmhouses"; large mansions that have nothing to do with farming, but, building restrictions to do with farmland mean that they have to carry that name. The majority were built by DLF Limited, a developer that in the 1980s and 1990s seized the land from the farmers illegally and they are mostly used for weddings and as filmsets.[3] Until recently DFL was one of the patrons of the Kochi-Muziris Biennale that takes place in Kochi (Kerala) every two years, the so called "people's biennale". Chhatarpur Farm is green, quiet and expensive.

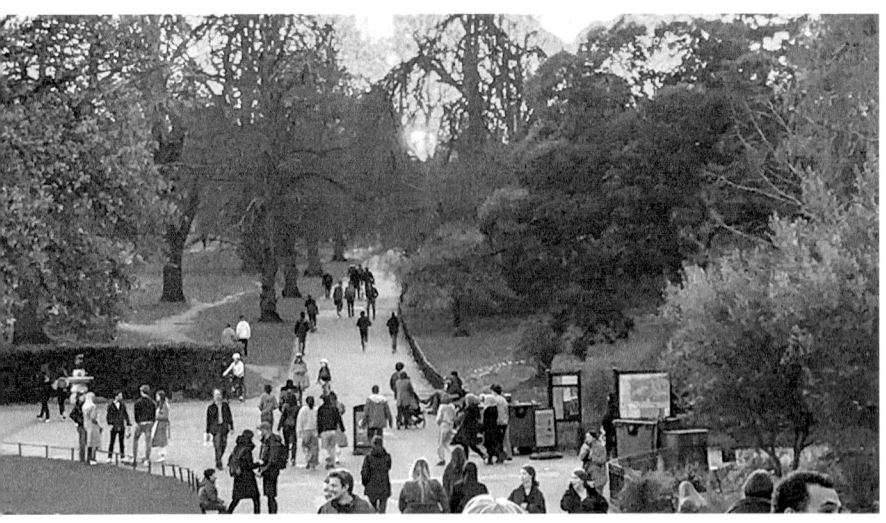

The Eastern side was built for the working classes. It sprawls all the way up from the main road to the old farming village of Maidan Garhi and it is populated with

17 MAY 2020

JA. *Just finished the coffee I brought back to London with me from Delhi!*

AS. *Ohhh Jasone that's disaster, I'm going to Devans tomorrow to buy some, mine also finished.*

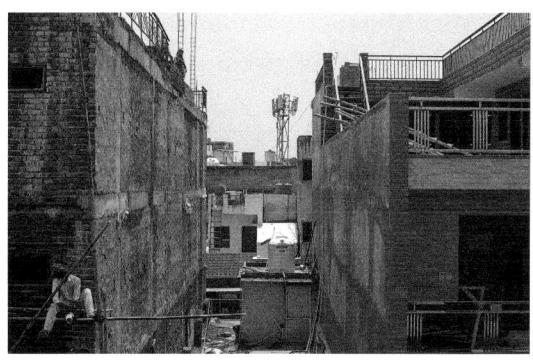

19 MAY 2020

AS. *Good morning Jasone I got my cofeeeee, let me know when you are free need to discuss something*

JA. *Morning Ashish sure, it's early here, let me finish my yoga and I will call you.*

AS. *Absolutely, coffee is my asana, but sorry no electricity now, I'll call you when power is back.*

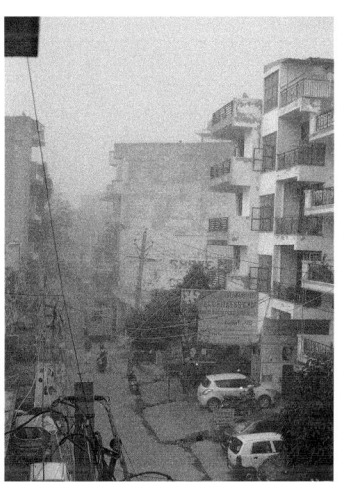

shops of building materials, wood and metal workshops and blocks of flats. Ashish and Jasone are based here. Many of the "colonies" built here were also constructed illegally, this time on land grabbed from the nearby Ignou University.

As a result, hundreds of flats are not recognised by the Delhi municipality and services such as electricity, water, collection of rubbish etc. are managed by the landlords or the neighbours themselves.

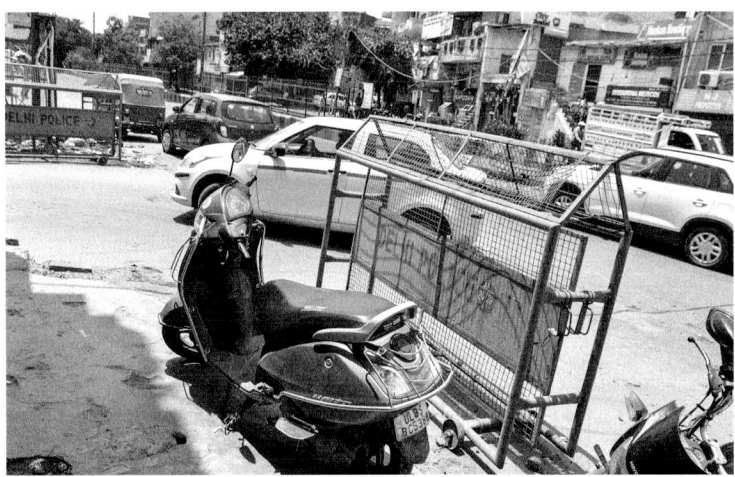

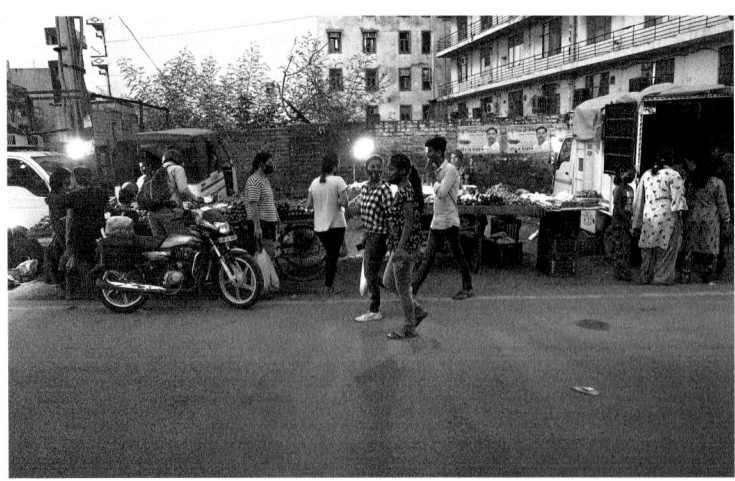

8 AUGUST 2020

JA. *Hi there, the Guardian says today 'India plans to cut ancient forest to create 40 new coalfields. Narendra Modi's dream of a "self-reliant India' comes at a terrible price for its indigenous population." Besides the human suffering, weird thing to do when the world is trying to cut down toxic emissions!*

AS. *Yup, I told you he is an asshole.*

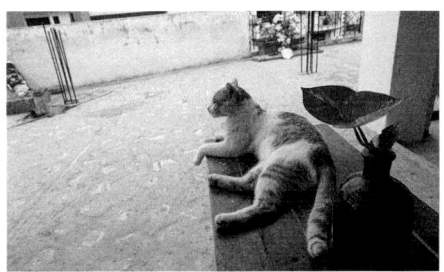

24 AUGUST 2020

JA. *Hi Ashish how is it going? Your Blink project's website running? I can't wait to see.*

AS. *Ohhhh Jasone I was just thinking of messaging you while having tea, what are you doing?*

JA. *I'm in the kitchen.*

AS. *Let me know after you cook if you will be free let's FaceTime.*

JA. *Sure, 10 min and I will call you.*

AS. *Cool.*

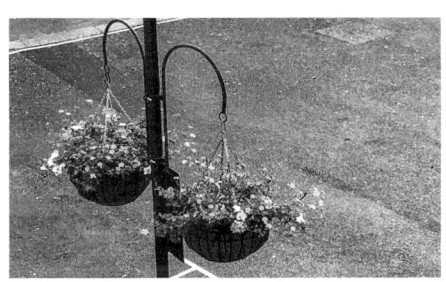

The Eastern side of Chhatarpur is noisy, dirty and densely populated and yet as a community it feels real. Made of the stuff that things are made of. Children play in the street and people know each other. In the evening, the main road smells of samosas, South Indian food and Tibetan dishes such as Momos and Veg Manchurian unheard of in China.

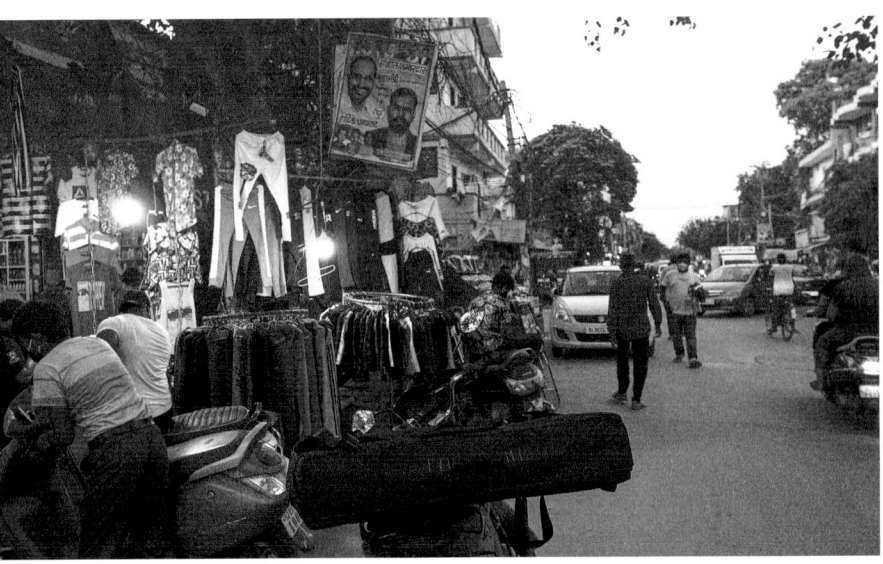

At the end of each day, hand-pulled carts set up shop on the side of the road and sell fruit and vegetables. The streets become even livelier, with neighbours, mostly women, descending from their homes to buy fresh ingredients for dinner. Sellers illuminate their produce with UV lamps and as the rays mix with the dust and pollution in the air, the evening acquires a bluish aura that is very distinctive.

During the health crisis all this movement and activity came to a stand-still and life froze. At the peak of the lockdowns (March 2020 and May 2021) people were only allowed outside one hour a day for groceries and basic shopping and without an official permit no traveling beyond the neighbourhood was permitted. As roads became more and more empty of people and activity, the city became

27 SEPTEMBER 2020

AS. *Hello Jasone how are you? How's your Ideas travel faster than light project going? send me some pics…want to see*

JA. *Sure give me a moment and I will show you. I was just looking at photos that I took in Delhi in January and look, a peacock in my terrace!*

AS. *Yes they live in Maidangarhi and they hang around the neighbourhood.*

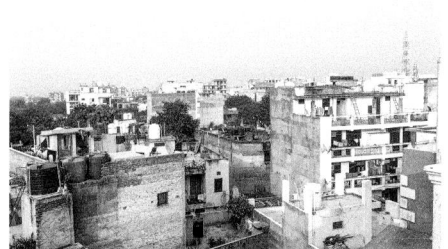
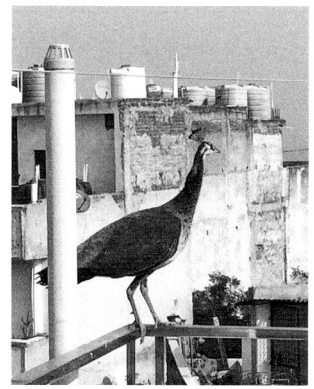
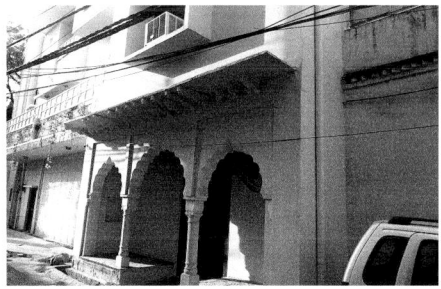
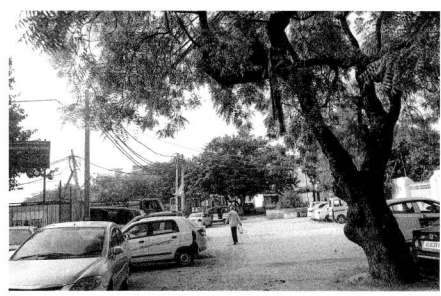

9 OCTOBER 2020

JA. *Hi Ashish, I was just reading that the Maidan Garhi area is mostly populated by Jat people…they are farmers right? Is Jat a caste?*

AS. *Yes originally Maidan Garhi'ans were farmers but now many have become property dealers.*

motionless. It looked beautiful and unfamiliar. This prompted Jasone to develop an idea for an exhibition under the title 8 × 4. It glows light, which she co-curated with Ashish in the terrace of the Maze Collective Studio in November 2021, as soon as the situation allowed.[4]

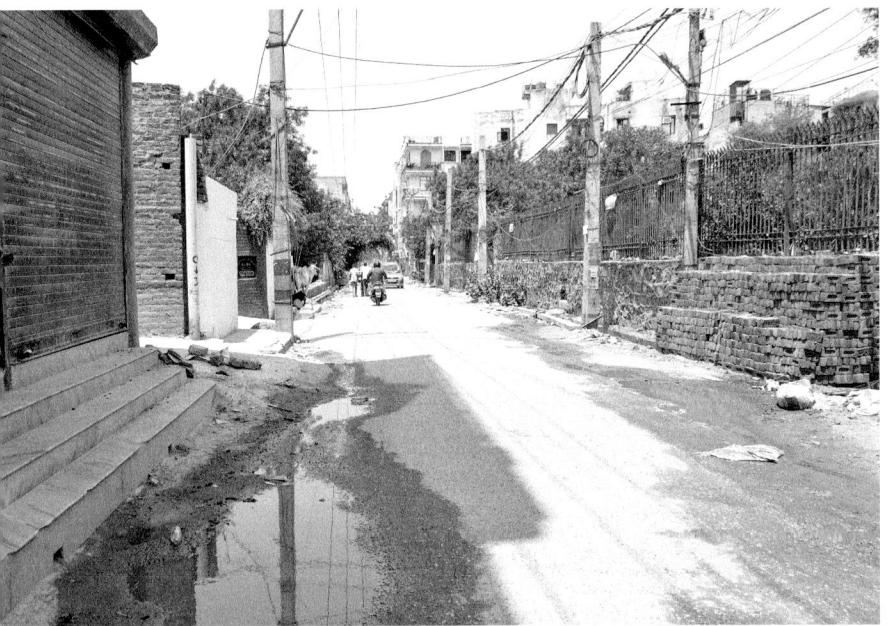

4 NOVEMBER 2020

JA. *Hi Ashish just saw your message. I was thinking of talking to you also, I have an idea for a project that we could do in your terrace, just tried you on FaceTime but not reply. I'm around.*
AS. *Sorry Jasone no electricity, will call you as soon as is back.*

24 DECEMBER 2020

AS. *Merry Christmas Jasone…have a healthy and rocking year. I am sending you a picture of our street, it's so quiet, I can hear birdsong, come soon.*

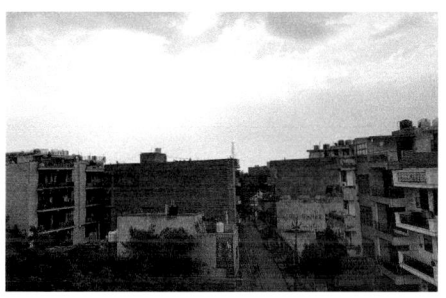

JA. *Thank you Ashish! Same to you, here is one of my Christmas tree in the balcony, come to see it on the flesh!*
AS. *I wish, Jasone.*

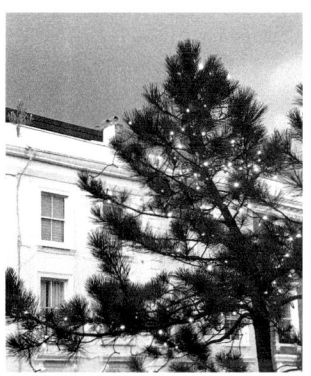

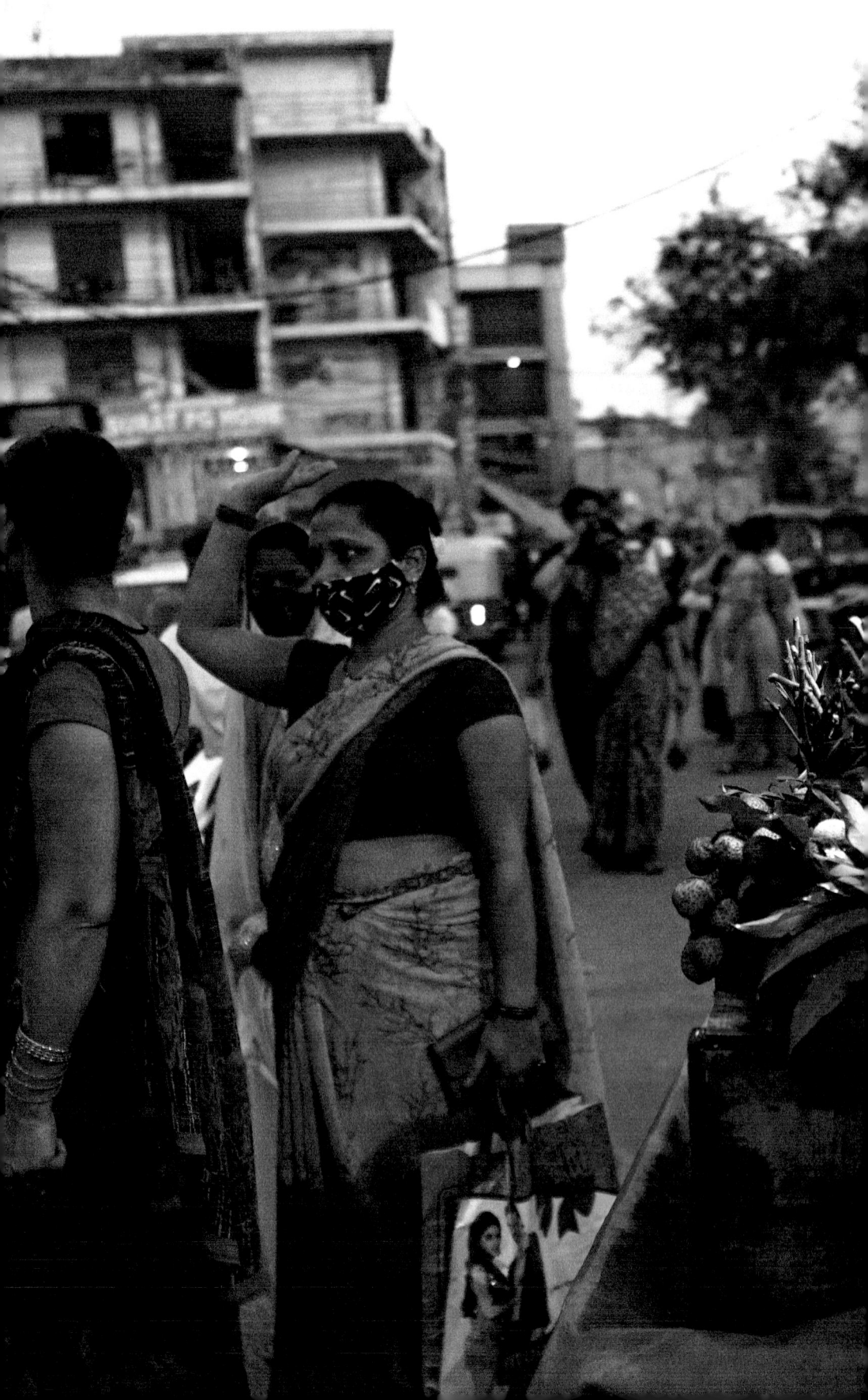

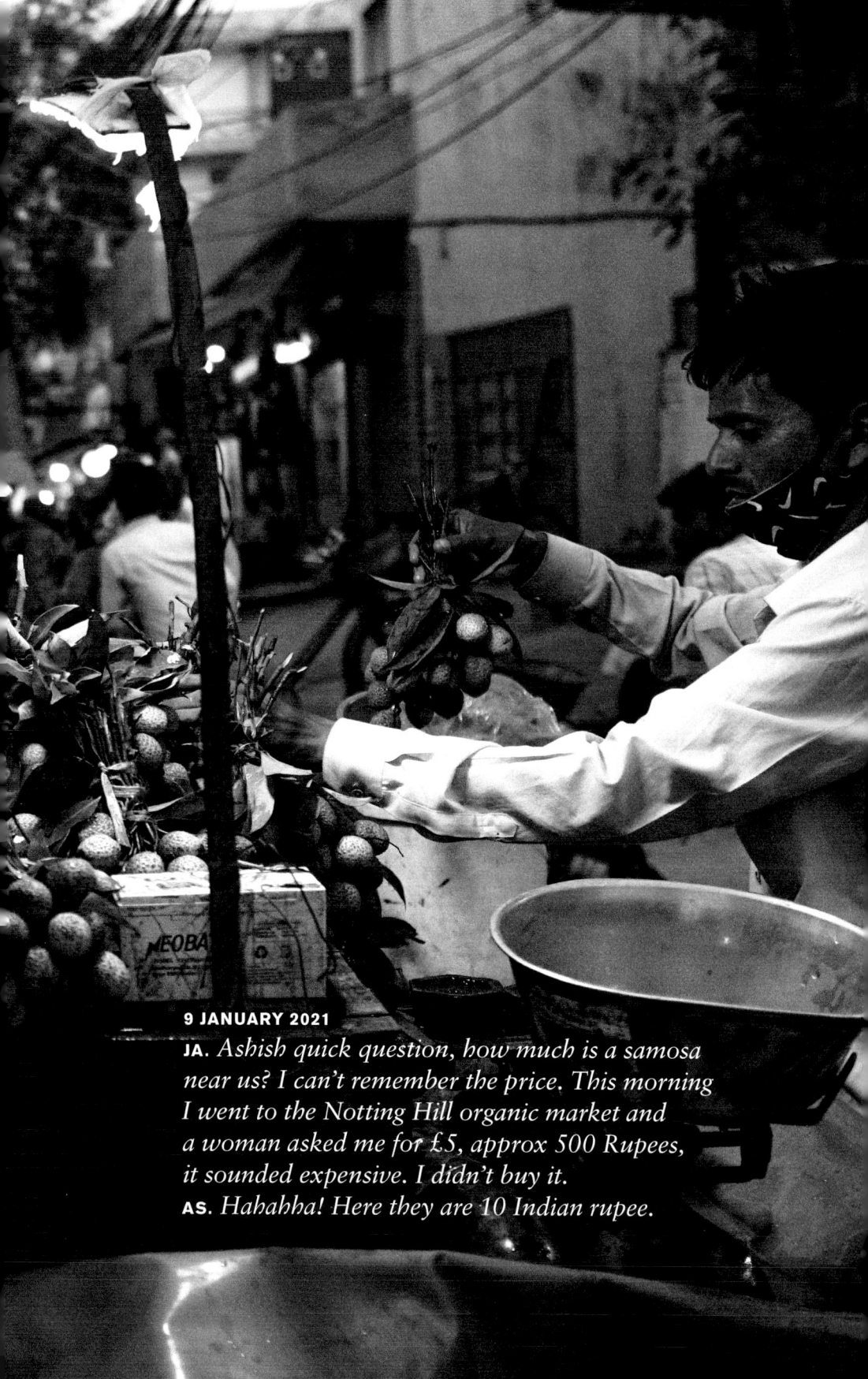

9 JANUARY 2021

JA. *Ashish quick question, how much is a samosa near us? I can't remember the price. This morning I went to the Notting Hill organic market and a woman asked me for £5, approx 500 Rupees, it sounded expensive. I didn't buy it.*

AS. *Hahahha! Here they are 10 Indian rupee.*

29 JANUARY 2021

JA. *Ashish today the paper says "Dramatic drop in COVID cases gives India hope of return to normal life" what you reckon?*

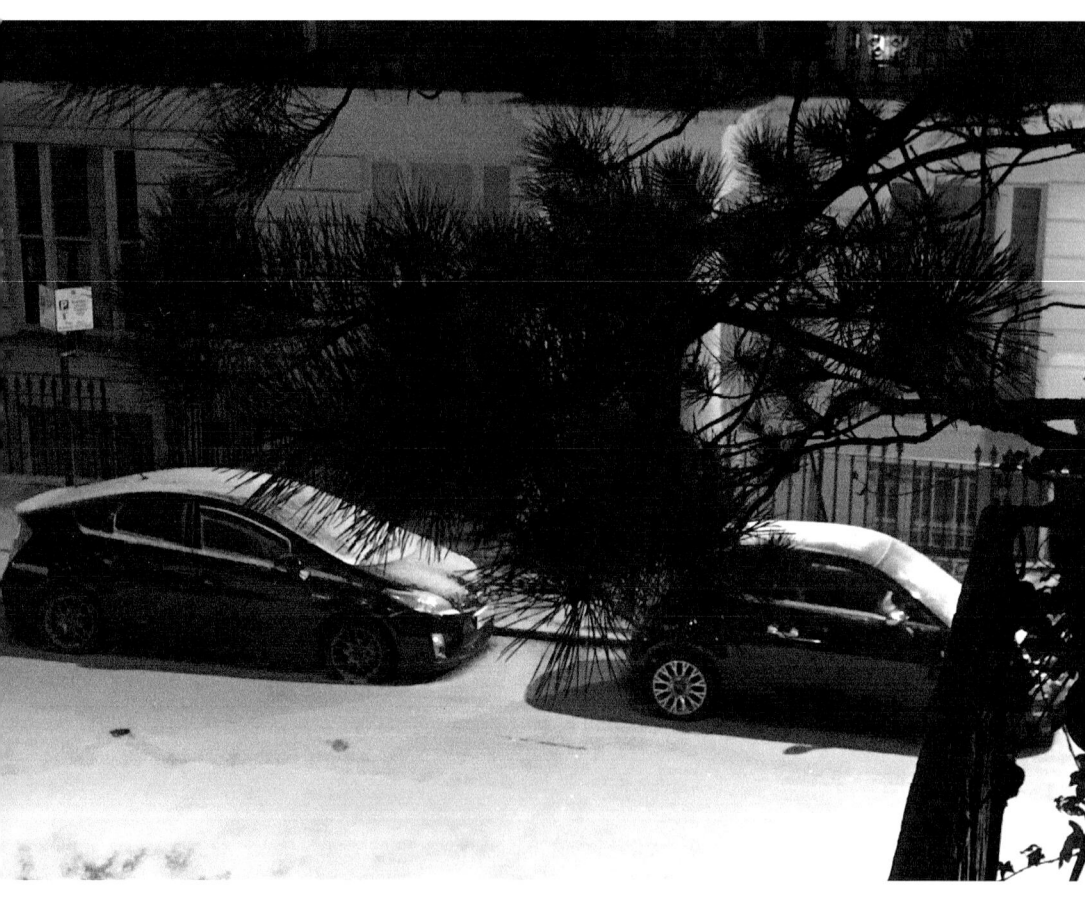

8 FEB 2021

JA. *Hi Ashish this is the view from my window at 3.00 am today finally show 2 degrees, so beautiful*
AS. *Ohhh Jasone I would die!*

ENDNOTES
1 See https://www.thehindu.com/news/national/pm-announces-21-day-lockdown-as-covid-19-toll-touches-10/article61958513.ece
2 See Ourworldindata.org
3 http://navdanya.org/site/attachments/category/11/Latest_Publications10.pdf
   https://www.indiatoday.in/magazine/investigation/story/19820515-nexus-between-politicians-and-bureaucrats-in-land-grab-operations-in-delhi-exposed-771787-2013-10-16
4 See https://www.ideastravelfasterthanlight.com/8x4-it-glows-light

Images: Ashish Sahoo and Jasone Miranda-Bilbao.
Text: Jasone Miranda-Bilbao.
Layout design: Devansh Sagar.

Swimming
in Venice

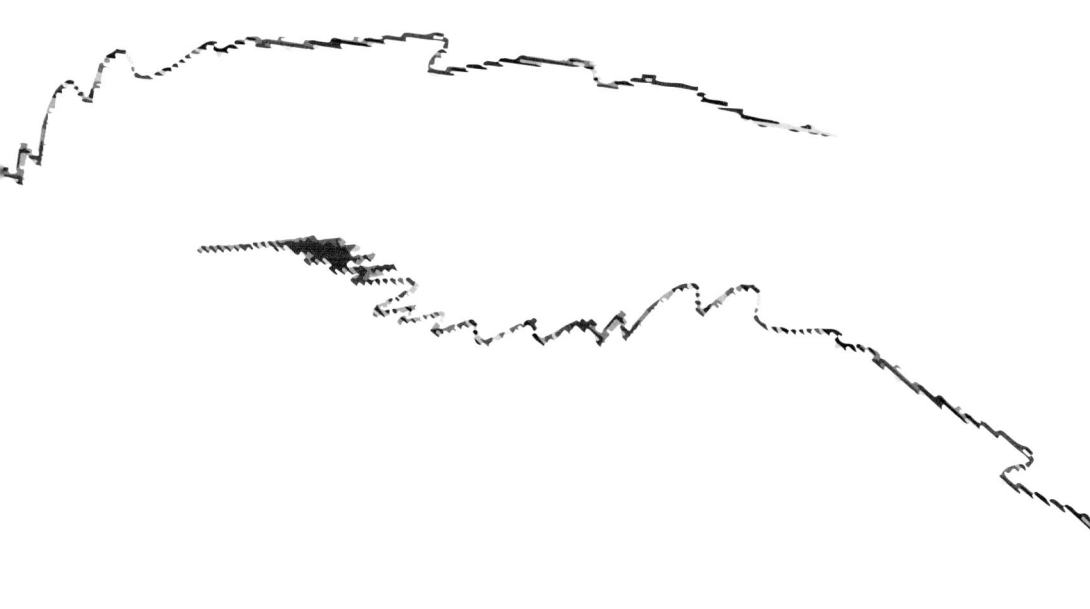

ANDREAS PHILIPPOPOULOS-MIHALOPOULOS
AND KATARINA ROTHFJELL

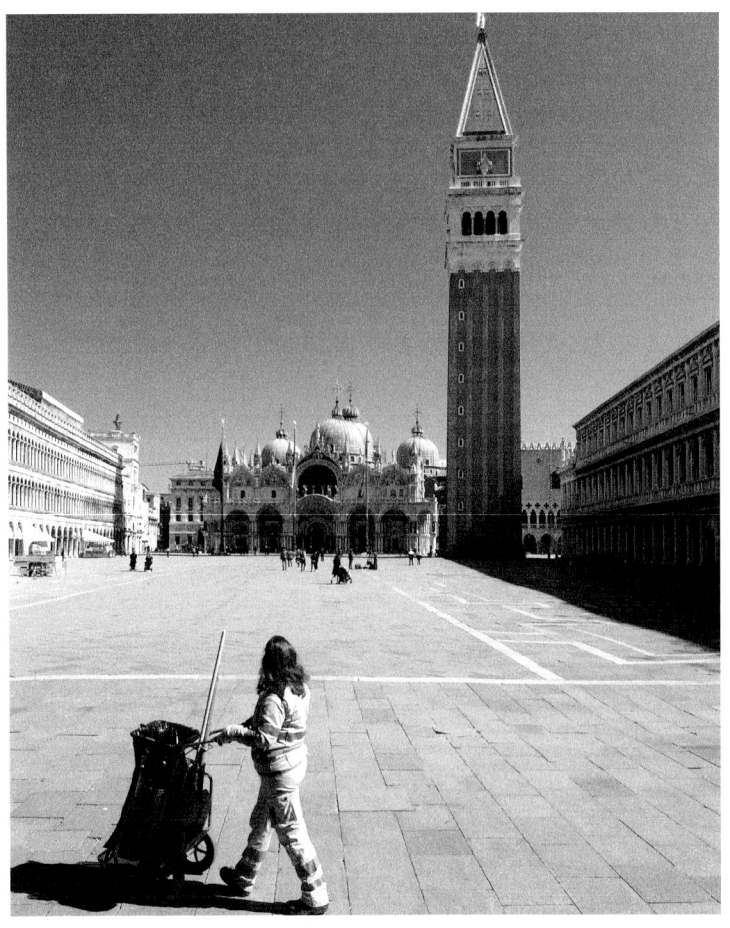

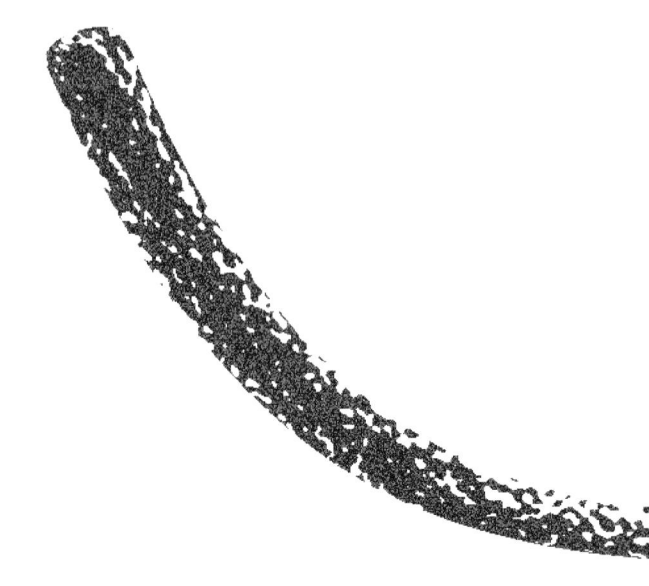

We are swimming at the beach in front of Saint Mark's Basilica (but we know, there is no beach in front of Saint Mark). The sound of Venice travels differently on the water, especially when you are so near the surface. Our bodies sometimes feel like gondolas, sliding and belonging, yet awkwardly elegant. We fall asleep on our backs, lulling city church bells, seagulls mating overhead, the Southern Lagoon a calm womb. When we wake up, we are alone in the Northern Lagoon, the other side of the city, in the middle of nothing, ourselves liquid, the water flat as the weather, silk skins mixing with taffeta algae.

Panic grips us. The only island here, we do not see but we know, is the San Michele cemetery, the walled container of cypresses, rotting bodies and aging Malvasia vineyards cultivated by Laguna nel Bicchiere, the "Lagoon in the Glass", whose wines still fuels local feasts and global protests. We are sinking and there is nothing to hold on to, until we orient ourselves. A little to the south the vaporetti of the Fondamenta Nòve come to sleep. We grab the edge of the platform. It is easy. We find a pair of oars and we pick them up. They will cover our nudity when we navigate the city to go back home to Castello. We start walking back. Like real Venetians, we disagree on the most direct (sempre dritto) route. She says, it's up the hill. He says, it's certainly not! We settle on a via media and get entangled in small courtyards with oysters and ostriches. We are approaching the Salizada dei Greci, the epicentre of the Greek community in Venice, but Greek ladies no longer chatter anywhere. Nothing guides us, no one is around who can give us directions. Up the hill, she says, almost randomly. Hills in Venice? The smell of the salt is stronger there. But where is the water, he wonders.

Renaissance Venetian painters fights water, as if they want to keep it out of the canvas. Water appears only in ceremonial cross-bearing or that one time when Tintoretto paints Susanna's reflection on the water to make her even more desirable to the spying elders. Or when the colours bleed into each other in defiance of Florentine outlines. Often one could not tell the difference between blood and water. We must wait for Canaletto and Guardi to see Venetian water. We must wait for the Grand Tour.

We have no time though. This is just our small return, from one water to another, from Venice-the-dream to Venice-the real. We cross bridges that have run aground, no water to span, no life to observe. Yet we are being observed from above: high up on an altana (that quintessential Venetian balcony in the sky reminding the city of the martyr of Sant'Andrea with its X-crosses used in its wooden balustrade) a woman not from Venice, a foresta as they say here, who has brought her own succulent forest from the main land (which she later on learnt to call it the way everyone else does in Venice terraferma, the land that doesn't move; this one word that splits the world into a moto perpetuo Venetian mosaic and everything else fixed and failing to move itself or anyone else and mixed it with lemon trees and mountain herbs), is looking at us from above. She has the same look as Veronese's Venice (and later on Tiepolo's) as she deigns to look down from the heights of the ceiling at Doge's Palace, her face in the shade, her brilliance incontestable, her glory unostentatious in a rare moment of Venetian modesty. Our observer from above dries her hair in the early morning sun like Venetian ladies used to, amidst the cured meats and the laundry. She exhales that breeze redolent of a freedom that Venice so generously seems to offer. This is our chosen home: a melancholy, sinking island, planetary dying observed, and yet: it imparts such inebriating happiness that we all dance while waiting for the end. The woman on the altana doesn't invite us up. She is not allowed. And we are still naked.

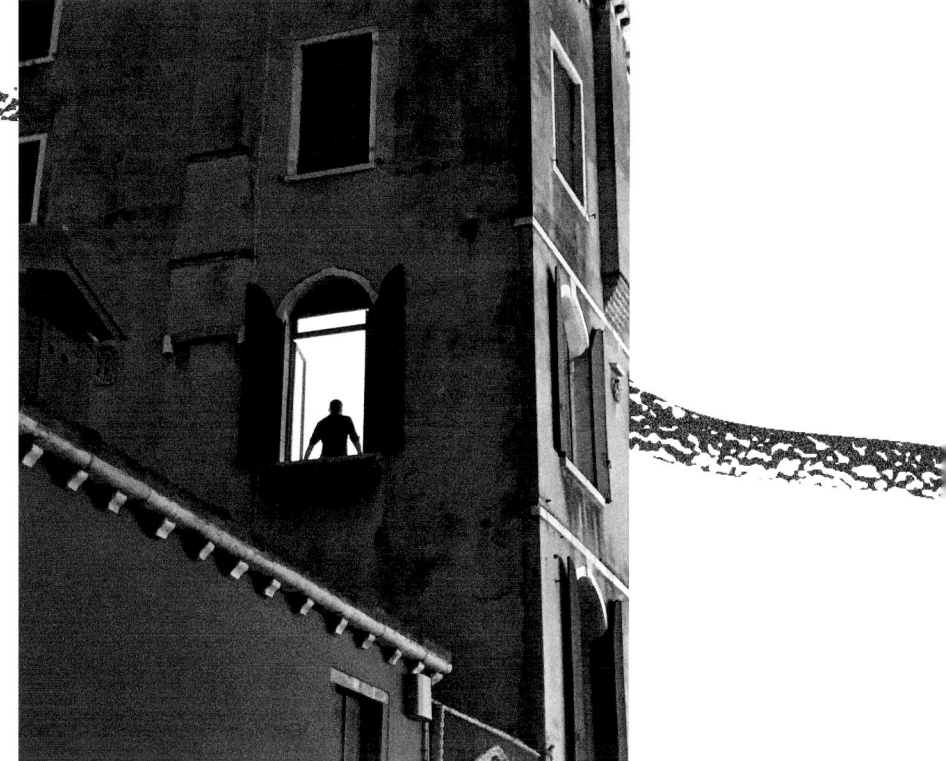

We walk for centuries, every hour marked by church bells. Venice does not need clocks. Most of them have stopped working. But in 2020, bells and clocks that have always guided the public flows of the city, are abruptly replaced by individually carved timings, determined by devices that ask one to choose between pharmacy, supermarket and, for the lucky ones, dog walking. Venice in lockdown is not Venice: a city whose heavily made-up face has been turned towards global tourism for the past few centuries, and has increasingly relied almost absolutely on it, in the process shedding all other aspects of what a city is, has found itself without a mirror.

Is even the fog even thicker than usual? It would seem so. Venice is having an identity crisis. Shops vanish one after the other, artists frantically imprint their prayers for their salvation from the plague on huge canvases, cruise ships turn into floating prisons for 40 days (the Venetian quarantena, the fortieth day when goods and crew were released in the city), and aeroplanes morph into huge cargos moving sick to the Lazareto island, last port in one's life, leaving them there to die.

Christian temporality is paramount. Christianity dissimulating as city, dissimulating as political power. We meet some friends by the church of San Pantalon. Ah, the church is open, quite rare that, we must walk in, Fumiani's largest baroque painting in the world on its ceiling, if you think there is no god you might reconsider after seeing this, he says jokingly. But they don't want to enter. We are atheists, we do not like religious art, they say. Christianity perverted everything, it is true, but also became the city and its art. He is perplexed. Maybe we could go to the 2015 Art Biennale then, when Santa Maria della Misericordia was converted into a working mosque as part of the Iceland pavilion? It's Friday and the mosque is heaving. We must be quick because it will be shut down due to protests in less than ten days after

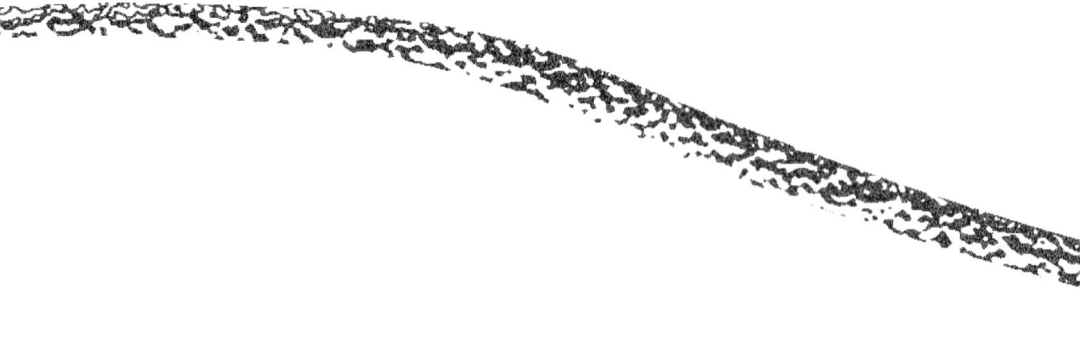

its opening. But they dither, it is still religious art, is it not. So we miss our window but we are not worried. We have become experts in dissimulation: we dissimulate our nakedness behind the oars; we dissimulate our indifferent brick buildings with elaborate stucco and istria stone facades; and we dissimulate water with paved-over *calli*, *salizade*, *campi*, *fondamenta* and above all *rio tera*, the rivers of the city filled with earth. We are walking on water all the time, where others before us were floating by, using only the water entrances to their homes. Our routes are determined by water: the city is a collection of islands, the bridges feeble attempts at dissimulating its fragmentation. This is an urban archipelago. But we still see no water.

Oh wait, here it is. Pellucid, luculent, glass-like deliquescence, full of tasty minerals, encased in transparent plastic. "Ara vien qua," the man on the boat calls us in Venetian, "per piacer el me daga na man?" He needs help unloading the water bottles for the supermarket. Venetians drink mostly bottled water because they cannot find any other. Even the water coming from the Dolomites straight to their taps is apparently not good enough. The boat keeps on thumping the fondamenta to the rhythm of the canal wavelets, the motor quiet but still gurgling, the boat man's throaty voice projected across the sound, raucous flow without double consonants or Ls – nothing to stop their voices from flowing across those linguistic lagunas, the whack of the merchandise dropping on the ground, the rolling sound of the wheeled carrello, the typical shopping trolley whose sound on the pavement is so very different to the tourist sound of the wheeled suitcase, ah you have a trolley, you try to dissimulate as local. But you will never be one.

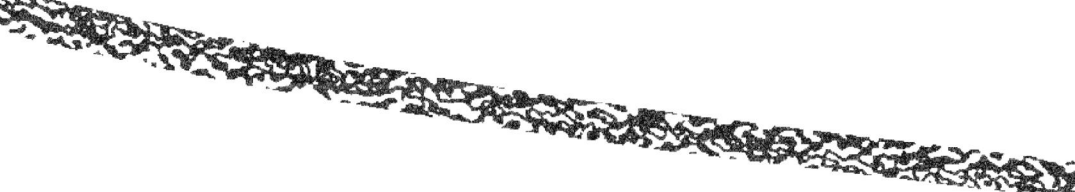

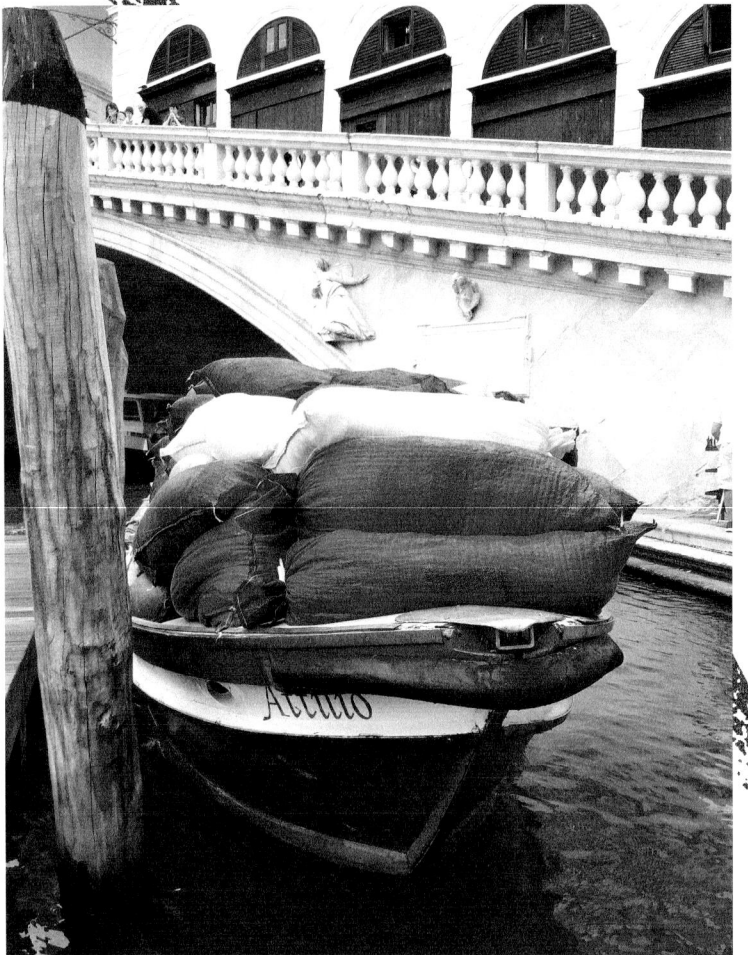

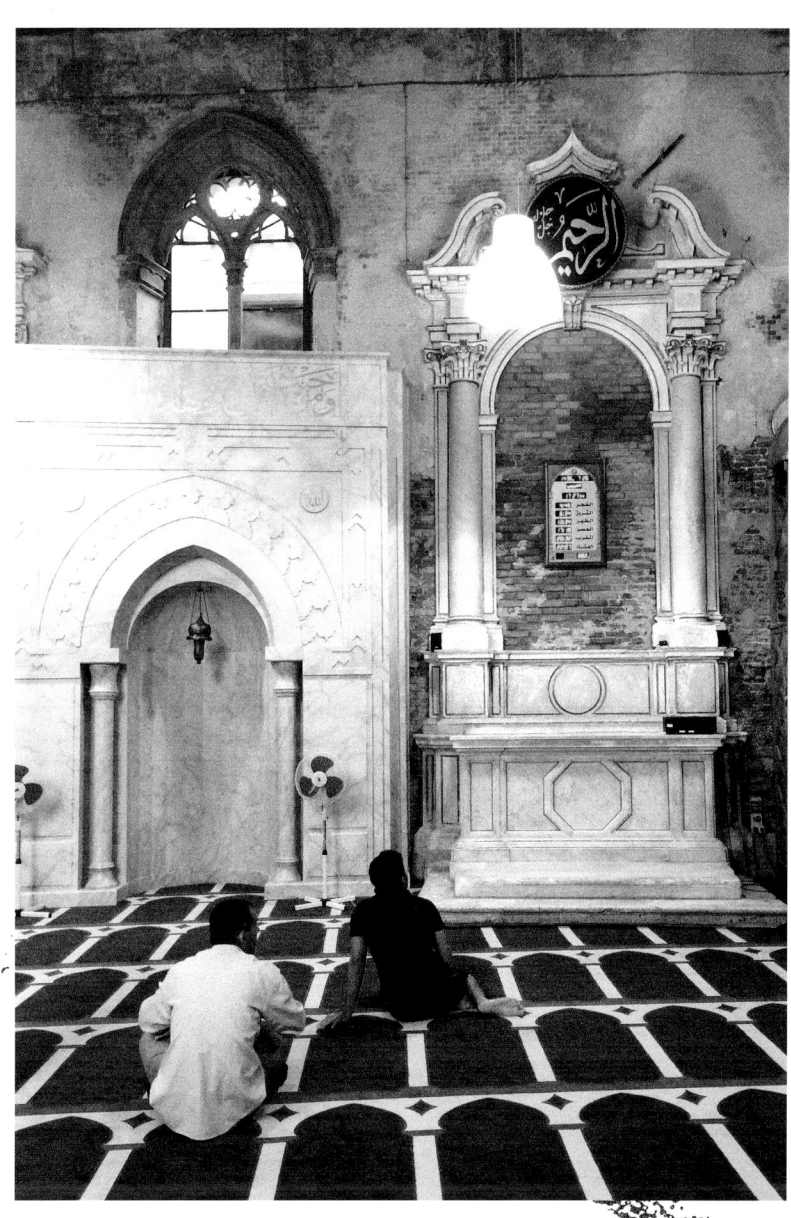

It is 22nd of February 2020. The first and most severe COVID-19 lockdown. The Carnevale ends abruptly. From one day to the next, medical masks replace the Venetian ones. We are comfortable in this dissimulation too, even though we are not allowed out. Where is home? No one can say. Venice is often a refuge, the whole city a home of hide-outs, side streets that only the ones in the know take, drawn shutters and hushed kitchen lunches. But the hide-outs quickly turn labyrinthine. Solitude is sometimes a choice but loneliness descends like a cupola of humidity on the city, a silent plague that painfully rests on bridges with its back bent, perched on a rotting bricola, those wooden poles in the middle of the lagoon that indicate the navigable canals in the shallow lagoon waters. COVID just pushed all that deeper inside. The chattering ladies have all disappeared. Only supermarket and pharmacy employees are around, and of course the ubiquitous, energetic young guys who transport food. Venice becomes the city of lost steps. Our feet are still wet. Our footprints darken the whole city. They don't seem to dry, nothing dries easily here, too humid, everything stays as it was put. The sweat remains too. The skin of the young Moldavian guy who is putting up the scaffolding turns into a mirror, reflections and ripples, spectral speculation, muscles and clouds, a tattoo or two, broad smile that opens into the new Venetian vernacular, an east-European accented flow of open vowels. Selina, the fruttivendola of the Salizada dei Greci, surrounded by fresh fruit and tourist-coloured pastas, asks him in her Bollywood soprano Italian, "what do you do yesterday," she has no past or future tenses, "it's always a long present inviting you to sing-along," and the Moldavian scaffolder obliges.

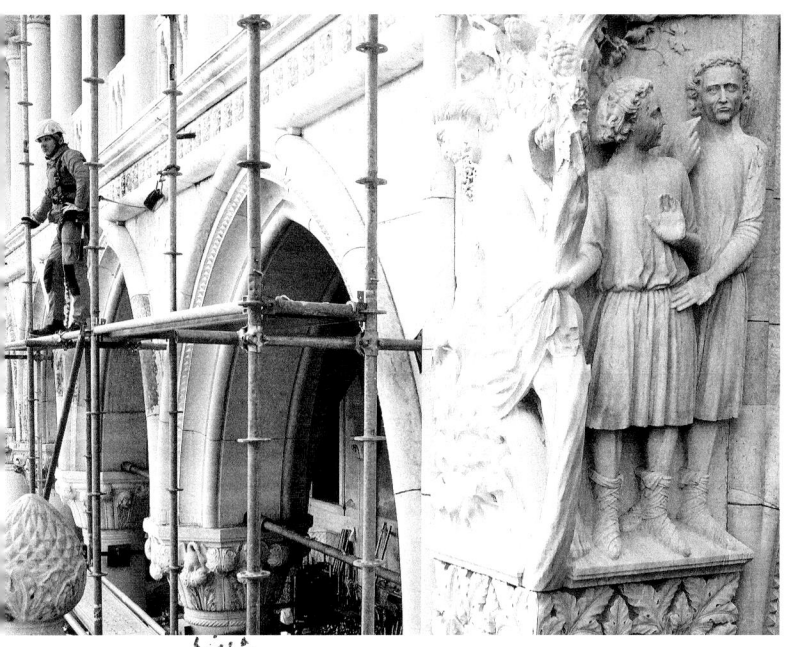

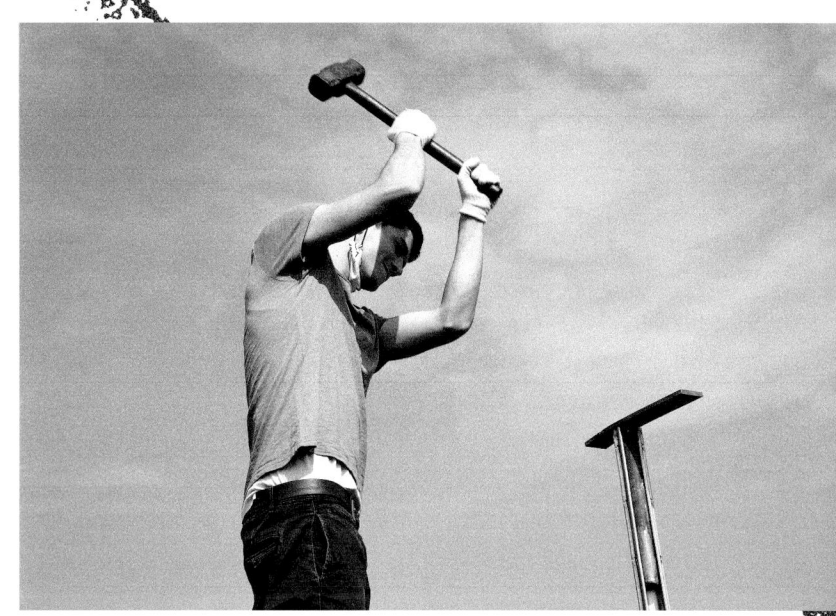

Will there be statues of Moldavians and Bangladeshis holding torches in gold servant uniforms and orientalist turbans in the future? The new exotic in Venice is us. Naked middle category of not quite aliens, yet never locals. We live here, we have chosen the city as our second or even first home, yet we are not counted amidst the residents on the sad countdown counter of the Rialto pharmacy, whose total sum invariably drops by a few thousands every year. We are only 50,000 now living in Venice, but we are not part of that figure. We are sandwiched between the two velocities that make up the city: the local one that hardly ever ventures outside their sestiere, one of the six labyrinths contained by the city waters; and the international art and money scene, flapping peacocks landing once every couple of years, eating at chic restaurants, or occasionally deigning to take a croissant and coffee at Pasticceria Chiusso, tempted by the waft of oven baked venetian fugassa – the sweet fluffy cake that has nothing to do with the focaccias we all know and happily dip in olive oil. Another dissimulation.

Can you hear that? Finally, water roaring our way, we think. Foamy volumes spreading their depths on the horizon. The rape has started and the city bends over. This is the new water. XXL cruise ships throwing their weight where we used to swim, our womb and our sacrum, disgorging pollution and spewing spermatozoa into the tiny alleyways: wired-up groups of voyeurs splattered all over the fake masks, sticky drippings from the stuccoed facades. We join another stream, No Grande Navi, this is the counterflow made up by locals who oppose the large ships, we carry inflatable animals, prehistoric beasts ready to dive in the canal and carry us all against the cruise ships.

We become one with the city, its decay becomes our opportunity. The crowds are siphoning us towards the Piazza – the only piazza in the city, since the rest are all called campi. It is the lowest part of the city, where waters from the whole planet whirl in one vast eye. All bodies are pulled in the spin.

Whatever one does, one cannot avoid the piazza. It is the first spot in Venice to flood – whether by tourists or waters. We want to swig an ombra ("shadow"), a tiny amount of red wine that used to perk up Venetians. In a city of light and gold, the ombra of San Marc's tower dragging itself slowly across the piazza, was the moving hangout of the wine merchants, whose wine remained always cool despite the humid heat. But we are still naked and we will not be allowed there. There are strict rules all over the city, and even stricter on the piazza. We raise our hands before our faces, we try to resist the pull, and just like that we embody the map of Venice: two hands folding into each, one mirroring the other, a cartographic speculation kept apart by the 3.8 km of Canalazo, the Grand Canal alla Venexiana.

Hands are our favourite extension while we walk around Venice. We touch everything and everything touches back. A red-haired lady touches a rusty iron ring on the wall by the little bridge leading to the Campielo de la Cason. Why did you touch this, we ask. She says in that characteristic way that Italians sometimes have, speaking while taking leave, the voice raising above the distance, her back firmly turned to us, "toccare ferro porta fortuna," touching iron brings good luck. A father losing his eyesight is still feeling the city around him, the way it touches his skin with its bells and breezes. He never carries a stick. His two sons help him around, three identical lockdown haircuts walking within the allowed 200 metres around their home in Santa Elena. The father is still seeing the city through his uselessly open eyes. During lockdown, he is surrounded by words, learned shelves of wisdom lining the walls of his apartment, touched only by memory. We touch the green marble tondo on the facade of the hospital, because it can heal our wounds. We touch the Thessaly marbles on the Church of the Miracoli, all looted from Greece, a marble reserved for emperors and appropriated by the Doge, because we know that miracles are granted when the body becomes coextensive with this former potent Republic of Serenissima.

The fossils frozen in the marble extend our touch across the Planet. We feel strangely central: this city is the unmistakeable global symbol of climate change. Venice's future touches the collective soul in ways that other symbols fail.

We will never reach home. We have walked for many lives, clumsily hiding our skin, tracing water where there is none. But something saves us from the despair of the itinerant. The salizada opens up underneath our feet. The effect is less gaping and more withdrawing, like the heavy velvet curtain of the Opera of the Fenice. For a brief moment we think we are back to normal. Is that the metaphor of the Fenice, another appropriated symbol perfectly integrated in the Venetian fold? The Arabic phoenix is reborn from its ashes, surrounded by scents of cinnamon and myrrh even when burning to cinders. We fly high. We are riding a hot air balloon above the city, taking in the city as the city would like to be seen, an empire of baroque whirls taming the Adriatic and the world beyond that. We can see the small streets teeming with exhausted crowds, guzzling cruise ships lining up in the Giudecca channel, and hundreds of flights trailing the sky. We hear the cry: we are still an empire.

Is this back to normal?

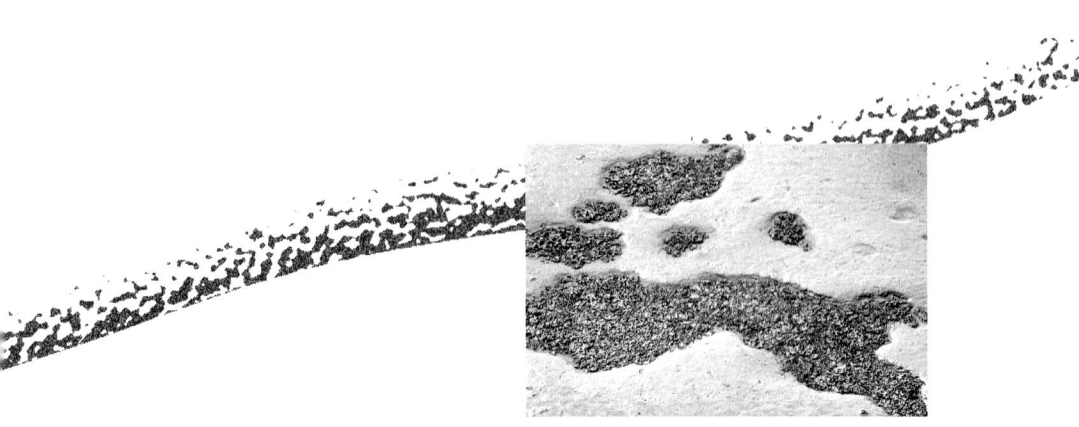

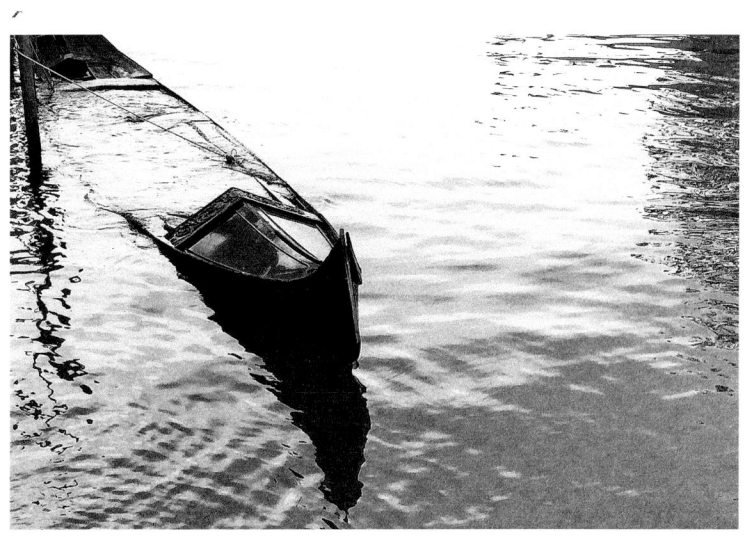

We have no time to look at what is revealed. We are
already plunging. We have become Venetians after all
because we have never learnt how to swim. Green, semi-
translucent lagoon water enters our nostrils. We just about
have time to hear what the roadworks man says when he
hits another big water closet deposit from the surrounding
houses: "siamo letteralmente nella merda." ("We are literally
in shit"). We swim in our gently denatured excreta, all green
algae and putrefaction, trying to rise up to the surface.
We are sinking. All around us, the mossy facades of the
Venetian palazzi finally settling into the mud. The architecture
returns to the primordial green with what seems like an
aerated relief. Venice, the lynchpin of the planet's destiny,
is finally resting.

Court Circular
SE11

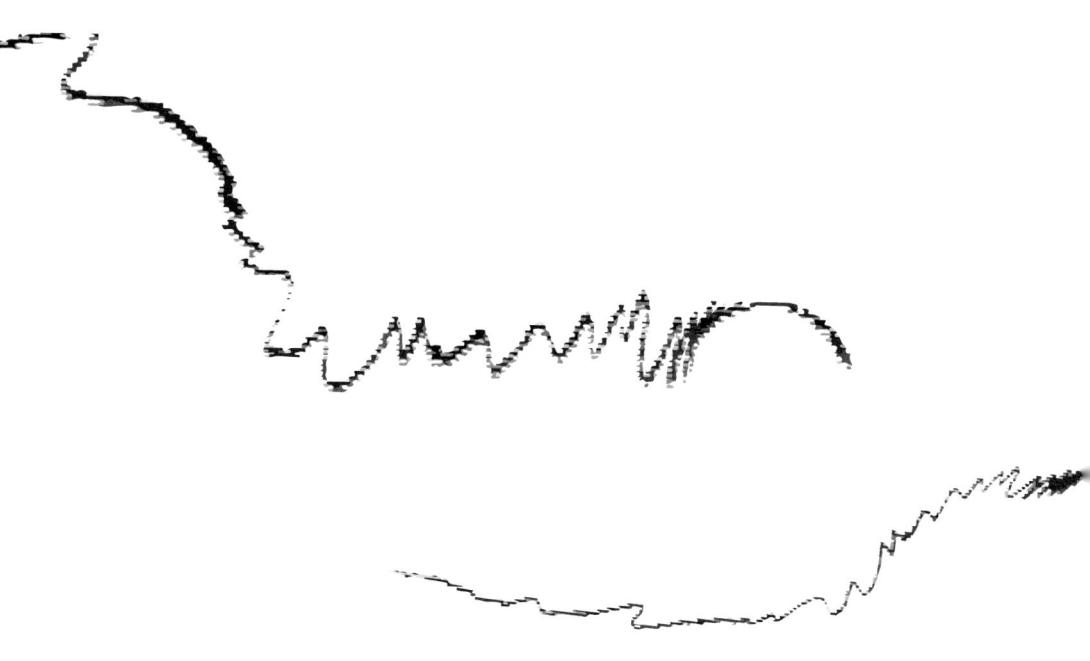

SIMON KING AND CORINNE NOBLE

INVITATION
J.V., MARCH 4TH, 2020

Dear N&K,

I hope despite the worrying news about COVID-19 you are both well.

I'm writing to formally invite N&K to participate in a group show scheduled to open at the old Lambeth County Court, Cleaver Square in Kennington SE11 in late May.

As part of this proposal, I've been thinking about how the work can best engage with the historical context of the space e.g. what it means for artists to appropriate it. I think it would be a very good fit for N&K – perhaps to situate work in the space, or create a group walk in the neighbourhood that engages with the theme.

Some background about the courthouse – since the 1930s it had mostly dealt with social housing claims and eviction cases but was controversially decommissioned a few years ago as a 'cost efficiency'. The space is now managed by ASC who rent out cubicle studios to artists. The space, as you can imagine, is unique – we have two courtrooms available to us as well as the main art-deco hall of the courthouse. What about coming over sometime to have a look and discuss possible ways in which we could do something together?

I look forward to hearing from you soon.
J

N., MARCH 5TH, 2020

Dear J,

*What a wonderful space and premise
for an exhibition!*

*Perhaps antique postcards offer a way forward to
weave with the history and location. Perhaps N&K
can create a short walk around the space interspersed
by topical cards. I can begin by collecting a small
number of antique postcards that depict law courts.
These cards could be a means of bridging the subject
of the court with an artistically-styled artifact –
we'd use these to prompt discussions and
observations along the walk.*

DISPOSITION

Perhaps the idea of disposition is not really so mysterious.
A ball at the top of an inclined plane possesses a disposition.
The geometry of the ball and its relative position are the
simple markers of potential agency. Even without rolling
down the incline, the ball is actively doing something by
occupying its position. Disposition, in common parlance,
usually describes an unfolding relationship between potentials.
It describes a tendency, activity, faculty or property in either
beings or objects – a propensity within a context.[1]

GROUNDS

N: Following on from J's invitation, and as we discussed,
I have the working title 'Holding Courts' and a few questions
to keep in mind. What are your first impressions on seeing
the image? How do you think the image might relate to the
title? And, if you can think of an alternative or permutation
to the title, what would it be?

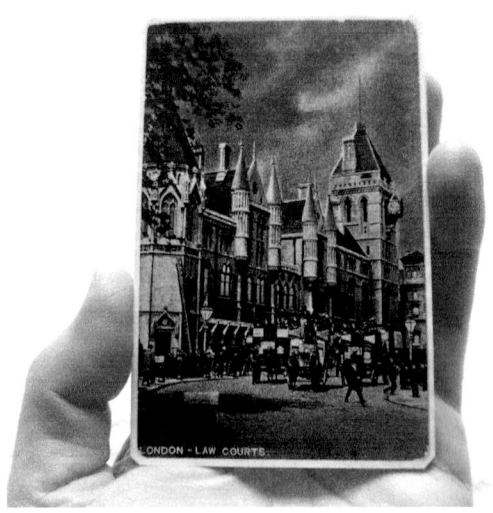

PURSUANCE

K: My first impression is to do with the Chancery Division
being located in this building which is also the site of the

Jarndyce *v* Jarndyce case, the labyrinthine inheritance suit at the heart of Charles Dickens' novel *Bleak House.* It also reminded me of the time in my twenties I was a solicitor's clerk and then a law student in and out of the Inns of Court which, even then, felt like stepping back into the Victorian era. 'Holding court' is something that happens literally within the building, but it is also what happens in the courtyard media gatherings following a landmark judgement.

***

N: You've moved away from the image and entered a literary and judicial labyrinth! Straight away targeting the scene-within-the-scene and raiding the memory banks. Yet, no mention of the hand, the scale of the postcard, or the colour? Perhaps this nicely captures our different tendencies – how typically, you look 'in-to' something (historical research) and I look 'on-to' it (appearance, what is present).

Here's what I'll point out – it's my left hand cradling a scaled-down version of an antique postcard. Behind the scenes, my right hand operates the camera (interesting, perhaps, it's the right hand that's raised in court as someone is sworn in to give evidence). The hand is far bigger than the building, there's something strange to weigh up there – imagine how that would be in reality?

Hands, holding, passing hand-to-hand, that's on my mind. How and why are these ephemeral things 'handed down'? All the hands that must have held this postcard along the way over time and all the homes that have handled and stored it before it reached me. I connect that with the suit in Bleak House because it goes on and on, and the message on the reverse grows ever more mysterious. We're left with something that holds only traces, whispers… and is wonderfully open to speculation.

***

ᴋ: Yes, the 'in-to' and the 'on-to', our two ways of seeing that occasionally come to the fore and interweave. The playing card size in respect to Lewis Carroll's Alice and the Queen of Hearts could be part of a magician's box of tricks featuring King, Queen and Knave as diamonds, hearts, clubs and spades. These lend themselves well to an underlying motif. The colouring is interesting too. An overall bluish grey tinge – perhaps reflecting what looks a cloudy or stormy day – but on closer scrutiny, the yellow on the lamps, suggesting that it is at dusk. It's also noteworthy that yellow is used sparingly, and red, the only other primary colour, seems to be part of the livery of the horse-drawn carriage. Did the sender perhaps add these colours to the original postcard? Do they have any overall significance?

I really like the relay of hands holding and the swearing of oath positioning of the hand and card.

'Holding Court' recalling the fixed expression must have its origins in the practice of the royal court, for example, of Elizabeth I, to sit in different parts of the realm. Another line is 'court' as a verb used, for example, in the context of *eros* – it has connotations of seduction and manipulation for me, 'the court of appeal' perhaps, so that could be an interesting line of thinking.

***

ᴋ: I've been reading *The People's War* by Angus Calder, and his chapter on the beginning of the London Blitz in September 1940. This passage resonates in relation to the location of the Royal Courts of Justice:

'At the hub of the wheel lay the twin cities of London and Westminster. With Whitehall, Bloomsbury, Fleet Street, St Paul's, the Bank of England, the central area still concentrated within its few square miles Britain's cultural past, its commercial presence and its legislative future. The raider could be sure that whatever he struck there was of objective or sentimental importance, and later this would become the most heavily blitzed area of all.'

Maybe there is also something in the idea of 'twin cities' ... 'legislative future' ... 'objective or sentimental importance'.

***

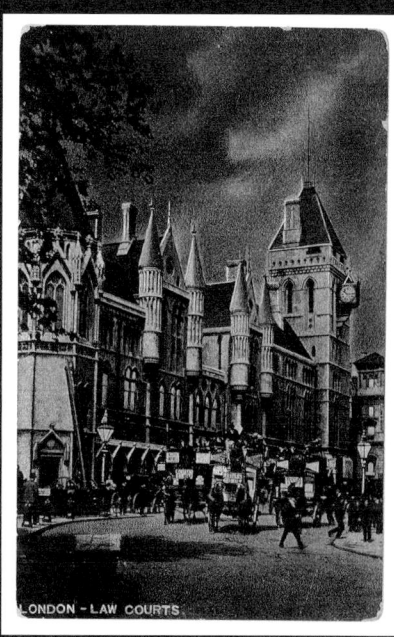

EVIDENCE

N: Have a closer look at this real-sized card image. It's been in a personal archive for over 100 years which suggests it has some 'sentimental importance'.

The shades of this postcard appear to indicate a night scene. Why is there a crowd and so many horse-drawn buses here so late at night? Looking closer, certain elements don't add up, for instance, the tree to the upper left is in silhouette, yet also casting a shadow on the ground. The streetlamps and window in the distance gleam yellow as if lit, but the figures nearby don't seem to throw shadows that relate to their light. I can only think this is a painted scene

where the added darkness is an artistic device played like
a card. Going back to the theme of 'anxiety', the uncanniness
of this picture seems pertinent, and the closure of the
Lambeth court (no legislative future there!). And, of course,
in what you were reading about the Blitz – the anxiety of
what the night would deliver.

Turning the card over, what do you make of the pencil
marks – thinking of anxiety, are there potential traces of
that in these too? I like the detail of it being from the 'Ducal
Series' (ducal = duke) – not quite part of the card suit, but
a player in court, nonetheless.

***

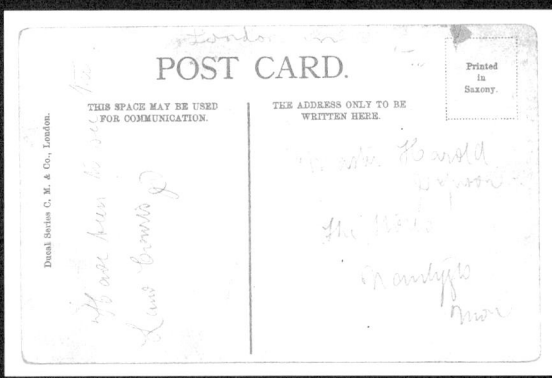

κ: I like your speculation – 'a tension between …' and the
connection to the theme of 'anxiety'. The scrawled, barely
decipherable handwriting has the quality of being written
in haste. Can you make out the address and is the recipient
'Master Harold Johnson' do you think?

Resonances for me in 'Ducal' and 'Printed in Saxony'.
Angus Calder's reference to 'making necessary repairs at
once to culturally important ruins' like the Royal Courts of
Justice. By a few leaps and bounds this leads me to filmmakers
Powell and Pressburger and *The Life and Death of Colonel
Blimp*, to the onset of the Second World War and the out-of-
kilter chivalric world of the protagonists depicted in that film.

***

N: The resonance of the final line from Calder is remarkable! And too, the resonance of the final line from Calder – 'There was havoc in the Inns of Court.' The words 'havoc' and 'court, sit on opposite benches in my mind, whereas there are clear parallels in the photos.

'Have been to see the Law Courts…'. Interesting it's in pencil – informal, provisional (yet followed with the writer's initials, as if certified). Is the medium (graphite not ink) that you detect the haste in? Perhaps it was written hastily, or amidst a flurry of other activity. I can't untangle the address (perhaps if I were working in an Edwardian sorting office there'd be an anxiety in that.

The message reverberates with my arrangement with J to meet on site – we cancelled this due to him self-isolating – how now can I SEE the court? I'm thinking about walking all the way there to take some photographs. We should think about where this walk should/would start. Ground this in reality.

***

K: Really glad that you are going at last to walk the route. I look forward to hearing more.

When I met with J at the court a week or so before lockdown, I brought with me a copy of *Capitalist Realism* by Mark Fisher. As we walked around the space with his son, I read aloud the passage, which I had come across coincidentally, about acquittal and surveillance control via Kafka's *The Trial*. It seemed to have an obvious parallel in the setting (and my past experience of eviction in this place!) as well as to the show's theme of anxiety. Fisher writes about the protracted legal wrangling in Kafka's novel which, for me, has its counterpart in *Bleak House*. What Fisher says about cybernetic power and control societies also reverberates with our new-found 'working from home' mode.

***

N: Take a look at this second postcard. It's shot from an elevated angle, unlike the first scene where the photographer must've been on the ground. Seen from height, the figures on the pavements are black marks, like small short ink-strokes – notations. Data. It's not quite a bird's-eye view of the street but it's a survey, nonetheless. I wonder what the vantage point was in the, apparently, middle of the street? Was the camera in someone's hand, or raised in a balloon? I recall other postcards we've come across which use a method of encoding the message – i.e. mirror writing. How historic correspondences were surveilled in their time, and by whom, and the potential for anxiety this might raise.

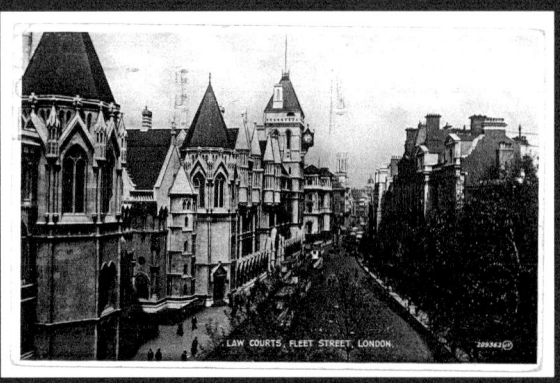

On the reverse, another pencil message, to Miss Weighill in North Yorkshire, from Auntie in Shepherd's Bush, January 1932: '*I have tried to get you a card of Marble Arch but have not succeeded we are all very well return Sunday. Auntie*'. I wonder how much effort (or anxiety) Auntie had expended in the search for a card of Marble Arch, and why it may have been more desirable than the one sent?

The cancellation mark states – 'IT'S QUICKER TO TELEPHONE'.

There's no house name or number for the addressee, simply the village name. Presumably everyone knew each other then, so it was unnecessary.

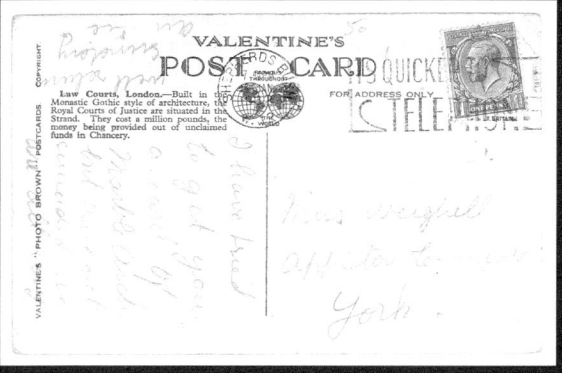

K: 'IT'S QUICKER TO TELEPHONE' almost reads like an admonishment. Does this 'public service' message reflect an increasing (presumably middle class) take up of domestic telephones in the 1930s?

Notations, notaries, note-taking (the solicitor's clerk sitting behind counsel). The figures remind me of Lowry in their outline. I think the camera may have been fixed to a rostrum and this was originally a commission of some sort to promote this symbol of the legal system.

There seems to be some bleaching of the skyline in the middle distance with the effect of bringing the building into sharp relief.

It's a 'Valentine's' postcard - perhaps the company had niched origins.

Is Miss Weighill a student of some sort, for example, of architecture? The postcard after all details the 'Monastic Gothic Style' of the courts and this might have been a familiar language. Was her aunt on a brief visit to London and the clock was ticking on her finding a postcard of the Marble Arch on a stationer's carousel (hence the hasty-seeming pencilled scrawl of her handwriting?).

I love the detail of it costing a million pounds and that this magical sum came from 'unclaimed funds from Chancery'. What were the stories behind these cumulative sums I wonder?

***

DISCOVERY

N: Just returned from my visit to Cleaver Square. Two things stood out, firstly, the orderliness of the adjacent streets, and secondly, the number and quality of historic painted street signs remaining on the walls. These signs, many retaining parts of letters and words in the paint, are what we are often drawn to when we walk, struck me this time as semi-erased/reworked paintings. This tension I perceived there put me in mind of what Brian Dillon has written on the subject of 'erasure'. I thought back to the first postcard (Law Courts at 'night') where the address on the reverse is undecipherable. What does it mean to dissolve an address? To 'not be able to place' something? Or even, to 're-place' it?

Back to 'IT'S QUICKER TO TELEPHONE'. The irony of that as a cancellation mark on a posted card! I wonder whether Miss Weighill had a telephone at all then, in a small village in the midst of the North York Moors. Interestingly, one of the first buildings I encountered on the walk from Kennington was a telephone exchange (entirely at odds design-wise with the surrounding architecture). Could that be a stopping point I wonder?

Mention of Lowry-like figures is pertinent because Lowry worked as a rent collector. There's a painting by him, *The Removal* (1928) depicting an eviction. Perhaps these strands could weave back to what J tells us about Lambeth County Court in his invitation. I'm also thinking that the historic street-based painted place names could be documented in a series of photographs or postcards.

***

K: I've been listening (somewhat distractedly) to Claire Tomalin's *Charles Dickens – A Life* on the radio. My ears prick up at the mention of his house in Doughty Street, transporting me to our Bloomsbury walk, with the location in that street of Doughty Court, a radical set of legal chambers. As Tomalin recounts, the writer's father John was constantly trying to keep one step ahead of his creditors when Dickens was a boy. Until they catch up with him and he finds himself in Marshalsea Debtor's Prison. When Charles visited John there for the first time, he found his father in an unexpectedly upbeat mood. It was on this occasion apparently that John Dickens spoke about the delicate balance between happiness and misery (or perhaps we could say anxiety?) caused by having sufficient yearly income or not having it. This of course made its way into Dickens' novel *David Copperfield* – in the famous words of Mr Micawber.

So, a lateral connection to Lowry's *The Removal* but also to this pandemic, and the depressing prognosis for UK employment particularly the financial security of the precariat, the furloughed, and the likely permanently laid off as UK businesses go to the wall.

***

OBLIGATION

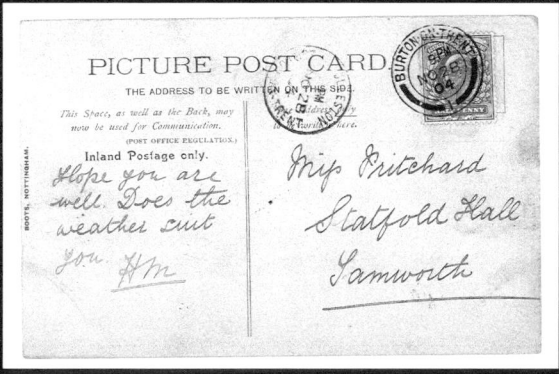

N: '*Hope you are well*' says HM's message of 28 November. I'm disposed to wonder what, in 1904, Boots the Chemist of Nottingham (the cards' publisher) might have prescribed for a customer experiencing anxiety?

What stands out is a peculiar colour chemistry – a hazy cyan watercolour sky and an otherworldly pinkish glow seemingly radiating from the building to the cobbles. Dream-like hues suffusing the air around a jagged fortress-like edifice. The blank canvas of the pavement in front of the courts, the spartan, sweeping expanse of highly ordered stones in the foreground... it all seems so surfaced, durable, robust, intact, grid-like, no room for weeds, nature, greenery, or creaturely things. This is an entirely human-dominated realm.

***

N: The ghostly embossed stamp on the envelope.
The traces of Veronal in the glass vessel.
The residue of street names...
There's something in the crumbling white paint of the signage in the photo below that for me, connects with the touches of powder lingering in the antique bottle.
Emptiness, removal, erasure, amnesia... almost.
A painted window to the past.

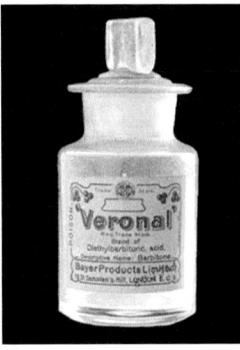
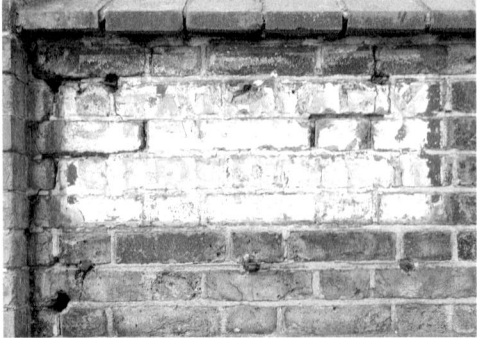

***

K: Yes, what is crucial in our method is that 'something in', the angle which leads us here and there, inexorably, down another rabbit hole. Such connective ellipses come into play as we divine the ghost signs that are everywhere around us when we walk together. Ingold's 'clues to whereabouts and expectations' that we make out in the parsing of and passing on of text, image and memory seems particularly pertinent to this rumination or rummaging.

I love the crumbly white-painted obliteration in your street sign, just one of many that we have taken over the last few years. *'Oublier'* – 'to forget' is the narcotic grain in obliterate and oblivion. The latter particularly, recalling your words 'emptiness, removal, erasure, amnesia' is what someone might have sought from a powder of Veronal in 1904.

***

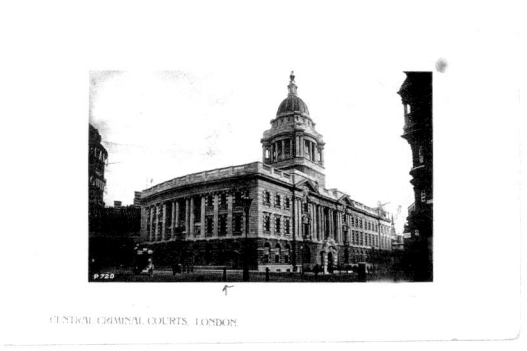

CENTRAL CRIMINAL COURTS, LONDON

N: The final card. Something from the 'SUNK GEM SERIES' – a glazed (varnished) white card with indented monochrome image of the Central Criminal Courts, London. The spacious indent framing the photographic scene prompts me to think of a moat on all sides of a castle. Certainly, the photographer captures the imposing edifice from a suitably timorous, upward-angled view. There are also what appear to be two small ink marks (lower middle and middle right). Are they some kind of 'x marks the spot' through which the sender nudges the receiver's memory?

On the reverse, the most expansive communication we've seen in these cards yet. I read *'Dear Walker'* where really, it's more likely to be 'Walter'. I'm going to leave it as 'Walker'…

***

K: More familiarly the courts are known as the Old Bailey. Did you know about Dead Man's Walk? I've found this from Dan Brown, editor of the Londonist website:

> *'Dead Man's Walk is a passage-cum-tunnel at the back of the Old Bailey, off limits to the public. It's a relic from the days of the notorious Newgate Gaol, which previously stood on this site. Condemned criminals would walk along the passage on the way to the private gallows.*
>
> *The passage contains a series of brick arches that get progressively narrower as the gallows site is approached. It must have been a terrifying final walk for the doomed of Newgate'.*

'Progressively narrower', the Dead Man's Walk, the dead walking, walking with the dead, the dear departed, the dear walker, all the people that walk with us. That correspondence again. That fleeting cognition. Perhaps 'W', as you say, standing for 'Walker' and not 'Walter'. 'Dear Walker'!
I think we have another possibility for our title.

ENDNOTES
1   Keller Easterling, Extrastatecraft: The Power of Infrastructure Space, (London: Verson, 2016), p. 72.

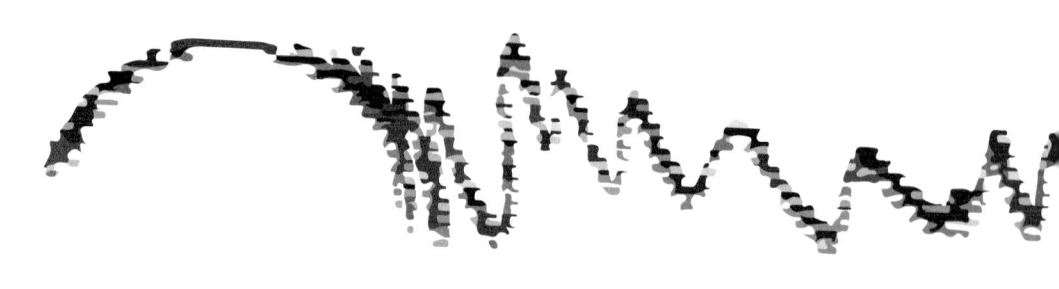

Night Walking in Lockdown

Meditation
on a Night Walk

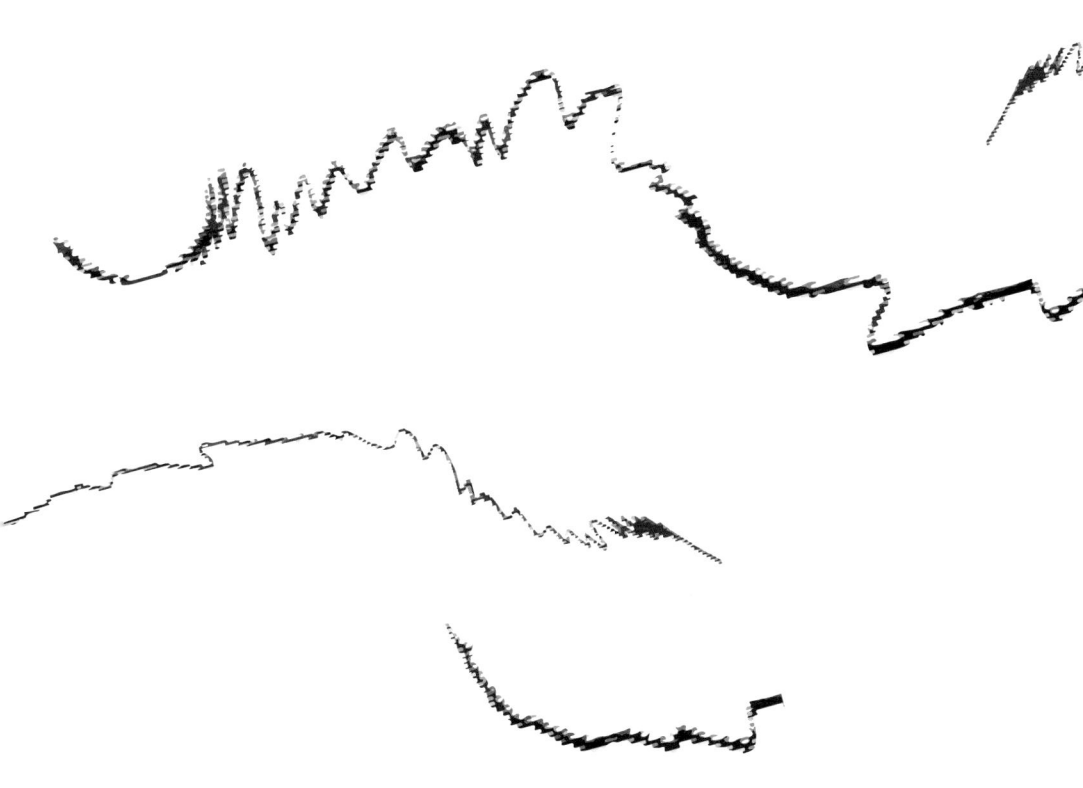

JONATHAN SKINNER

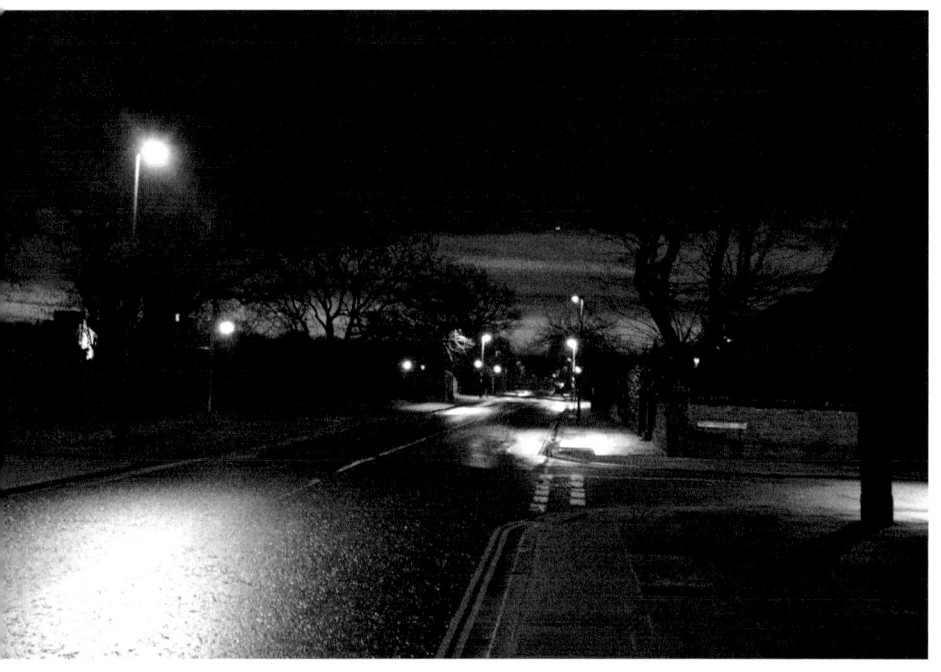

One hundred years of lockdown! As if? If only I had known that magical realism was real. But such hindsight is difficult whilst walking in the dark. I barely know where I am going anymore. And it's the same walk around the block that I took with my dog, day and night – or rather those in-between times just after sunrise and sunset. Now its dark dark. Ominous dark. The one I still avoid if I can. So this is a walk by necessity, but not essential travel. Essential exercise in the dark? Doubly masked: mind and body.

Last night the school gates on the other side of the road "chink chinked". I jumped out of my skin and faced-off the phantom school kids. We live opposite their playing fields and tennis courts and I swear I heard them evacuating like it was the end of a school day. But it was midnight, the flag clacking against the flagpole, and the automatic gates re-setting themselves when nobody is meant to be around. I didn't even feel that I was meant to be around, and I live here. But the gate opened wide and then closed again just after I passed it on the other side of the road. For the first time I was not glad that I was the only person walking these streets. Tomorrow night: no headphones blocking my anxieties with LBC Radio streaming into my consciousness, and maybe a t-shirt on the other way round to fool those foxes and adolescents. That was what I learned from my fieldwork in the Caribbean, an anthropologist conversing about the jumbies and how they couldn't follow you if your clothes were back to front. The automatic gates chinking late at night have replaced the bottles dangling and clanking in the wind. I walked a bit faster down the road. I skipped the pavement joins. My calves tightened as my heart tensed and released, and an adrenalin shot rolled out through my exo-skeleton. I listened more intently. I checked my steps for echoes. I glanced around. The fact that there was nothing and no one about allowed me to check my pace. But no cars? The silence deafened me. The deserted streets alarmed me. I sought comfort in the lights coming from the windows of the houses

I passed – computer gaming, tv, just a warmly lit room. This was my twenty minutes outside of the house, outside one of them. This must have been what it looked like when the tea-time strollers passed our house, the pandemic flâneurs – high-end south west London souls, trim, health conscious and in no need of masks. Up the street to Hounslow they all wore masks; down the street to Kingston, the masks were infra dig. The virus daren't pass them. Wealth = immunity. Up north they socially distanced. Not here on my streets. This was why I was now out at midnight.

***

Devika Chawla (2013) is a communications scholar living and working in Indiana. She hails from India and walks daily. Walking is her special, thoughtful time, a 'sacred hour' in the evening that serves as a bridge – to her past, and to her mother country. She grew up walking and finds that the action prepares her, domesticates her landscape, taming the tribulations of her living-working conditions. It echoes anthropologist and Israeli tour guide Jackie Feldman's (2007: 356) descriptions of the 'tiyul' (journey/hike) through the landscape to learn from it and love to it and to establish a political presence, to re-occupy it. Chawla (2013: 167) draws from Rebecca Solnit's (200: 5) evolutionary meditation on walking, *Wanderlust: A History of Walking*, where she suggests '[t]he rhythm of walking generates a kind of rhythm of thinking'. Feldman draws from French sociologist and anthropologist Pierre Bourdieu and his notes from fieldwork amongst the Kabyle of Algeria where he observed and pictured peasants working and walking and thus – yoked to ethnic (and French-colonial) dispositions – mode of thinking. Bourdieu (1995: 93–94, author's emphases) writes from his fieldnotes: 'Bodily *hexis* is political mythology realized, *em-bodied*, turned into a permanent disposition, a durable manner of standing, speaking, and thereby of *feeling* and *thinking*'. Bourdieu continues with a characterisation of the peasant 'at walk': the measured pace of 'a man who knows where he is going and knows he will arrive in time' versus the hesitant gait of 'half-hearted promises' (Bourdieu 1995: 94). For Feldman (2007: 361, 368) there is a Protestant body hexis, and engagement with the land, and the guides and pilgrims to the Holy Lands have a common group habitus 'present but submerged'. Feldman (2016: 62–63) elaborates in his monograph, *A Jewish Guide in the Holy Land: How Christian Pilgrims Made Me an Israeli*, the guide and pilgrim walk and in that act, one of spiritual practice, there is an appropriation of well-worn paths and well-thumbed Bibles, the two blending and merging as 'embodied text'. The Land of the Bible, and the pilgrim are both made by walking.

Walking makes a place, and walking makes a person for these academics. The rhythms and styles of the walking are distinct and durable dispositions, just like a writing style of rhetoric has a habitus according to postcolonial critic Michael Niblett (2016). Niblett contends that we make implicit use of text governed by the unconscious. Just below the surface, submerged like a lymph node, there is a disposition to speak just as there is to walk; it is like proprioception but without the nervous system. This social science disposition of the body, an internal layer – an infer-skeleton – infects academia. It is all so, so 'perfectly predictable' (Bourdieu 1995: 15). There are 'mental dispositions' – schemes of perception and thought; there are physical dispositions – 'postures and stances, ways of standing, sitting, looking, speaking, or walking' (Bourdieu 1995: 15). Life must have been ever so dry and repetitive, like an endless, Remainer's rant. Only Pierre can see it. And that is because he has 'objectivated' (2003) himself and walks as a shepherd of sociologists with his 'cleft habitus' for support. This habitus shifts between the individual and the community. It appeals to himself as a country-born individual and academic outsider, as well as everyone else with family and class ties, especially 'to the manor-born' (cf. Reay 2004: 434). Tim Edensor (2007: 218) picks up and runs with the jackboots of an idea, appropriating it, running the gauntlet and deploying it for those around him with an 'urban habitus' – desensitised, inured twenty-first century peasants of the city living with convention, restriction, order. For Edensor, the pavement–the streets of London, including south by south west – is best cracked and crumbled. The walking is best appreciated wherever it is when it is picking a path through industrial ruins, non-linear, unruly aesthetics, inefficient and thus anti-capitalist. I take all of this in my stride.

For anthropologist Tim Ingold (2000: 144), we inhabit and embody our environments as much as our selves. Our perceptions of place are relative to others, and our identities are characters, trails, pathways that we leave on and around others. It is intersecting and rhizomatic for Ingold who criticises the Western notion of walking. For him, 'we think of walking as the spatiotemporal displacement of already completed beings from one point to another' (2000: 144). A more expansive re-conceptualisation of walking he prefers is 'the movement of [a] substantive formation within an environment' (Ingold 2000: 144) to which we can include humans, animals, roots and runners. If it lives and breathes and moves, then it can be considered to be walking, from his anthropological position. Such germinating propositions miss the ruminating, the disjointed thoughts that pass untampered through my strides, reactive, unpredictable intrusions, an introspective, tropical undergrowth. They don't distinguish between the thoughts and the senses because they come out of the same communitarian alliance. Ingold, for example – a distinct and eminent academic, a 'body-person' (2000: 162) dwelling in our world – reviews Bourdieu's theory of practice, his habitus as 'a pattern of thought-feeling', a skill that is found to 'subsist' in practical activity. It is how we find our bearings in our environment. 'Embodied mind' and 'enminded body': the thought and the action are indivisible and both are social activities, Ingold (2000: 171) declares. 'We are social beings because we walk', Ingold later reiterates with his colleague Jo Lee Vergunst (2008: 2) in *Ways of Walking*. This all repudiates the 'isolated, self-contained individual', the night walker, the day-dreaming rambler; even the ethnographer of mobilities and temporalities such as Katrin Lund (2019) and colleagues walking across Iceland to retrace and recreate a poet's long past stomp across the landscape, reciting his work as they go. And, yet, here I am.

Where is the self-consciousness in walking? The 'intelligent wandering' (cf. Rojek 1993: 112) associated not just with the Grand Tour but le petite turn around the block? Or the trudging through hospital corridors with the hospital porter examined by Nigel Rapport to show an uncontained living of resistance to reduction; Bob the bodybuilder and hospital porter juggles identities, bodies and movements to control his work and leisure domains, to remain elusive and 'elsewhere' (Rapport 2009: 103). Frédéric Gros (2015) presents *A Philosophy of Walking*, or rather the philosophers on walking. It is 'suspensive freedom' (Gros 2015: 3) – not the moment of weight transfer from leg to leg as in Argentine tango – but a moment of escape from constraint. Walking is self-liberating, simple and spontaneous. But contra Bourdieu et al. it is also ahistorical ('the walking body has not history, it is just an eddy in the stream of immemorial life' [Gros 2015: 7]). The immediacy of walking – of the pace in the present rather than the plod with the past – erodes the walk as an accumulation of sediment in the body, clogged up, fettered, enslaved. For Gros it is an act of escapism. When you walk out that door, you walk away from yourself rather than to meet yourself (Gros 2015: 6). Nevertheless, Gros accepts Nietzsche's romantic climbs, Rousseau's solitary murmurings, Thoreau's rewildings, the subversion of Benjamin's urban flâneur strolling against the tide. For me, these camouflaged walks in a time of COVID have disjointed intrusions about them, thoughts reactive to each other, consecutive internal meanderings that contrast with the progressive steps taken by the rest of me. Beneath the surface is a sizzling, crackling stream-of-consciousness inner dialogue to my footfall. Both steps and thoughts are ponderous but creative, unique, expansive and individual for all their similarities and patterns and postures. Each walk around the block follows the same pavement, takes the same time and passes the same houses. These are not simple nightly re-enactments but complex generative turns, to use a Steiner (2002: 139) expression from his seemingly structuralist but ultimately erroneously titled *Grammars of Creation*. They are gentle, creative steps influenced by language and physique, learning and lore, but they abide in me, compromised.

***

At the bottom of this part of the road, past the four schools all in neat little rows on my left, past the vets with its now-outside waiting room, the road junction allows me to walk back on myself in a V. It's a dangerous, blind corner for pedestrians. Joggers, foxes, and the unmasked may be on the other side closing the distance with myself, blindly. Our breath might mingle? They might infect me? Technically it would be a re-infection after my COVID-Christmas; thank you Track 'n' Trace for the Christmas Eve 'ping'. That week I would have been breaking the law if I'd done this same walk as of tonight. Or maybe I could have slipped out without my phone, and masked up to avoid the schools' surveillance cameras? But clearing the corner could put me in proximity with a new variant: the Kentish Olde Towne, the Brazilian Go-Go, the South African Township. They sound like small breweries to me, something to get drunk on. But I hold my breath instead. I won't even get drunk on the air.

My rule of thumb is that if you can smell someone, then you should not be inhaling. It could be in their exhalations. The trouble is that I'm enjoying the return of my smell and it's particularly acute after Santa took it away over Christmas.

I spent that week face-planting my Vick's jar, and finger-tip tasting the Marmite each morning. I'd already infected my wife, but she was still keeping her distance.

Rounding the corner, is like lurching to the right. It requires a walking recalibration. Now, I don't feel that I walk steadily when I night-walk. It's more of rocksteady, a rolling gait that feels a tad more from some sides-to-sides. The weight builds to the left one the outward leg. And it is added to on the inward stretch. By now I'm in a rhythm and my breathing is steady – I'm calmer coming home down a residential street. In and out. Left and right. Arms might come out of their pockets now and start to swing. Perhaps this is the unbalancing? I'm not sure if it can be seen. But I feel it acutely. My gaze turns inwards, introspective, feeling the gait as lumbering and excessive, feeling a different roll off my feet – my right angle more 'blocky' from tendonitis down the Achilles tendon, the left free and easy. The toes roll outwards from big to little. The bigger they are, the stronger their grip and the more distinct the feel. They pick up the surface changes in the tarmac, the cracks and crenellations in the crazy-paving left by the council, the errant pebbles from a posh driveway.

It's staring slightly ahead with my head slightly bowed and the lights glinting towards me and the drop to my left after a sharp right turn that I spook myself yet again, with a reminder to an old ear infection. Ménière's disease I call it. Stress, my best man diagnosed me. It's a slipping, tilting, falling feeling as though gravity is to my side and not beneath me. Vertiginous? It comes with an acid-like refocus on leaves in the trees, acute awareness of lines and boundaries, and an overwhelming sense of perspective out to trick me especially when railway tracks come at me as I walk towards them or the path converges in front of me, as I head my way forwards. This is when my breathing shifts and I use my diaphragm with my lungs to add a litre and ward off a creeping numbing fuzziness rolling up my chin into my face.

My cheeks turn into puffer fish and I dance off into a different consciousness if I am not too careful. My wife's trick is to count my breathing. It's a distraction that keeps me breathing, and walking. I then wander and wonder and walk. I change tenses and time zones in my memories: going to work by train in Bangor-Belfast commutes; Bruce teaching me his waltz in Oxford and giving me his memory of waltzing down the street. One, two, three. One, two, three. We're travelling to my special places, my comfort zones. I'm warm all over, basking under a Caribbean sun, lying on a deck, dribbling at the small fish below me between the slats. I'm in a tutorial with my desk lamp to brighten the place and stop any spinning when I glance up at the walls. There are walls on my right and a pavement drop on my left. I keep it that way, regularly. It's not deliberate but it happens all the same. Bruce would be walking differently, I muse, with exaggerated heels and toes and rises and falls as he went down that Oxford street. Did he linger between counts? Did his feet close and the weight change through the hips? That would unbalance me here and now in my midnight walk.

**

Dancing has inflamed the fascia in my right foot. Impact has aggravated tendonitis into the ankle. And age and diet have contributed to calcification in the heel with a painful bone spur. An MRI has also shown up a chip in the front from an old, severe ankle sprain from running through a Romanian village in the dark. When standing, the right foot is now at full dorsiflexion – think squatting all the time. When loaded with weight, working as a fulcrum, the heel-off phase of my gait is impeded. After a game of tennis, inflammation of the heel thickens the tendon so there is no flexibility and I limp like Quasimodo: the foot needs dragging behind me for a day to recover. Forget about the elevation and push-off phase in 'normal' walking. Its store of elastic energy has been run dry: the early flatfoot phase of the step jars with impact, and as the weight passes forward into the late flatfoot phase to push off the heel, there is no movement or push. The over-developed metatarsals grip and rotate and compress into a critical toe-off. Steroid injections into the Achilles heel give temporary relief, and sometimesmedication, until my body builds up a tolerance to them. Ultrasound reduces the inflammation. Wrapping the heel in cabbage leaves overnight using clingfilm, and walking in seaweed for their iodine content have been popular local vernacular remedies. I like to joke that I can then have stewed cabbage for breakfast. Stretching with a Salomon boot keeping the heel at 90° helps after an old basketball injury – a break from landing on an opponent's foot and rolling off. We lost and I spent a month at my parents' home convalescing.

Moving up the body, the knees have worn cartilage and crack and pop under duress. The hip is tight. The lower back on the left turns to chronic lower back pain if I don't walk around the block every day. The right arm no longer swings freely, locking in the elbow from falling off a bicycle once. Sometimes it needs shaking to eventually straighten with a ghastly crack. The neck has reduced range from whiplash in car accidents and the top vertebrae popped out falling down a flight of stairs. The nose is broken and curves to the right with breathing different from one nostril to the other–usually it's from the mouth engaging with the diaphragm – a leftover from playing the flute. Another basketball injury. Not to mention the spiralling fracture in my left thumb – basketball again. That one required an insurance disclaimer to go cross-country skiing at school.

The local massage specialist explains the lower back pain as a tightness from the opposite side of the body. It needs a set of stretches. The PT in the gym explains the ankle difficulties as a lack of calf muscle in the right leg from relying on the good left. They prescribe controlled calf-raising and lowering over the edge of a pavement. The next danger is on-coming traffic. Back home, my spritely masseuse used to walk around the walls of the massage room with her elbow jammed into my back to keep me more supple, to work out the knot, to drain out my lymph nodes. Her accomplice, a gifted body and mind therapist used to whisper affirmations in my ear in-between unthreading the congealed tendon into my heel. She was an expert, humming, feeling with sure hands where everything was and should be. BUPA vs NHS. She could diagnose a pedestrian at twenty paces, seeing a different walk in every person: pronations, flexions, contractions, extensions, under-developments, over-developments, wear and tear. Sometimes I see passers-by like her as injured figures telling a story. Theirs is a controlled falling, a practiced propulsion as legs catch the rest of the body, an evolutionary traspie.

Our walk harnesses gravity unless the step is made in space such as Buzz Aldrin's zero gravity bounce on the moon – a flat imprint with roll through the foot or toe-off. Journalist and world walker Paul Salopek (2013) rather charmingly describes the walk as 'iambic teetering'. Out in space, the no-atmosphere imprint is preserved for inter-planetary posterity. Our walk on earth uses hip abductors to stabilise the pelvis, and with spinal extension we stand upright in a neutral position, handsfree. The biomechanical movement is efficient allowing energy resources to be diverted to the brain (cf. Earls 2014). It evolved with *Australopithecus'* departure from the tree canopy for colonisation of savanna environments, leaving the trees for provisioning. This evolutionary adaptation is suggested by the world's oldest footprint site, the Laetoli Footprint Trails – the paleontological find by the Leakey family of some of the earliest hominin footprints. Here are tracks from our ancestors near to the Olduvai Gorge in northern Tanzania from approximately 3.5 million years ago: *Australopithecus* afarensis. They show bipedalism, a capacity predominant from *homo erectus* to *homo sapiens*. These footprints were preserved in ash followed by light rain. Research into their impressions by David Raichlen et al. in

2010 show a strong and heavy heel strike from the deep impressions, followed by lateral push from the heel to the base of the lateral metatarsal. There is a well-developed, medial longitudinal arch in the print with an adducted big toe, and a second deep impression made by the big toe which suggests a forwards roll of the foot and 'toe off'. With no 'knuckle drags' nearby, a one metre gait equivalent to a normal step, and the arch in the sole of the foot, all suggest a walk more human-like than ape-like. The arches of my own feet have a collapse in them ameliorated by heel pads and supports to build up the left side by half a centimetre. I nevertheless re-created the footsteps when visiting this first walking museum in Tanzania whilst on safari. We drove all the way and walked infrequently.

***

The memories warm me and flood in from different directions. They fend of the dark. But an uneven pavement, a tilt and a crack catch my metatarsals with a refined jolt. There's a pause in my breath past the bus stop with its bins and circle tobacco stains and stubs on top. A minor gasp as I unreleased my lungs in the march up the road. Turning right puts me back on track for home: two turns to sanctuary; brief observations that the coast is clear. It's a new pavement, harder edges, posts to stop the buses from mounting in their lazy turning circles. This is the Beachy Head part of the walk. It follows the sliding and slipping sensations. I have to cross over the drop – usually I wait for a driveway to soften the moment. It takes me back to my visit to the cliffs. I revisit in my head, occasionally. We have a family ban on my return. I've written about it and reviewed the photographs from the day. It's a narrative of awe: awesome to awful. We called in a jumper – not the woolly version but an unfortunate lost soul who had stepped determinedly off the awful margin. My colleague writes about these breakpoints: those who typically visit the edges to get a better appreciation of their lives and then they return from the brink. It's a celebration moment. Only this one wasn't. It was tragic. The triangulation points of a frame broached the skyline as the rescue teams abseiled down the cliff face, risking their lives for the lives lost. That takes me back to camp when the children's harnesses were so large we had to wrap them twice around the body and hold our breath again.

All this passes through my head at warp speed as I transition the pavement onto the tarmac. Cautiously, I double check to my left and my right. There is a one in ten minute chance that the 111 will be rounding the corner, veering away from the pavement's bolsters. Sometimes we wave to the drivers. Our neighbours worked the buses; inspectors. They live on the final corner and when gardening they pause mid-prune to watch the driver's technique, the push and the pull, the rotation, the speed, the traffic, the acknowledgement. The inspection over, they return to the snipping and the big red bus sails on down the road.

The bus is complemented by the post box. It stands on the corner of the road. Returning home, I turn on the inside. Leaving home I am on its outside next to the road. It feels like cutting corners. A large dark hedge on my left shoulder, the little red post box on my right with the road. I've never seen it in use. It's a relic of orderliness, a street ruin. Passing it, behind me I leave the expensive houses, well aware that some of the windows in them are open – a cross-current? Once a laser followed me on the ground. I turned and it was gone. Its memory shines alongside me. It's here that I once saw the Red Arrows flying towards Buckingham Palace. I got back inside the house to watch them fly over the other residentials. Sometimes, pre-COVID the music from cover concerts wafts up and bounces off the houses and the little red box, or a rackety-rumble from the trains in the background, or once even a cheer from the horse racing. But now, it's all quiet.

REFERENCES

Chawla, D. (2013) 'Walk, Walking, Talking, Home', in S. Jones, T. Adams, C. Ellis (eds), *Handbook of Autoethography*. London: Routledge, pp. 162–172.

Bourdieu, P. (2003) 'Participant Objectivation', *Journal of the Royal Anthropological Institute* 9(2): 281–294.

Bourdieu, P. (1995) *Outline of a Theory of Practice*. Cambridge: Cambridge University Press.

Earls, J. (2014) 'The Functional Anatomy of Walking', *Positive Health Online*, Issue 216, August 2014, http://www.positivehealth.com/article/anatomy-and-physiology/the-functional-anatomy-of-walking.

Edensor, T. (2007) 'Sensing the Ruin', *Senses & Society* 2(2): 217–232.

Feldman, J. (2016) *A Jewish Guide in the Holy Land: How Christian Pilgrims Made Me an Israeli*. Bloomington: Indiana University Press.

Feldman, J. (2007) 'Constructing a shared Bible Land: Jewish Israeli guiding performances for Protestant pilgrims', *American Ethnologist* 34(2): 351–374.

Gros, F. (2015) *A Philosophy of Walking*. London: Verso.

Ingold, T. (2000) *The Perception of the Environment: Essays in Livelihood, Dwelling and Skill*. London: Routledge.

Ingold, T. and J. Vergunst (2008) 'Introduction', in T. Ingold and J. Vergunst (eds), *Ways of Walking: Ethnography and Practice on Foot*. Farnham: Ashgate Publishing Limited, pp. 1–20.

Lund, K. (2019) 'Connecting Temporalities: Walking Through Narratives of Guilt and Passion', in I. Jenkins and K. Lund (eds), *Literary Tourism: Theories, Practice and Case Studies*, pp.36–45.

Niblett, M. (2016) 'Style as Habitus: World Literature, Decolonisation and Caribbean Voices', in R. Dalleo (Ed.), *Bourdieu and Postcolonial Studies*. Liverpool: Liverpool University Press, pp.119–136.

Raichlen, D., A. Gordon, W. Harcourt-Smith, A. Foster, and W. Haas (2010) 'Laetoli Footprints Preserve Earliest Direct Evidence of Human-Like Bipedal Biomechanics', *PLoS ONE* 5(3): e9769. doi:10.1371/journal.pone.0009769.g001.

Rapport, N. (2009) *Of Orderlies and Men: Hospital Porters Achieving Wellness at Work*. Durham, NC: Carolina Academic Press.

Reay, D. (2004) 'It's all becoming a habitus': beyond the habitual use of habitus in educational research', *British Journal of Sociology of Education* 25(4): 431-444.

Rojek, C. (1993) *Ways of Escape: Modern Transformations in Leisure and Travel*. Basingstoke: The Macmillan Press Ltd.

Salopek, P. (2013) 'To walk the world: part one', *National Geographic*, December 2013, https://www.nationalgeographic.com/magazine/article/out-of-eden.

Solnit, R. (2000) *Wanderlust: A History of Walking*. New York: Penguin.

Steiner, G. (2002) *Grammars of Creation*. London: Faber & Faber.

Melbourne:
Mantra Bell City Hotel

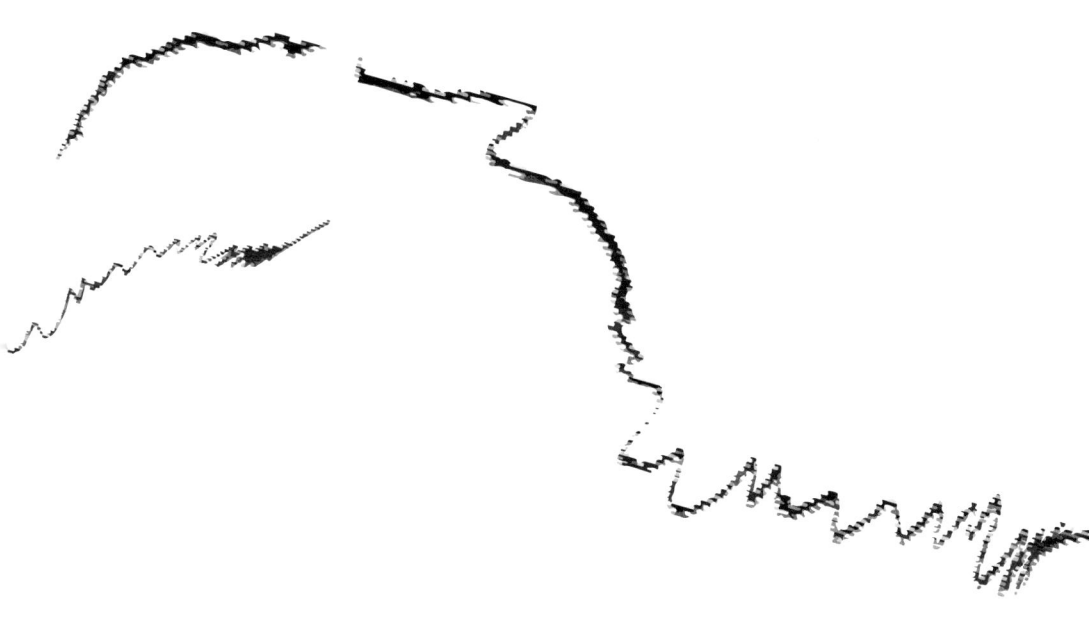

JACQUELINE FELSTEAD

Preface: On the night of 25 January 2021 a walk of the periphery of the Accor-owned Mantra Bell City Hotel was shared live on Zoom to a community who, via a split screen, could also see footage from past walks at the Hotel – secret investigations – undertaken since October 2020. This furtive walking, within our constrained allowable travel radius during COVID lockdown, took place in response to the indefinite detention of refugees on the Mantra Hotel's third floor. This essay begins with an account of the footage, that was shared during our virtual walk in the darkness, and it closes with what we encountered entering the Mantra – a space that had simultaneously functioned as both an upper-class hotel in the midst of refurbishment and a prison – 'live' at first light.

10 DECEMBER 2020

Hi everyone, hello it is an unusual time. I haven't come for a while because of COVID-19, now it's gone back to normal. That's good, thank you God. I have something to say today especially on Human Rights Day because I never expect that I am going to see them on the window in front of me, my friends, after – it's just a long time for 7 years. My heart is broken. I don't have any words today really, my words is really my tears.[1]

We love you.

Sometimes I feel as if we are stuck inside an aquarium. We exist in this small enclosure where we are watched constantly. We can see the outside world but cannot touch it, we cannot live in it, we can only observe it.[2]

Shame!

Today it is my day, it is your day, it is everyone's day.[3]

25 JANUARY 2021

We walk the periphery of Melbourne's Mantra Bell City Hotel tonight while speaking to footage of the hotel's inner workings shot surreptitiously by day. Formerly a hospital, the 1950s nurses' swimming pool within apparently transports one's mind away from the six lanes of traffic at the hotel's suburban entrance.

Until very recently, Mantra was a prison for over 60 refugees detained indefinitely on its third floor. These men, detained at Mantra for 16 months, had begun their detention 7 years earlier at Manus Island Regional Processing Centre. They had been brought to Australia through 'Medevac' legislation, which briefly gave doctors the authority to send asylum seekers from Australia's offshore detention centres in Papua New Guinea (PNG) and Nauru to Australia for medical treatment. With the repeal of this legislation, these refugees were left imprisoned in publicly unknown sites, like this hotel.

The Mantra is a *black site*, the site of *black ops* that are not listed on any government website. The daylight refracting from the hotel's glass exterior contributed to the concealment of the workings inside, whereby a private institution was used to conduct public business so contentious that it typically takes place offshore. During lockdown the hotel was within the 5km radius that my immediate community could walk.[4] In a period in which public protest had been largely impossible, walking this perimeter was a means of acknowledging this black site, a secret, and keeping its infrastructure on the radar of our collective consciousness.

I need to give some background to explain the significance of having 'medevaced' refugees in indefinite detention in our neighbourhood during COVID-19, and I'll give this background as we walk. In 2013, Australia's offshore detention centres for detaining asylum seekers were reopened, when Prime Minister Kevin Rudd announced that asylum seekers who came to Australia by boat would be detained offshore, and that they would never be settled in Australia, even as genuine refugees. [5] By 2014, 3,127 people, including children, had been indefinitely detained in Australia's offshore centres.[6] They were from Iran, Sri Lanka, Pakistan, Afghanistan, Somalia, Iraq, India, Bangladesh, Nepal, Lebanon and Sudan and a large percentage were stateless. Since 2014, the media have been discouraged from reporting, ostensibly for the safety of those detained.[7] The 2015 Australian Border Force Act prohibited workers from leaking information about detention conditions.[8] By 2016, there were 2,000 classified reports of abuse on Nauru. Since, 13 people have died in detention including by suicide and from delayed medical treatment. One man, 24 year-old Reza Barati was murdered at Manus Island Regional Processing Centre. Offshore and out-of-sight refugees have been detained since 2013, people of all ages and backgrounds, who had committed no criminal offence – but then they were here. The Mantra is a significant daily reminder, despite its being a 'black site' – that is, the location of an unacknowledged military operation. This detention facility wasn't listed on any government website, but *we know* and we traversed it, marking out its infrastructure.

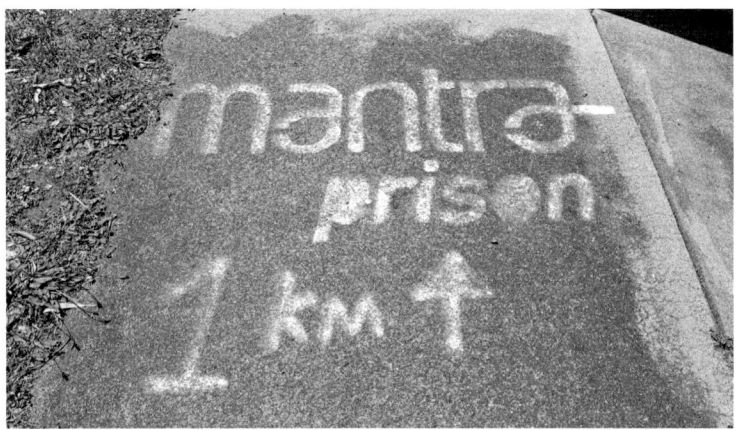

18 NOVEMBER 2020

Beginning at the *Mantra Prison 1km* stencilled to the
pavement, we walk past such everyday places. Preston and
Northcote Community Hospital (PANCH) once stood
on the Mantra site. Now its Health Service is opposite the
hotel's main entrance and its banner reads *Refugees Are
Welcome Here* in a face-off against the hotel's billboards
reading *Weddings from $99** and *Team building from $58**.
Mantra's Break Free and Bell City Hotels are all grey and
orange splashes where their mirrored surfaces don't meet
the sky. Reportedly, there is little possibility of isolation
within during the pandemic.

19 NOVEMBER 2020

Scout the grounds behind the facade and find a new
basketball court with no sign of use enclosed by hurricane
fencing, bamboo tall, blue sky and a young man gazing
from the third floor.

Marching boldly in, glass doors open to Mantra Bell
reception and unattributed paintings reference Indigenous art
processes. There are hydrangeas, a closed hairdresser and
a temporary wall with pictorial signs: wait, sanitise. At the
counter I inquire about wedding receptions and am told to
phone. Around the onsite post office advertising passports,
across the carpark and below to an elevator. Here I find that
I can only go up – but this is the out-of-sight place where visitors
of detainees are met by security and led along a disorienting
underground route to a room with a table tennis table.
The advertised Chill Restaurant is a building site, a chandelier
floats upstairs, the coffee shop van plays jazz to no-one.

The other fenced-off hotel building reads *Break Free.*
Both hotels are owned by Accor, a French company who
opened 10 new hotels in 2020 during the global pandemic.
It is well documented that the Australian government has paid
extraordinary amounts of money to private companies to
detain refugees, but the amount here is unknown. A woman

asks me to leave. Walking down the street the man from reception comes out to say 'I need permission', that 'it's private property' and that I should not have entered and photographed, maybe he's Immigration, maybe he's the Hotel.

10 DECEMBER 2020

On the night of Human Rights Day people gather outside for the *Hologram and In Person Rally*, holding candles distributed by Amnesty International and waving to the men gathered at the third floor windows.[9] Excerpts from speeches are shared as we walk in the night. 'Moz from Mantra' picks up his mobile from his third-floor room and, broadcast through the system on the street, starts with the Acknowledgement of Country, continuing 'I hope one day to be free and learn more about your beautiful culture. On Human Rights Day I would like to acknowledge that Indigenous rights and refugee rights are inherently linked... Despite the COVID-19 restrictions we see that everyday people are protesting for us and fighting for our freedom...' The prevention of the *Migration Amendment (Prohibiting Items in Immigration Detention Facilities) Bill 2020* had stopped the imminent banning of mobile phones, SIM cards and internet-capable devices. This bill would have expanded search and seizure powers in relation to immigration detainees, including allowing for the use of detector dogs.[10]

Michael Green helps form an image of who is inside. Michael was smuggled in to Manus Island Regional Processing Centre in 2017. It had been forcibly closed after PNG ruled that Australian offshore detention procedures were illegal. Four hundred detained people, making a stand through staying at the centre, were left without food, water, electricity and medical care for 24 days. At night, in the heat, they sat in the dark or dragged beds out into the open. They built devices to capture water and divvied up smuggled food by a system according to country groups, arranging supplies according to their numbers.[11]

13 DECEMBER 2020

Online a family room is available. Together we can walk the second and fourth floors as paying guests while the refugees are imprisoned on the third – one guard per two people. The trick is to be guests, which we are.

The swipe card key says to 'Discover your true potential.' The building map laminated to the room's desk shows three corridors leading from a central point, like a panopticon. but central isn't a guard tower, at least on this floor. The kids stare at the sixth-floor view. Emmett comments that it's beautiful, that there is no beach, but stands still in wonder at 'all the houses and cars from up here, and the police.'

The parallels with the film *The Shining* come up in our night walk, and are due to more than just the apparent emptiness of the hotel, which we wander following Audrey's child-like sense of proper direction, looking for the entrances to the third.[12] Mentally, the third floor, where the refugees are imprisoned, functions in a manner not unlike Room 237 in *The Shining*, in that it is a place that you shouldn't go and an anchor through which all architecture comes to be defined: the spot where punishment occurs. The corridors seem to recede and Mantra transforms quickly into a maze or, as Simon suggests, as we walk in the dark online, a labyrinth. Some doors open, others don't and some doors that open from one side do not open from the other. This combination of architectural deterrents and surveillance remind one of the Castle Keep in Kafka's *The Burrow*. In this story, an underground maze is made by a paranoid creature wanting to confuse an unseen enemy and deny them the pleasures of home. Down the fire escape we pass one entry to the third floor, a frosted glass door guarded by a woman seated in a yellow vest with her curly hair pressed against the pane. On another stairwell a third-floor door is thick wood with a prominent lock. We try not to be noticed and no-one comes.

Paying hotel guests can often go where they like – here employment relies on the success of this expensive family hotel

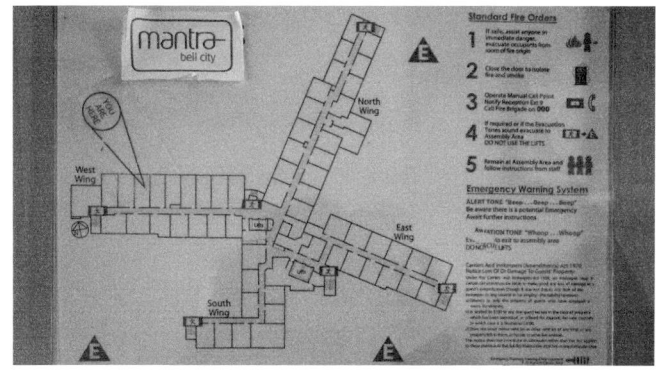

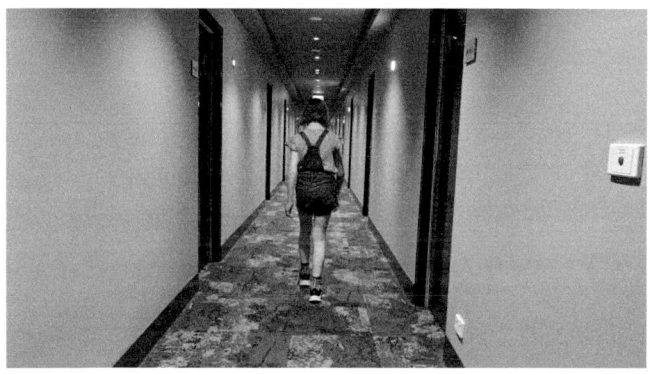

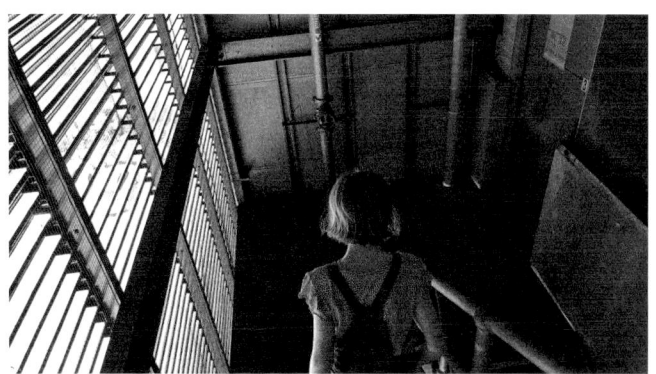

during the global pandemic – and it has been left unsaid by the impeccable staff that here one shouldn't wander. Instead the construction fences that deter one from a building site double as devices to shepherd guests away from the prison. But, someone has left a tin in the doorway of the second floor fire escape and there is access to the floor below those imprisoned. It takes a while to piece together the logic of this floor which is under construction. In each south-facing room a feature wall has a wallpaper that is a section of a picture, pink flowers from a tree in bloom against a blue sky.. Every room section differs. In one room too are the pillars of a building. In another it becomes apparent that this floor beneath the prisoners' feet is an artist's impression of Preston Town Hall. This local centre of government is aesthetically deconstructed across the whole level, a symbol of law, democracy and tax.

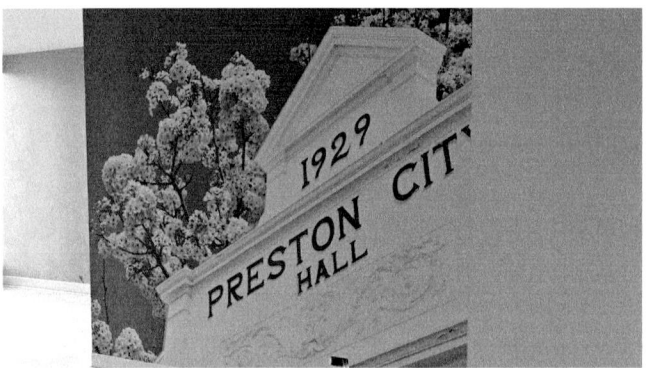

The lift takes longer and a man appears, initially in our lift – a person whose presence seems calculated. The multiple swipe cards we have for the lift and room keep failing and need to be reset. The staff member who advised me in the evening to *not* find the pool, to *not* go to the gym and that I would find the transformation they are doing to the hotel 'breathtaking', coincidentally appears suddenly from the neighbouring room with a room key-card when mine fails, and opens my door so easily.

In the night I make three-dimensional models of the minute details of this transformation. A door in a temporary wall opens to a staircase. The top empty floor has an outside garden with artificial grass viewable through a locked door. Descending, the fourth-floor too is under refurbishment and its windows give an approximation of the view from the third. Those imprisoned would see the taunt of the city skyline from the windows of the south-facing rooms, the 'Asylum Seekers Welcome Here' sign on PANCH to the north. This is the 'fish bowl...'

14 DECEMBER 2020

The lift door opens on Floor 3 to let someone in, my children both presume it's the ground floor and try to walk through. They are deftly placed back into the lift by alert men in fluorescent vests.

Similar experiences of the labyrinth-like quality of the Mantra have been recounted by visitors to refugees, that is, before visits were suspended due to the global pandemic. The suspicion is that the journey is a ploy to conceal the direct route.

Reception says to wait around the corner out of sight. After a long time someone comes and leads you down and then into a lift to the basement car park, you lose your bearings and walk a surprisingly long way and are led into a foyer just below ground, perhaps under another building. There is the table tennis table and the two security guards, a man and woman, escorting your detained friend. You chat, play table tennis until your friend needs to go to the toilet. He is unable to be dissuaded by the guards who call down a male security guard. Two male guards accompany him to the toilet which is in the same room, the door 10 metres away. The visit ends suddenly. Michael confides 'it's a strange experience, you think about the other guests and if they know, probably in certain circles people still don't know. A prison and a hotel and a black site and accessible.'[13] There are 6000 people who have come to Australia since 2013 and some were detained indefinitely and others weren't. Michael adds 'imagine every day, every waking moment, to know that there's no – even according to the logic of the system – there's no sense to it…'

16 DECEMBER 2020

The men are moved to the Park Hotel, Carlton. What is unusual isn't that they are moved but that people know about it. That the public bear witness to the buses leaving.

That night the Mantra seems deserted. Mifumi recalls the men's desperate pleas to be released before catching COVID. The swimming pool for nurses does exist. Liz remembers when the hotel was 'nice, sunny, happy.' She remembers the raves before that and the hospital earlier still. 'So this: my grandmother died up on that floor, my best friend was born here, Matt's eldest was born in the whitest room he'd ever seen, he had plastic surgery after being stabbed. They had a babies' room where we would look at the babies. I had my stomach pumped here, did my brother's kneecap here, had chewing gum removed from by brother's bum here…' The third floor beds are already thrown out, piling up by the gate. We are witness to a swift erasure.

25 JANUARY 2020 6AM EST

Now having walked the deserted grounds in the cover of night with our virtual walkers online, in the quiet of first light together we enter the Mantra Bell City Hotel reception.

The foyer *has* become The Hotel, refurbished beyond recognition; its gleaming surfaces announce 'Money!' An immaculately attired hotel worker is glimpsed on the other side of the building, her singularity indicating that something is amiss. Outside, on a national holiday and with the easing of restrictions, the city has assumed much of its old self, but not here. Perhaps advertised rooms are not really available or the hotel pretends to be full.

Perhaps it is that we have the good conscience to stay away from the Mantra Bell and 'Break-free' because it held asylum seekers in indefinite detention. That through the global pandemic we had our own tiny, comparatively infinitesimal, taste of lockdown, of not being able to see those whom we love and of being confined in close quarters. But I know there *are* people staying here, but perhaps these are the kind that want their doors shut and don't want to be a bother.

The hotel has differing streams of engagement, or rather, different streams of entitlement. Historically, the Mantra has two hotels next to each other, one upmarket and the other often block-booked for government social housing, including forensic psychiatric release. My own entitlement stream still has an inbox full of requests for review and recommendation. The new foyer announces that they invested in the base rate of $230 AUD per night. It's only via collective memory, and the tape recording we have just shared, that the thinness of this facade can be pinned down.

We come back to *The Shining*. Like the hotel in the film, nothing has stuck to these surfaces, or perhaps it is this infrastructure of surface, the hotel's cultivated thin veneer, that brings about specific events. One way of reading the film is that it is the Overlook Hotel's cultivation of itself that has such dire consequences, directing both performance and punishment. The apparition of the bartender tells Jack Torrance that his credit is fine, but then the butler, Delbert Grady, informs him it is time his wilful wife and child were corrected, that the child is 'attempting to bring in an outsider'[14] – the question of race burns brightly here too – how are outsiders defined, treated and kept on 'the out'? Here it *is* the punishment that funds the barman, and my own credit (which as I am reminded by the Black Lives Matter movement is inherently race-related), is fine here too.

Unseen decision makers – elusive figures – command the morphing of the space from hotel to prison to hotel.

Now even the internal laminate is coated to refract; like the mirrored glass exterior, it can make the political transformations required of postmodern architectural space. Little can be pinned to rebounding light; it's orchestrated to draw attention away from itself. Still, underneath must be that makeshift lobby, sufficient for the needs of every case worker, guard and builder, and that glowing pink neon sign of the well-equipped but superfluous beauty salon which was inaccessible for the detained majority. Now a feature salon, viewable from both interior and exterior, opens over the top of a monolith whose make-over is financed by indefinite detention, during a difficult financial time, with a population in isolation and borders shut. It's a microcosmic economics – in return for provision of services detaining refugees already in need of medical care and with little possibility of social distancing; during the global pandemic, substantial (but unknown) funds are received, and a considerable hotel refurbishment is undertaken, as the hotel prepares itself for brighter times. Accor opened up 10 new hotels worldwide, including Raffles Bali, during the global pandemic. The old Mantra is hard to make out here, the refurbishment is reminiscent of the dismantling of Manus Island Regional Processing Centre (MIRCP) which also happened after its closure. Still here we find clues of it, walking in the dim morning light.

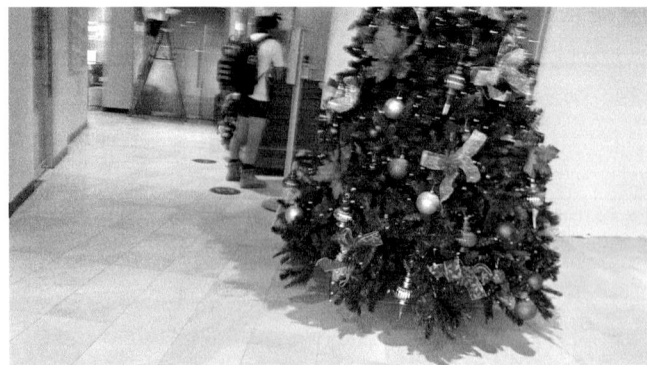

New beds are stacked in the recent basketball court. Used beds, presumably those of the asylum seekers, were stacked in the Mantra carpark on December 16th, the very same night these refugees were moved. This was three weeks ago, and we have just rewatched it while standing in the dark in the same carpark spot. The very existence of the basketball court in which these new beds are stacked may be due to the findings of the Australian Human Rights Commission who in 2019, considering the Mantra's use as an alternative place of detention, had required open spaces. The Commission had not entered since due to COVID. Purportedly new spaces were little used because detainees had to apply to use them, they couldn't just be outside. Either way, the fence around the pristine court has been removed and it is surely an attraction for new hotel guests.

There is another trace too, a feeling to be heeded. As Dick Hallorann says to young Danny Torrance, 'Well you know Doc, when something happens it can leave a trace of itself behind. Say, like, if someone burns toast, well maybe things that happen leave other kinds of traces behind…I think a lot of things happen right here in this particular hotel over the years and not all of them was good'.[15] The last walk of the Mantra takes place, although the refugees are no longer there, because of an indelible mark on civic conscience.

Today, an unknown number of refugees remain in indefinite detention in black sites across Australia and offshore. It is like night has descended, in that, in the dark, there are spaces that you know exist but you can't see. Sometimes in the dark things give the impression of being able to transform their shape, and this is a time when hotels can double as black-site prisons. We never get into that third floor but know that it is there and map the outskirts in the dark with our feet, and we mark out its morphing infrastructure with our conversation.

In-person walkers: Jacqueline Felstead, Mifumi Obata, Elizabeth Robertson, and Daniella Ruffino.

ENDNOTES

1. Betelhem Zeleke, speech, *Hologram and In Person Rally, Human Rights Day: Free the Refugees – 7 Years Too Long in Detention*, 10 December 2020.
2. Mostafa Azimitabar, speech, *Hologram and In Person Rally, Human Rights Day: Free the Refugees – 7 Years Too Long in Detention*, 10 December 2020.
3. Thanush Selvarasa, speech, *Hologram and In Person Rally, Human Rights Day: Free the Refugees – 7 Years Too Long in Detention* 10 December 2020.
4. Melbourne Australia was in lock down from 7 July to 28 October 2020.
5. Australia does not have a Bill of Rights.
6. These centres were, initially, Nauru Australian Immigration Detention Centre and Manus Island Regional Processing Centre, PNG.
7. Paul Toohey, "That sinking feeling Asylum seekers and the search for the Indonesian Solution," *Quarterly Essay*, Issue 53, 2014.
8. Hannah Ryan, Nick Evershed, Andy Ball, Nell Geraets, and Alexandra Spring "Interactive timeline: what happened to every person caught up in Australia's offshore processing regime" *The Guardian*, 10 December 2020. See https://www.theguardian.com/australia-news/ng-interactive/2020/dec/10/timeline-australia-offshore-immigration-detention-system-program-census-of-asylum-seekers-refugees
9. Protestors had previously been fined for allegedly compromising COVID restrictions.
10. For more information, see https://www.aph.gov.au/Parliamentary_Business/Bills_Legislation/bd/bd2021a/21bd002
11. Conversation with Michael Green, 20 January 2021.
12. Kubrick (1980).
13. Conversation with Michael Green, 20 January 2021.
14. Kubrick (1980).
15. Derrida's notion of hauntology is relevant, whereby something that is no longer affects both the present and one's ability to move forward into a changed future. Derrida (2006) argues such spectres require parlance, they need to be spoken to. See Derrida (2006) and Mark Fisher (2014).

REFERENCES

Derrida, J., Kamuf, P., Magnus, B., and Cullenberg, S. (2006). *Specters of Marx: The State of the Debt, the Work of Mourning and the New International.*, New York: Routledge.

Fisher, M. (2014). *Ghosts of My Life: Writings on Depression, Hauntology and Lost Futures.* Winchester: Zero Books.

Kafka, F. (2018). "The Burrow," in *Metamorphosis and Other Stories.* London: Vintage.

Kubrick, Stanley. (1980). *The Shining.* Los Angeles, CA: Warner Bros.

Migration Amendment (Prohibiting Items in Immigration Detention Facilities) Bill 2020. (2020, August 5). Retrieved from https://www.aph.gov.au/Parliamentary_Business/Bills_Legislation/bd/bd2021a/21bd002

Ryan, H., Evershed, N., Ball, A., Geraets, N. and Spring, A . (2020, 10 December). "Interactive timeline: what happened to every person caught up in Australia's offshore processing regime" *The Guardian.* See https://www.theguardian.com/australia-news/ng-interactive/2020/dec/10/timeline-australia-offshore-immigration-detention-system-program-census-of-asylum-seekers-refugees

Toohey, Paul, 2014. "That sinking feeling Asylum seekers and the search for the Indonesian Solution," *Quarterly Essay*, Issue 53 (2014).

Biographies

EDITORS

Jaspar Joseph-Lester is a London-based artist. His work explores the conflicting ideological frameworks embodied in representations of modernity, urban renewal, regeneration and social organisation as a means to better understand how art practice can redefine master plans and regeneration schemes that determine the cultural life of our cities. He has exhibited his work internationally and is author of *Revisiting the Bonaventure Hotel* (Copy Press, 2012). Joseph-Lester is Professor of Critical Spatial Practice at the Royal College of Art.

Ahuvia Kahane is Regius Professor of Greek, A. G. Leventis Professor of Greek Culture and Fellow of Trinity College Dublin. His research interests include temporality, complexity theory, ancient literature and the relations between antiquity, modernity and contemporary critical thought. His book *Epic, Novel and the Progress of Antiquity* (Bloomsbury) is in press. Forthcoming work includes (ed.) *A Cultural History of Time in the Ancient World* (Bloomsbury), *Orality and the Formula* (de Gruyter), and 'Ancient Narrative Time' (in *A Handbook of Ancient Literary Theory*, Oxford).

Simon King is a London-based writer and walking artist undertaking a practice-based PhD at Birkbeck, University of London. His research investigates the infrastructures of creative and critical practice in relation to walking, dialogue and social engagement. He is the co-founder with Jaspar Joseph-Lester of the cross-disciplinary Walkative project at the RCA and has worked collaboratively since 2017 with the artist Corinne Noble to create participatory group walks that have an overarching theme or narrative and a distinctive methodology.

Esther Leslie is Professor of Political Aesthetics at Birkbeck, University of London. Her books include various studies of Walter Benjamin, *Hollywood Flatlands: Animation, Critical Theory and the Avant Garde* (2002); *Synthetic Worlds: Nature, Art and the Chemical Industry* (2005); *Derelicts* (2014): *Liquid Crystals: The Science and Art of a Fluid Form* (2016): and *The Rise and Fall of Imperial Chemical Industries: Synthetics, Sensism and the Environment* (2023). Work on the biopolitical economy of dairy, with Melanie Jackson, includes *Deeper in the Pyramid* (2018/2023). A study of anti-fascist radio pioneer Ernst Schoen (written with Sam Dolbear) appeared in 2023, *Dissonant Waves: Ernst Schoen and Experimental Sound in the Twentieth Century.*

CONTRIBUTORS:

Anna Ådahl is a Swedish artist and researcher working in various mediums such as film, installations and performance. She uses the editing tools of assemblage and montage where found footage meets newly produced images, where ready-mades are used as props in spatial narratives and the body is used as an investigative tool in staged performances. Her PhD at the Royal College of Art (2022) addressed the aesthetics and politics of today's post digital crowds. She is currently pursuing a postdoc and is running a funded (Swedish Research Council) practice-led fine art research project in collaboration with Stefan Jonsson at the Royal Institute of Art, Stockholm/LiU, titled *Collective Agency in an Era of Authoritarian Automation.* Her work has been shown at Pylon Lab, Dresden; Impakt, Utrecht; Whitechapel Gallery, London; Moderna Muséet (part of the collection), Stockholm; LIAF, Norway; CCA Derry-Londonderry amongst others.

Ryan Bishop is Professor of Global Arts and Politics, Director of Research in the Department of Art and Media

Technology Research Group at the Winchester School of Art, University of Southampton (UK). He co-edits the journal *Cultural Politics* (Duke University Press) and the book series 'Technicities' (Edinburgh University Press).

Jacqueline Felstead is an artist and researcher. She employs photography, moving image, sculpture and media technologies to focus on the relationship of simulated environments to lived experience. She holds an MFA from Monash University and completed her PhD, titled *Loss in a Simulated Environment* at the Victorian College of Art, University of Melbourne where she taught in sculpture. Felstead was awarded the Anne & Gordon Samstag International Visual Arts Scholarship which funded associate research at Royal College Art, London. She has undertaken residencies at Banff Centre, Canada and Objectifs, Singapore with the support of Asialink and Australia Council.

Duncan Hay is a Senior Research Fellow at the Bartlett Centre for Advanced Spatial Analysis UCL, London. Hay is a digital humanities specialist whose research examines the intersection of culture, space and technology. He received his PhD in 2012 in English Literature from Manchester University, where his thesis looked at the writing of the London-based writer Iain Sinclair in relationship to the theories of urban space developed by the twentieth century European avant-gardes. He is currently project lead on Memory Mapper, an open-source web toolkit for mapping culture and place.

Norman M. Klein is an urban and cultural historian who is identified very much with Los Angeles. Among his best known work: *History of Forgetting: Los Angeles and the Erasure of Memory*; *The Vatican To Vegas: The History of Special Effects*; *The Imaginary 20th Century*; *Tales of the Floating Class*. Klein is a professor in the School of Critical Studies, at California Institute of the Arts, Los Angeles.

Robin Kirsten is an artist, who completed a practice-based PhD at the Royal College of Art, funded by the Techne AHRC Doctoral Training Partnership. Recent projects in 2020 include a collaborative theatre piece, *Nothing is Here*, and a solo exhibition of three hypothetical museums, *Studies for a Museum*. Kirsten's practice and research is framed by his interest in the self-generating museum, which he models from a building block he calls the Universal Object.

Antonia Low is a Berlin-based artist and Professor at Staatliche Akademie der Bildenden Künste Stuttgart. Her art practice is concerned with the interaction between architecture, materiality, aesthetics and history. Low studied Fine Arts at Kunstakademie Münster, and Goldsmiths, University of London. Her published monographs include *Der verlorene Raum* (Kettler Verlag); *Inventar* (The Greenbox Verlag); *Low Deluxe* (Argobooks).

Fiachra Mac Góráin is Associate Professor of Classics at University College London. He holds a BA from Trinity College Dublin, and an MSt and DPhil from the University of Oxford. He has published on Virgil, Varro, and Dionysus, and is currently working on a book entitled *Virgil's Dionysus*.

Jasone Miranda-Bilbao is an artist who works in various media. She received a PhD from Goldsmiths, University of London in 2007 and since then has lived and worked between London and Delhi. She exhibits her work internationally and in 2015 she set up the ongoing curatorial project *Ideas travel faster than light* that has led to collaborations amongst artists from India and the UK and others.

Virginia Nimarkoh is an artist and activist. Her art practice has explored ideas of utopia, particularly in relation to community action, architecture, and public space. She took part in (Re:)Thinking the Street: Urban Encounters at Tate Britain. She currently runs Lambeth Larder Community Food Resource, a food insecurity social enterprise. The Museum of London commissioned Virginia Nimarkoh and Fan Sissoko to work with The Advocacy Academy to create We The People (2019), an intergenerational short film, exploring active citizenship in Brixton, south London.

Corinne Elinor Noble is a London-based artist, originally from Yorkshire. A graduate of Chelsea College of Art (BA Painting) and the Royal College of Art (MA Printmaking) her linear drawings, hand-sewn books, wooden constructions and walks find inspiration in familiar fragments: found rocks, antique postcards, household bricks and historic photographs. Since 2017 she has collaborated with the writer Simon King, as N&K, to create and lead imaginative group walks.

Andreas Philippopoulos-Mihalopoulos is an academic/artist/fiction author. He is Professor of Law and Theory at the University of Westminster, and Director of The Westminster Law & Theory Lab. His academic books include the *Absent Environments* (2007), and *Spatial Justice: Body Lawscape Atmosphere* (2014). collection of short stories, *The Book of Water*, is published in Greek and English. His art practice includes performance, picpoetry, sculpture and painting. His work has been presented at Palais de Tokyo, the Tate Modern, Inhotim Instituto de Arte Contemporânea Brazil, the 58th Venice Art Biennale 2019, the 16th Venice Architecture Biennale 2016, Arebyte Gallery. Philippopoulos-Mihalopoulos currently collaborates with Danielle Arnaud Gallery.

Nicholas Ferguson is an artist based in London. His research examines the relationship between art, space and power, with recent and ongoing projects focusing on London

Heathrow, its neighbourhoods and airspace. He is Associate Dean for Research at Richmond American University and Senior Lecturer in Critical and Historical Studies at Kingston University.

Katarina Rothfjell was born in Stockholm and is inspired by her Danish-Norrland Swedish cultural heritage. While studying art history at Stockholms Universitet she began to undertake freelance photo collaborations with designers Camilla Thulin, Anna Holtblad and Gunnel Sahlin. Following coverage of her work in the Danish press, she studied in London and Paris before working at Dansmuséet Stockholm as an archivist, darkroom technician and event organiser for curators Bengt and Lilavati Häger. At Studio Bo Appeltofft she developed her knowledge of interior design-food-fashion photography before moving to Venice in the early 1990s. Rothfjell's main sources of inspiration are artisan traditions, design, fashion, film and nature and her professional skills include glass-design, photo reportage, cultural events commissioned by international agencies and private assignments.

Ashish Sahoo is an artist based in Delhi.He graduated in Sculpture from the Kala Bhavan, Visva Bharati University, Shantiniketan (India) and later from Delhi College of Art. He works predominantly with photography and runs the artist project, the Maze Collective Studio. In 2017, he won the prestigious photography award "Umrao Singh Shergill."

AbdouMaliq Simone is senior professorial fellow at the Urban Institute at the University of Sheffield, co-director of the Beyond Inhabitation Lab at Polytechnic University of Turin, and author of *For the City Yet to Come: Changing African Life in Four Cities* (2004), *Improvised Lives: Rhythms of Endurance in an Urban South* (2018), and *Jakarta: Drawing the City Near* (2014)

Jonathan Skinner is Reader in the Anthropology of Events at the University of Surrey. He has interests in festivals, dark tourism, social dancing, and walking and tour guiding. He has undertaken research in the Caribbean, the US and UK and is the co-editor of *Leisure and Death: An Anthropological Tour of Risk, Death, and Dying* (2018), winner of the Ed Bruner New Book Award.

Index

Acknowledgements

We would like to thank our contributors for their involvement in *Walking in Cities: Navigating Post-Pandemic Environments*. We would also like to thank the Research Office and the School of Arts and Humanities at the Royal College of Art, under the stewardship of Dr Emma Wakelin, Professor Ken Neil and Professor Rachel Garfield. The Department of Classics and Research Accounts at Trinity College Dublin has also provided generous support for which we are enormously grateful. Samuel Jones has once again worked beyond the call of duty to design a compelling and thoughtful publication. Christine Shuttleworth has helped considerably by providing us with an excellent index. We would also like to thank Routledge for their continued support, in particular Kate Schell and Selena Hostetler for their patience and encouragement over the years of development. Finally, we would like to thank The People's Museum: Somers Town and Iris Watson.

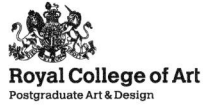

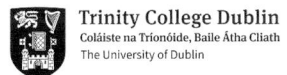

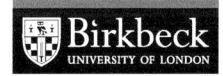

Walking in Cities:
Navigating Post-Pandemic
Urban Enviornments

Editors
    Jaspar Joesph-Lester
    Ahuvia Kahane
    Simon King
    Esther Leslie

Indexer
    Christine Shuttleworth

Design
    Samuel Jones

First published 2024